solo/black/woman

scripts, interviews, and essays

Edited by E. Patrick Johnson
and Ramón H. Rivera-Servera

Foreword by D. Soyini Madison

D0761317

NORTHWESTERN UNIVERSITY PRESS
EVANSTON, ILLINOIS

Northwestern University Press
www.nupress.northwestern.edu

This book has been published with the support of the Andrew W. Mellon Foundation.

Library of Congress Cataloging-in-Publication Data

Solo/black/woman : scripts, interviews, and essays / edited by E. Patrick Johnson and Ramón H. Rivera-Servera.
pages cm.
"The publication also includes a DVD of video samples for each of the performances documented, discussed, and analyzed within"—Introduction.
ISBN-13: 978-0-8101-2947-4 (pbk. : alk. paper)
ISBN-10: 0-8101-2947-7 (pbk. : alk. paper)
1. Monologues, American—21st century. 2. African American women dramatists. 3. African American actresses. 4. American drama—African American authors. 5. American drama—Women authors. 6. African American women—Social conditions—Drama. 7. McCauley, Robbie. Sugar. 8. Jones, Rhodessa. Big-butt girls, hard-headed women. 9. Davis-Bellamy, Nancy Cheryll. Passing solo. 10. Cooper-Anifowoshe, Edris. Adventures of a black girl in search of academic clarity and inclusion. 11. Bridgforth, Sharon. Delta dandi. 12. Robinson, Stacey Karen. Quiet frenzy. 13. DeBerry, Misty. Milkweed. I. Johnson, E. Patrick, 1967– II. Rivera-Servera, Ramón H., 1973– III. McCauley, Robbie. Sugar. IV. Jones, Rhodessa. Big-butt girls, hard-headed women. V. Davis-Bellamy, Nancy Cheryll. Passing solo. VI. Cooper-Anifowoshe, Edris. Adventures of a black girl in search of academic clarity and inclusion. VII. Bridgforth, Sharon. Delta dandi. VIII. Robinson, Stacey Karen. Quiet frenzy. IX. DeBerry, Misty. Milkweed.
PS627.M63S65 2013
812.0450806—dc23

2013016091

For
Sarah M. Johnson
and
Mamá Cruz

CONTENTS

FOREWORD

D. Soyini Madison

Why perform alone onstage? Why pay attention to a black woman? Movie audiences travel in throngs to multiplex cinemas to sit before an encompassing screen—lit up, writ large—surrounded by booming sonics and the high-tech, surface projections of grand fantasy and hyperreality. As one noted cultural critic stated, "Movies? Yes, but theater, no. It's not my form." The screen is everywhere, mega large and nano small. We are engaged and enraptured at every turn by screens. They are our entertainment and our saving grace. But there are those special moments when we escape the screen and find great pleasure in the "liveness" of the theater. Enter the celebrated American musical and the stage-show spectacle where dance, song, and rhythm culminate in virtuosic showmanship and where bright lights, big sets, and luscious costumes adorn the musicality of the stage. But there is also that population of more elite theatergoers who might flinch at the musical, for they are connoisseurs of the classics that embrace the high culture of opera and the canons, old and new, of literary drama. And there are still others who turn from the highbrow conclaves of "serious" theater to the lowbrow locales of belly laughs and carnival joy, and, here, whether it is the chitlin' circuit or vaudeville antics, the carnivalesque stage is powered by call-and-response entertainment.

I have listed a hodgepodge of performance experiences, technologically projected and viscerally present, constituting highbrow taste and lowbrow talents, not so much to emphasize their differences, because I understand they often intersect variously and simultaneously as they are consumed and appreciated in this fractured, time/space compressed, and multisampled (post)postmodern epoch. I list them to make the point that the human attention span has limited capacity in an era where the objects of our attention are boundless and the demands excessive. Choice and attention require effort. How do performances of solo black women capture our attention? In this contemporary moment of choice excess, why would anyone choose to spend time in this way?

This is a question I've asked since the early 1970s when black women, with nascent recognition and support, were beginning to stand alone onstage as dramatic actors. This is a question arising from my experience, reminiscences, and once youthful nerve. *Sister Son/ji*, written by Sonia Sanchez, was my first solo performance. Under the direction of Val Gray Ward, it was produced at the Kuumba Workshop and in Chicago in 1976. The play depicts stages in the life of a black, revolutionary woman through flashbacks of resisting racism, betrayal by black male revolutionaries, and ending in her triumph over loss, rejection, and isolation. The Chicago playwright and author Useni Eugene Perkins wrote my second solo performance, *Our Sun-Backed Lips Will Kiss the Earth*, in 1978. The play captured various scenes of noted black women in African and African American history and toured for over five years across the country at college campuses, churches, and community theaters.

Upon reflection, what I remember from these experiences over thirty years ago, as a solo, black, woman performer, and what I realize now, writing this foreword, as a teacher and scholar of performance is that when a black woman stands onstage alone, she must become the consummate griot, the epic storyteller, the virtuosic alchemist letting loose blood, red, woman cycles of hard truth, unabashed literacies, and black female abjection. Like the griot, she is reader, singer, keeper, and destroyer of the record. She brushes the dust off the record book and opens it with purpose. This is a radical act of grand proportion and courage. She reclaims the record, holds the book to her ear, and listens to the spectrum of its horrors as well as its glorious triumphs. She lifts the pages and translates the strained whispers from this timeworn record of misnamed black women and the nameless forgotten. She enters page and sound of unending black-woman-stories of broken bones, broken hearts, and lives rebounded and renewed. She is an alchemist of translation and remembering. She blends her own sweet words into the record book. She lifts pages and whispers into performance. She is sound and meaning. She tells the story in motion. The room overflows with her aliveness, holding fast our breathless attention, because the storyteller is essential.

Our existence depends on the teller of stories. We have no choice; we are made this way.

She stands alone. She holds our fresh curiosity inside her story. We do not look away. We do not stop listening. We are in lockdown within the grip of her unfolding tale. We do not want her to let us go. Our desire is to know what happens next. We are drawn into the pleasure and pathos of empathy and the tense immediacy of lyrical description. Our desire is to gaze, without interruption or distraction, at the mysteries of this virtuosic performer. We are attentive and trusting inside the pages and whispers of the record book she conjured with her virtuosity. We only need her, her alone, for the story. We can only imagine this story, this unfolding life, through this solo performer, because this is how the story came into being for us. We are all presence by the solo-ness in solo performance, because the skilled, solo performer has made us experience and believe that the story cannot be performed any other way. It is virtuosic because it is solo and it is solo because it is virtuosic.

Solo black women (SBW) complicate the redundancy of performativity and the talk about it through black female stylizations that are not contingent upon naturalized repetitions, but on the unnaturalized, resistant, Africanist, gestural economies across black female circum-Atlantics. The gift of SBW is that, inside performance, these black female performativities are not necessarily revealed as naturalized repetitions that shape identity, because their alterity is illuminated and their stylized acts are constantly teasing identity. What is gifted to us in SBW that lies beyond performativity is a *complex mix and blend* of discursive circulations, gestural economies, and historical affects that break up repetition and scatter style across hearts and minds making black female performativity contingent, otherworldly, and radically contextual.

To respeak performativity through performance, solo black women attend to the fact of blackness and the hauntings of black female abjection. *When and where she enters her race enters with her* is always marked as abject. Abjection is the shadow looming over the record book. You can see it hovering over the page and hear it choking the whispers in scenes of abjection: you serve empire, capital, production, and phallic violence; you are reasonless; you are empty of meaning and history; you are an ugly, broken, voiced thing. In SBW performance, these scenes of abjection are on trial in the bush, in the field, on the street, in the cave, in the cell, at the kitchen table, and in otherwise spaces. The solo black woman holds the record book inside her performance and inherits the griot's mission as keeper of the village history—the talking book—and as excavator in the genealogy of its members—all of us. The griot's song is a subversive, black, feminist epic where its lyrics are sustained by performatives that hail love stories that break down doors and by hard, whipping, backtalk that shames the power gods. Black female abjection is left shaking and impotent on the stage floor.

The SBW performs across the palimpsests of griot resurfacings and the sonic reach of Africanist cosmopolitanisms that charge her imagination. The SBW passes the record book, like a talking stick, onto the stage floor. She performs chords in winged, tongued epics of black, feminist futures for the whole village to imagine and to plot. We are held in rapt attention, defying distraction, in the solo performance of her multitudes.

INTRODUCTION

E. Patrick Johnson and Ramón H. Rivera-Servera

The anthology *solo/black/woman* brings together seven solo performance texts by a trailblazing cohort of feminist performance artists of the African diaspora, accompanied by critical essays about their work, and interviews with the artists by leading scholars of black feminist performance. This multigenerational group includes veteran performers Robbie McCauley and Rhodessa Jones, whose careers helped shape the booming field of monologue-based solo performance art in the 1980s; theater practitioners Nancy Cheryll Davis-Bellamy and Edris Cooper-Anifowoshe, who have assumed solo voices as significant aspects of their trajectory as ensemble artists at community, university, and professional venues from the 1980s onward; critically acclaimed performer Sharon Bridgforth, who pushed the boundaries of the practice in the 1990s; and, emerging young artists Stacey Robinson and Misty DeBerry, who continue to mine the wealth of possibilities and directions this realm of performance activity might engender. The collection showcases the range of aesthetic approaches as well as thematic foci undertaken by black feminist solo performers over the past thirty years. It also introduces key concepts and approaches to the understanding of this significant body of work. The publication includes a DVD of video samples for each of the performances documented, discussed, and analyzed within.

This publication is the product of a performance-based editorial process. Generously funded by the Mellon Foundation's Universities and Their Presses program, Northwestern University Press, and Northwestern University's School of Communication, the Performance Encounters Series out of which *solo/black/woman* emerged sought to develop processes of publication about performance that could integrate productively the challenges of documenting live art, the scholarly and pedagogical goals of publication, and time-based media platforms. We saw this as a unique opportunity to develop an ambitious performance documentation and analysis project that relied on the "performance encounter" as a mode of knowledge production. As co-curators and coeditors whose own scholarship has been shaped by our own encounters with the beauty, richness, urgency, pleasure, and political promise of black feminist performance, we sought to produce substantive exchanges between performers, scholars, and audience members at our campus and the community-at-large that could mine the opportunity to stage and document these performances and collectively develop discourse around them in the very liveness of the shared event. The result was a publication plan that centered on performance as both the object and the method of study.

Over the course of four years, we invited each of the artists included in this volume to present their solo performances as part of the Department of Performance Studies public programs season. We commissioned scholars in the field of black feminist and queer performance to attend the public showcases, lead postperformance talk-backs, and formally interview the artists or develop a critical essay about the performance witnessed as part of the series. We approached the short residencies by artists and scholars on our campus as our publication laboratory, staging conversations in performance spaces and classrooms, coffee shops and restaurants, intent on fostering deep dialogue and engagement with the multiple voices that intersected with each respective piece. All the performance texts, interviews, essays, and video samples included in this volume result from the shared few days of the performance residency. That is, they all represent different ways of documenting, reflecting upon, and analyzing the same performance event. In doing so, we do not pretend to fix performance or even fetishize the singularity of the "unique version" of the art object. Instead, we are invested in advancing a multi-vocal and multi-perspectival approach to performance that is cognizant of the partiality of any single source and the richness of their interrelation.

The insistence on the encounter with each of these performances in the liveness of the staged production and cognate programming is also born out of an investment in securing the viability of this work in the form it was conceived, in circulating it among audiences as it was intended, and in sustaining the performer's practice. In this sense, the archival efforts of the publication were also conceived to exercise each of these women's significant performance repertoires before an audience. In fact, some of the pieces included here (Rhodessa Jones and Sharon Bridgforth) were actually reperformed for inclusion in this collection after having been retired or significantly reconceived. Other pieces were reworked in the process of editing and rehearsal that the invitation to participate in this project initiated (Robbie McCauley).

Even though the solo performer appears to be the only body on the stage, she is never alone. Performance, as many of us have argued, invests in primarily collective experiences that far exceed the binary plurality of the performer/audience relationship. It is in large part the intention of this collection to situate each performance within its social world, to understand how the women artists whose work you will encounter here emerge from, develop work in relationship to, and labor to sustain or form communities around black experience from a feminist, and at times queer, perspective. But our work on *solo/black/woman* was also about recognizing, and at times extending, the already existing networks of influence, mentorship, and support among exponents of solo black feminist performance in the United States and those who study it. It is in hopes that the reader might find in this publication an abundance of models from which to conceive and sustain black feminist performance practices as well as a variety of examples on how to rigorously engage these works in scholarly, activist, and pedagogical contexts that we imagine the "encounters" that constitute this project as continuing, multiplying.

It is the longevity of a contested "tradition" but also the vitality, versatility, and innovation of contemporary practice, already intimated in the multigenerational and formal range of the practice evidenced in this volume, that we believe solo black feminist performance demands our consideration as an indispensable subgenre of performance art. It is our contention that the fields of theater and performance studies have yet to sufficiently engage both the archives and repertoires of black feminist solo performance. To our knowledge, *solo/black/woman* is the first publication devoted to black feminist solo performance. However, as we explain in the section that follows, the women included in this volume are part of a long history of black women who have practiced solo performance in the United States.

The work of black women performers, playwrights, and critics in the African diaspora represents a diverse and critical component of black arts and letters. Although often overshadowed by the work of their male counterparts, black women artists' and critics' contributions to the black aesthetic reflect a deep and abiding commitment to the liberation of black people in general and to black women in particular. Given the policing of black literary production from the late eighteenth century in the context of slavery to the late nineteenth century in the context of Jim Crow, however, black women's artistry did not circulate far beyond its community's boundaries, forestalling for decades what would eventually become a wellspring of proto-feminist artistry. While there were exceptions like Phyllis Wheatley's book of poetry, *Poems on Various Subjects, Religious, Moral* (1773) and Harriet Jacob's novel *Incidents in the Life of a Slave Girl* (1861), both of these were *literary* examples rather than plays or performance scripts. Black women playwrights and performers would not get recognition until much later.

The Harlem Renaissance of the 1920s was especially significant to the emergence of black women performers who received critical attention. The genre of music in particular provided a platform for solo work by women. Josephine Baker, Gladys Bentley, Jackie "Moms" Mabley, Bessie Smith, Billie Holiday, and a host of others enjoyed great success during this period, which demonstrated that black women could not only enjoy commercial success, but also write and produce their own work. Baker and Bentley in particular, whose acts included dance and skits, represented an early model of solo performance work by black women that incorporated elements of theater during a time when music was one of the few vehicles for black female solo work. These two women performers also pushed the boundaries of performance through their appropriation of racist stereotypes in the case of Baker, and gender play in the case of Bentley. Similarly, Jackie "Moms" Mabley, who enjoyed a fifty-year career in standup comedy, pushed boundaries as the first to do lesbian-themed comedy (perhaps a prototype for the standup of contemporary black lesbians like Wanda Sykes). And while black women playwrights were beginning to produce important work and gaining more recognition during this period, the genre in which black women creative artists flourished was fiction. For example, fiction writers such as Georgia Douglass, Nella Larson, Alice Dunbar-Nelson, Jessie Fauset, and Zora

Neale Hurston eventually became part of the black literary canon. The only exception was Hurston's play *Color Struck* (1925) and cowritten play *Mule Bone* (1930), with Langston Hughes, neither of which enjoyed commercial success.

Indeed, it was not until the 1950s and 1960s that the voices of black women playwrights begin to reach wider audiences and enjoy mainstream commercial success and crossover appeal. For example, Alice Childress's play *Trouble in Mind* won an Obie Award for best off-Broadway production in 1956. The watershed moment, however, came in 1959 when Lorraine Hansberry's *A Raisin in the Sun* became the first play written by a black woman to be produced on Broadway and to win the New York Drama Critics Award (paving the way for Lydia Diamond, Katori Hall, and Suzan-Lori Parks to be part of another "first" over fifty years later when all three had their plays produced on Broadway at the same time in 2011). This was followed by the success of Adrienne Kennedy's *Funnyhouse of a Negro* in 1964, which also won an Obie from *The Village Voice* for most distinguished play. All of these plays deal with racism in some form or fashion, whether it is the racism of theater itself in *Trouble in Mind*, housing discrimination and upward mobility in *Raisin*, or internalized racism in *Funnyhouse*. The key difference between plays such as these and those written by black men of this period, however, is each of them has an implicit feminist bent. Fueled both by the Black Arts Movement and feminist movement of the 1960s civil rights era, black women in particular were empowered to speak specifically to the intersections of race and gender in a context in which they confronted sexism within the civil rights and black arts movements and racism and classism within the broader feminist movement. Black women's artistic production during this period, then, catalyzed a critique from within and without, generating a powerful platform upon which to codify black feminist performance.

Much of this push for inclusion vis-à-vis artistry came from feminists of color, especially black and Latina activists—some of whom were also lesbian—who felt a particular urgency about the place of women in the struggle for equal and civil rights. In addition to poets and fiction writers such as Sonia Sanchez, Nikki Giovanni, Jane Cortez, Alice Walker, and Toni Morrison, were critics/artists such as Cherríe Moraga, Barbara Smith, Gloria Anzaldúa, Audre Lorde, Cheryl Clarke, Jewelle Gomez,

Beverly Smith, bell hooks, and Michelle Wallace among others. It was in this context that Ntozake Shange's choreopoem/play *for colored girls who have considered suicide when the rainbow is enuf* emerged. First performed at a women's bar, the Bacchanal, in Berkeley, California, *for colored girls* went on to be produced off-Broadway at the Anspacher Public Theater in 1976 and then on Broadway at the Booth Theater later that year, receiving a Tony nomination for best play. Shange's play is critical to any history of black feminist performance not only because of its explicit focus on the plight and rage of black women, its commercial success, and its critique of black male sexism, but also because of its shattering of the genre of what constitutes a "play" by bringing together twenty poems performed by seven women actors whose "characters" are simply a color of the rainbow (for example, "Lady in Red"). Each "Lady" tells of her struggle through poetry, music, and dance. Now considered a classic, *for colored girls* empowered a whole generation of black women artists to employ performance as a vehicle for social change and to push the boundaries of what constituted black theater. It is no coincidence, for example, that Robbie McCauley, whose work is featured in this volume, was a member of the original cast of *for colored girls* on Broadway, starring in the role of "Lady in Red." It is also no coincidence that Shange's work has a major influence on the work of other artists included in this volume, such as Stacey Robinson and Sharon Bridgforth, despite the fact that *for colored girls* is not a solo performance. Nonetheless, the chorus of voices of black women's experiences in *for colored girls* is a template for these solo artists to use their own bodies to embody multiple characters to render the multiplicity of their gender's oppression and/or liberation. In this way, black women solo artists' work in particular disrupts the "solo" versus "multiple" cast dichotomy, suggesting that black women share experiences based on their race and gender that are both unique and universal.

Over the past forty years black women performance artists have continued to build upon this rich history of black feminist performance—some explicitly embracing the "feminist" moniker while others either disavowed that characterization of their work or left such a designation to critics. Explicitly drawing on black feminism, scholar/artist Omi Joni Jones actually modeled how to embody theory in her solo show *sista docta*, which chronicles the racism and sexism she has experienced in the academy. The show's very title, with its use of the black vernacular spelling and connotation of "sister," juxtaposed with "docta," announces its feminist politics by calling attention to the irony that there are so few black women Ph.D.s. On the other hand, critically acclaimed actress, playwright, and professor Anna Deveare Smith has a body of work such as *Fires in the Mirror* and *Twilight: Los Angeles* that does not explicitly focus on women as much as race relations; yet, she is perhaps the best known of all solo black women theater practitioners. Nonetheless, Smith's politically charged shows certainly paved the way for younger black female solo artists like Sarah Jones, who has plays like *Women Can't Wait!* that focus on the oppression of women and others, or like *Bridge and Tunnel* that focus on the immigrant experience in the United States, but nonetheless has a strong cast of women characters. Whatever the case, the artists of today are indebted to those women who came before them in carving out a space for their work to exist.

It is also important to note how feminists have provided a space for such work to occur. For example, the grassroots activism of feminists of color provided venues for artists like Sharon Bridgforth to debut their work—not in commercial venues but in community spaces where audiences identified with and were affirmed by the work—while the early commercial success of Kennedy and Shange paved the way for someone like Whoopi Goldberg, whose one-woman show, *Whoopi,* debuted on Broadway in 1985 and for which she won a Tony. In between community and commercial venues are academic and local theater venues, where black feminist performance has historically been supported and has thrived. The academic tour circuit has helped propel and sustain black women's artistry as a pedagogical tool to introduce students to feminist theater and/or black feminism; and local and regional theaters, often started and run by black women artists, help incubate new work and sustain the archive. Each of the artists featured in *solo/black/woman* is a product of this history but represents the shifts and divergent interests of her individual historical moment; nonetheless, each artist's work sustains a focus on honoring the complexities of black women's experiences in the African diaspora.

To demonstrate the range of experiences and perspectives over the course of three generations of women, we have arranged this volume chronologically. That is, we begin with the most senior of the artists and end with the most junior. This arrangement is less about a focus on the artist's age as much as it is about establishing how one artist's work responds to a specific historical moment and how it in some cases cracks open a space for a successor's work to pick up where she left off.

We begin with Robbie McCauley, a pioneer of the genre who, as we indicated, appeared in the first Broadway production of *for colored girls.* Her body of solo work is always semiautobiographical and deals primarily with the history of her family within a broader context of the experiences of black people in the African diaspora. Her show *Sally's Rape,* for example, deals with the rape of McCauley's great-great-grandmother, who was a slave in Georgia. Like *Sally's Rape, Sugar* also deals with a trauma to McCauley's family, but this time one that she carries inside her body. While the show is about her struggle with diabetes, McCauley places the disease in the larger context of black people's relationship to the history of sugar and slavery. Sandra Richards's essay, "I've Got the Sweetest Hangover," amplifies McCauley's engagement with this history and focuses on how her body's presence holds and averts history in each performance of the show.

Rhodessa Jones has been performing for over forty years, but for the past thirty years she has been primarily concerned with working with incarcerated women through her Medea Project: Theater for Incarcerated Women, which she founded in 1989. Her show *Big-Butt Girls, Hard-Headed Women* grew out of her work with these women and chronicles her first encounter with incarcerated women when she began working in prisons as an aerobics instructor. Lisa Biggs's essay, "In the Space Between Living and Dying," discusses how Jones uses the show to represent incarcerated women as human and how play in particular provides a space for hope where little exists.

Although born in the Midwest in Detroit, Nancy Cheryll Davis-Bellamy has spent most of her career in Los Angeles where she founded the Towne Street Theatre in 1992, an African American community theater company devoted to producing work that effects social change and adapting classic African American literary texts for the stage. Originally produced as an ensemble adaptation of Nella Larson's 1927 novella *Passing* at Towne Street Theatre, Davis-Bellamy's *Passing Solo* embodies both of the main characters in the novel, Irene Westover Redfield and Clare Kendry Bellew, who both pass for white. While highlighting the explicit racial issues of skin color and self-hatred, Davis also animates the subtle subtextual sexual tensions bubbling at the surface of these two women's relationship that refracts a different "color" of passing. Bryant Keith Alexander's essay "Performing *Passing* and *Passing* as Performance" focuses on the psychology of performance, "the things that motivate how people think and how their cosmologies of knowing inform their behaviors." In so doing, Alexander attends to how Davis-Bellamy's performance amplifies how passing is not only the achievement of aspiring to whiteness, but also about escaping the constraints of blackness through tactical maneuvering and performance.

Another theater practitioner who turned to solo performance in the 1990s, Edris Cooper-Anifowoshe, developed her national profile as a director of theater. Her turn to solo performance was meant to generate a more intimate look at theater from an insider's perspective and more specifically her own through recounting her "adventures" in the world of theater training and in the profession. Thus, *Adventures of a Black Girl in Search of Academic Clarity and Inclusion* is an autobiographical meditation on how Cooper-Anifowoshe negotiates her desires of becoming a theater practitioner and scholar with her family's desire for her to be a respectable black person. Confronting the racism in the academy and the class cleavages in black communities, she seeks "clarity and inclusion" in both. Renée Alexander Craft's essay "How Does It Feel to Be a Problem?" suggests that *Adventures* is a rant against the marginalization of black aesthetics and experience from the American theatrical canon and that that critique is engaged through a postmodern performance aesthetic to layer her broader commentary about the experience of a black girl in a postsegregation America.

Although she began her career as primarily a poet and short-story writer, Sharon Bridgforth, highly influenced by the work of Laurie Carlos and others in the theatrical jazz aesthetic, turned to performance scripts as her primary mode of production. Bridgforth's work is deeply steeped in African cosmology, especially Yoruba religion, and African American worship practices such as conjuration, spirit possession, and the yet unborn are almost always featured. Her work is also decidedly queer and blurs the boundaries between the sacred and the profane, the spiritual and the sexual. This is the case in *delta dandi*, a weaving of poems, monologues, and songs that pursue the collective experience of

African American grief through the character "girl," a child who belongs to the spirit world. Stephanie Batiste's essay "Aquanova" understands Bridgforth's *delta dandi* under the rubric of the theatrical jazz aesthetic where dramatic action is rendered episodic, layered, contrapuntal in order to render a character like "girl" both specific and universal. According to Batiste, the multiplicity of voices "accomplish the capturing, collapsing, and extension of time such that the past, present, and future exist in the same moments, words, and gestures."

Playwright and performer Stacey Robinson is a New York–based artist who has also worked with Sharon Bridgforth and others within the theatrical jazz aesthetic. In *Quiet Frenzy* Robinson tells the story of LaShonda, who is still mourning the sudden death of her sister from a car accident and who, during a psychotic break, enters into a world where she encounters strangers, spirits, and magic—a journey she must take to become whole again. In her analysis Nadine George-Graves attends to the ways in which Robinson's body works semiotically in the performance space to deepen the connection between how the specific memories of loss narrated in LaShonda's story reverberate with the longer history of black trauma.

The youngest of our artists, Misty DeBerry is a Chicago-based performer who developed first as a performance poet whose work explores gender-based violence. Her solo performance work allows her a platform to integrate her activist and aesthetic interests, as well as her commitment to social advocacy for the disenfranchised—especially black girls and women. Thus, we see in *Milkweed* the story of three queer black women who are survivors of sexual abuse. Spun together through the omniscient narrator, Monarch, these stories of Bernadette, Stain, and Glow render a tale of trauma, struggle, but ultimately, hope and resilience. Francesca Royster's essay focuses specifically on performance as a mode of redressing past violence because of its focus on the body. She suggests that DeBerry "explores the ways that the experience of violence is always being processed in the body, that the body's knowledge must be trusted as we make sense of these experiences, and as we transmogrify them in our healing."

This volume emphasizes the performance encounter, in which meaning-making happens in the moment of performance. Improvisation, revelation, and communion all become possible during the encounter between a performer and her audience. The critical essays presented here are based on the live performances. Thus, in some instances, lines as they are quoted in the essays will differ from lines as they appear in the printed versions of the plays (or may not be found at all).

solo/black/woman

SUGAR
A WORK-IN-PROGRESS

Robbie McCauley

PRODUCTION HISTORY

Sugar was first performed in Boston, Massachusetts, by ArtsEmerson in January 2010. It was directed by Maureen Shea, with set design by Mirta Tocci, and music composed and performed by Chauncey Moore. Previous versions of the play were performed in Evanston, Illinois, at Northwestern University's Alvina Kraus Studio in October 2008 and at the John Warfield Center for African and African American Studies, University of Texas, Austin in February 2009.

PROLOGUE

LECTURE THOUGHTS

[*A podium or music stand is available way over left with a chair, a stool, and two tables. Up center is a table with covered boxes, down right of it one with a bag, avocado, sharp knife, and brown bread. A stool is up left, with a chair down left. Stage light is rising. House lights are dim. We hear Mick Jagger's recording of "Brown Sugar,"* ROBBIE *grooving singing dancing speaking with it.*]

ROBBIE: Shoot! I gotta focus on the lecture [*though she continues to groove*]. The three diabetes *d*'s . . . depression, denial, drink . . .

Triangles again, sugar, slaves, and rum

Life is bigger than biography
Sugar more than sweet . . .

The politics of sugar—the seduction of nations, of women, the wedding of chocolate, sugar, sex, with Africa, the Americas . . . and Europe

[*Music fades out.*]

SCENE 1

SWEET AND SOUR

[*Lights change to find* ROBBIE *talking to herself, sitting on the stool up left, periodically stretching.*]

ROBBIE: Laurie, me and our deep dark brother poet friend argued all night at the Orchidia (Ninth Street and Second Avenue early 70s Lower East Side) about Mick Jagger's song—us saying we'd take public praise of our magic beauty from whomever . . . ! but that was way back . . . [*Stands*] when me and Laurie would have nothing to do with who owned who as people to love, before Zake had us considering suicide, before our consciousness came of [*dancing images of map and body*] Columbus bumping into Santo Domingo looking for sugar in India and the rape of black women . . . understood as the rape of land for sweet, sweet O-ooo-Babybaby brown sugar, raped away from our lives, which became more than a metaphor which is what the brother, who later became my deep dark brown sugar daddy (whose poems I lost in the Colonnade the night I danced out loud on the table), was talking about.

[*She lies down.*]

I came to New York in 1965, the year aspartame was discovered by accident by a chemist—aspartame—180 times sweeter than sugar, and seemed to have no calories. I was 120 pounds back then with very skinny legs. [*Sits up.*] I can't start with Mick Jagger that song too controversial Upsouth. W/black poets in late night bars. Down South Black people busy couldn't "get no satisfaction"—Otis Redding.

[*She goes over to magazines.*]

[*To audience*] These magazines say all kinds of things . . . especially in Boston . . . I need four people in the audience to participate, four different sections.

[*She picks four different people from four different areas of the audience and asks them if they agree to answer her question. She improvises with the four people until she's satisfied they understand how to participate.*]

Answer this question with one word without using the word "good" or "bad."

I'll repeat that instruction: Answer this question with one word without using the word "good" or "bad."

[*Improvise clarifying the instructions, explaining that this is not a riddle, but that participants should speak the word from their guts.*]

OK, here's the question: What do you think of the American war with Iraq?

[*She repeats the words, making poetry and comments on making performance out of charged material.*]

[*There is a light at the stool where she stands formally reciting.*]

> At the Colonnade
> I was a terrible drunk
> no romance at all
> except for the night in the Colonnade
> when I lectured on the table, lost his poems, and took off my top.
> After, like all the others, he said he loved her best then,
> like all the others insisting I open something never closed,
> Wishing I'd give I'd give away my bits of freedom . . . all the violations I participated in . . . ?
> He and I knew we were killing each other.
> His poems.
> My life.
> His mother, the angel, fed me homemade cake
> told me to get away while I could,
> And my blood sugar didn' eem rise.

The men love drama, opera, tears. The first husband banged on my door so hard she called the police on a Black man . . . he laid on me after. I trusted myself. They did not kill him. He went away forever of course. What did he expect . . . with all the unspoken storms in my father's house?

I was only intellectual. A bang in the body, and thrusting like horses, all I needed and rage released.

Sex is different from kindness she always knew.

And shame more difficult than guilt.

Sugar carries shame.

The second husband, needed late night donuts from New York delis and my morning sugar'd be thick enough to suck out my teeth.

His extra women who had no shame gave me earrings, advice, and other gifts as if we were in some other country.

Doctors who'd never walked the swinging ropes kept pushing me on balance. What were they thinking as I found my way across mountains over deep waters?

No longer able to be rescued, I took charge, inspired by one of the extras who told me, "Diabetics sleep a lot."

SCENE 2

THINKING OUT LOUD

ROBBIE: Light change!

[*She is thinking out loud to audience.*]

In Minnesota I've had the scariest insulin shocks. Maybe it's the rigor/vigor it takes to live here. I hate those two words. They sound too much like nigger, like being required to work too hard just to live. Somebody just wrote a book giving white people the right to say that word, probably somebody who . . . that's all he could think to do . . . In universities things can get like that. I know.

[*She performs a recognition dance.*]

In Columbus, Ohio, there are over a million Black people with diabetes, many living in the neighborhood known as Near East. Columbus has the uneasy designation, the Black diabetic capital of the world. I didn't do the counting, so sue me for what I believe and accept. In Columbus, Georgia, my sweet cousin. Too much too soon to talk about. Question: How come more Black people with diabetes are disproportionately amputated? Disproportionately die. She loved "Dance of the Flowers." Department Slavery is unforgiveable.

Sister Julia in Ohio told how she was driving one day, and in the hospital the next day with a sore foot, and they were telling her she had to have it amputated. Well, first she was in shock, and she told it better than me.

[*In Ohio* JULIA *appears and tells her story.*]

ROBBIE: Now me, I'm not so much for religion. I prefer common decency. But too many things from my Christian background call me up. Even Marx himself said, *Religion is the sigh of the oppressed creature, the heart of a heartless world, and the soul of soulless conditions. It is the opium of the people.*

He said a lot more about stuff, that has been misquoted and badly executed, but I'm not here to go there. I know that traditional religion takes over when I fly. When the plane starts sinking and jumping, I do not pray, "From each according to his ability to each according to his need," I say O Lord, Jesus!

Speaking of decency—[ROBBIE *sits down on edge of stage right.*] Brother in Ohio . . . He said, [*becoming witness*] I hate this disease. It invaded my body without permission. It is an insidious, creeping tiresome thing. I did nothing to make this happen. I did everything they ask, and I was attacked anyway. I can't manage it. It goes up and down. I lose one hundred pounds, I exercise. I no longer have the disease for a while, and then for no reason it comes back. I hate it. And it has the unmitigated gall to attack my paltry sex life. And they tell me I have to take little pills (which I will take!). Just this morning I thought about going down to my car, turning it on, and playing my favorite music, but nobody would believe I wanted to die if I played that song, but I thought about that this morning, but then I thought I'd have to take my dog with me, 'cause nobody could take care of my dog like me, and I couldn't do that.

[*Light change.* ROBBIE *crawls to chair downstage left.*]

Anyway, the first one in Minnesota came in January '95, when I woke up and crawled to the refrigerator and drank some juice before taking my blood sugar—to find out that sucker was eighteen. [*Sits on chair.*] How I live through the brittle brutality is beyond me. Other times were even more dramatic. Way back when I drank, I barely remember what happened. Drunken blackouts in the middle of insulin shocks were the worst. I don't know if anybody's done any research on diabetes and drinking. Ever' body knows when I went . . . I went to AA and they told me to cure alcoholism I had to stop drinking. Now I don't know if I was an alcoholic, I always said after that I stopped drinking 'cause of the sugar. I stopped drinking right away so I wouldn't have to go to the meetings. The meetings confused me, me being a professional confessional type "a performer."

[*Light change.* ROBBIE *stands by left chair.*]

Standing on the bus one day, two thousand somethin', going to Boston, the Fungwah bus, fifteen dollars from New York at 1 P.M., had no business standing, but we're just crossing the Manhattan bridge. It's a great bus. I had on my fake ghetto cap, still not dressing my age. No matter where I am I act like I'm at home, and the driver . . . people call it the Chinatown bus because it goes from Chinatown to Chinatown Boston and New York. (I am just as racist as anyone.) It's quite an enterprise. I was on one of the larger ones, before I'd got a smaller bus, not many people, 4 P.M., twenty-five dollars. So on the one o'clock, fifteen-dollar bus, me acting like I'm at home . . . the driver like the thrillingly rebellious underground working class speed demon I have no business still fantasizing about, hit the brakes on the bridge, and I hit the floor on my back. [*Does a fall.*]

[*Light change. She grabs back to center.*]

I shouldn't be here. I'm older than all the wars. The reason I keep living is my stubbornness. Mother'n'em would've given up on me long ago. The day I told Daddy I had diabetes was the day he tore up the mimeographed Marxist flyers I'd brought home. I saw the righteous rage of an American patriot. Picking up the bits of paper, I looked in his face and said, I went to a clinic today and they told me I had diabetes. He said, you ain't got no diabetes, and he never mentioned it again. My mother's brother, Bud died at seventeen, or was it fourteen. The only boy so many myths, loved football so much he went out in a damp T-shirt to carry water for the real players at Spencer High, and got pneumonia. Whenever Mother talked about the death of her only brother, she only expressed sympathy for the nurse who had to go tell Ma Willie that her only son was dead.

[ROBBIE *falls with gesture showing inability to balance.*]

The first thing I heard was "your back!" "My arms," I hollered. A clean-cut white guy with earrings all over his face and two young women who'd been speaking Spanish stood weaving on the bumpy bus and pulled my arms, bless their hearts, hurt so bad I wanted to die, knew I wasn't dying, wanted to die of embarrassment. Some people from the back of the bus say, "You alright?" Stretched my arms out, "I'm a dancer," I said. From the back somebody say, "You better dance yourself to court." Sister wit her say, "I know what you talking 'bout." Nobody bothered to be a witness. Thank God I'd made a sandwich.

The cowboy/Chinese bus driver pulled over, hit the brakes way softer off the bridge. At least he's speaking English I thought just as racist as anyone. "I'm a dancer," I said still delirious. He drove a little more slowly. I did Alexander Technique thinking through, through my body. By the time my back started to feel longer and wider my brain was back and I checked my blood sugar which was 149 . . . , put my thumb on my pulse, figured vitals were OK. I shot up. "You're cool," one of the girls said, "my aunt's a diabetic." That's when I wept.

[*Light change up center. She pulls out needles, prepares insulin, shoots up during this story.*]

When my friend Nikos first met me, he thought I was a junkie. I remember flirtin'. He didn't tell me till years later. It was about 1987 and we were on a bus to march to Washington against the war in Nicaragua. It was my last big last march until appearing with a candle in Boston against Iraq. I found out later he wasn't straight. Now a friend I couldna got through a lot of wars without. Anyway back then, he told me later I pulled out my needle on the bus. I don't remember even doin' because it was always such a no-no, but he said the bus was dark, and another was helping me, 'cause I had to hold the needle up to the light to see the numbers on the like I'm doing now, but when I think about it, now I do it every now and then, especially on buses because tryin' to get up to get to the bathroom is dangerous. I think people should just do it discreetly when they have to, and it should be accepted, like nursing babies.

[*She moves to table over right, takes brown bread out of bag, cuts avocado in half, and puts sandwich together. By end of section she is improvising about how good avocados are. There is also orange juice available.*]

Ever since I can remember, I wanted to eat just salad. I wanted raw green things to clean out my body, which was slimy dark green and red mud inside. Instead I ate hot brown food, even the greens were too wet and full of fat white meat. Chocolate cake, chocolate ice cream, peaches and figs, dark bird legs. Wet bitter red drippings later in New York seemed to be the be-all, but I was looking for greens, dry and clean . . . I love avocado. I once lost a boyfriend over avocado 'cause he couldn't stand it.

[*She walks to chair downstage left, where she talks and eats.*]

The first diets said I could have a drink a day, said I could have a scoop of vanilla ice cream, said I could have a slice of angel food cake. The thing about diabetes is that you're addicted to sugar, like alcoholics are addicted to liquor, so you can't have any. America wants to keep people addicted. It helps capitalism.

[*She yoga stretches in all three spaces. Lights follow.*]

You know I was supposed to be dead . . . I was a child with it in Georgia. Used to have to pee all the time. From the first if it wasn't for the old ladies wondering if I didn't have sugar, 'cause my sores healed so slow, Ida never suspected. Didn't nobody want to hear nothing 'bout no chronic conditions for children, nothing where the children might die, just let it happen and blame on the Lord's clock. Just work till "One day she came home sat down and died." I had it a long time, but my mother fed us good—three squares a day. I'm so glad I ain't get diagnosed till I paid for it outta college. The Negro folks that raised me much as I was cared for and much as I was loved, the ignorance and despair woulda cut me up. Outta college I began to take care o' myself, like I saw fit, realized I wasn't tired and lazy all the time, or had some sex disease which all I was tested for. Once we visited Old Aunt Carrie who lived at the top of the hill where we waved at the train, where I knew that I'd be on that train one day. Aunt Carrie used saccharin. Random connections to trains and outdoor bathrooms made me know I had to go to college to get out, not to change the world, but then came the rest of the world and a sense of history.

Don't worry, I'm not gon' tell everything. I came mainly to tell on the people who for all those years ignored us in the medical profession. I do pretty good now on my own accord. I refused to let folks let me die. The first clinic I went to, I saved up for, and they had to take me because I insisted. Then I was given pills with out of control brittle diabetes, which back then everybody knew most often you needed insulin for, and was told after I ended up half dead in D.C. General because as everybody knows Providence Hospital told my father they couldn't let me in there even though I was dying, and my father jumped so bad with the people because he was saying "my child" thinking of his seven sisters and brothers who hadn't made it to adulthood because of neglect by the system even though that was one of the reasons their family stayed in the army—after they took me to D.C. General the first of many times cold in the ambulance, I overheard a nice doctor saying, "They should have given her insulin, she seems OK, they don't like to give Negroes hypodermic needles."

But I found it everybody! The *New England Journal of Medicine* told it, say the medical profession all those decades treated us different! Well, duh! But I'm glad it's on paper, because when I have to go for care now, people look at me, check my age, sometimes call other folk to look at me. A [*she mumbles her age playfully*] Black woman with diabetes and heart disease . . .

Daddy's heart it seems came down to me, with all its trouble. He didn't take care of his, but my pressure always been good. When I say that to the doctors, they look at me askance, 'cause black people and high blood goes together in their minds. It is pretty amazing how they have ways of looking at us. But the ways they've had of not looking at us is what I want to talk about.

[*She walks to podium.*]

White racism as we've said before is a condition . . . like diabetes. You may be born with a tendency for it, but you don't have to die of it. It can be managed. The symptoms come from excessive sugar, which is a metaphor for privilege. So balance the intake of privilege, and exercise the reality that white is not all that. [*to self*] Do metaphors have to logical?

[*She sits rocking downstage center.*]

I wanted, like my mother, to be stronger in old age. Had I been stronger, Ida stood stronger inside the contradictions of it, and let everybody know what need not happen. Ida looked whatchamacallum, can't say his name, the president who ain't, woulda looked him in the face and tol' him to shut up a long time ago, looked at 'em like the mythical ol' colored women I woulda been by now, used to do, woulda said we can change the world, look at us, still here, still clear, all the rhetoric would have served me, if it hadna been for Daddy's heart and the sugar and the wars, but myth is myth, and old time religion, the right thing to do, holding on, and keeping it real wins inside the harsh contradictions of brutal truth, real politics and dead children havin' me wake up weeping like my mother did that Wednesday September morning in 2001, not remembering the day before, both of us older colored women feeling like noncomplicit German grandmothers in 1938, ignoring the sound of so many trains, like any old women weeping in the middle of war.

[*Light change over right.*]

Is there a relationship between health and politics . . . ? The authorities, who own the future, now admit it's over. They know both China's capitalism and its medicine. My body is a city. I have stalked sidewalks with long white lovers, with panic and l'il deaths. Black cops harassed us just as well. The empirical fear of us has become an embodied phenomenon. My first poet love told me he feared himself. I keep surviving sugar and a breaking heart. If the future is over, maybe we can finally learn from the past. They're so connected, I'ont believe I can say no more till I fall down a minute.

[*Lights change all over off and on.*]

Once in Canada drunk at Stratford on the Avon . . . people there stood in lines to buy large amounts of liquor once a week. It was a semidry town with many drunks. Trying to kill myself, after being called names in the street, something I thought I was used to, I rode my bike into a tree. When I woke up in the hospital a soft hand was rubbing vitamin E oil on my face, all broken up. It will heal soon, she said. Afterwards I asked how much I owed. At the desk the people looked puzzled. Pay? Someone spoke to another. I'm working here I said, I'm from the U.S. She wants to pay someone said. So they wrote down some figures and said twelve dollars, and smiled at me as if they were doing me a favor. They were.

[*Light change, downstage center.*]

Now I am old in old-time terms, but my mother is over ninety, Aunt Jessie died at ninety-six, and Mother's older Sister Nell still wore high-heeled shoes till the day she died at eighty-nine, and alla the women in my family stayed pretty and active as they got up in age, so I didn't understand the little drag-ass energy going on with me. Of course sugar makes you tired.

[*Stalks about. Lights change.*]

One morning recently I got the swimming in the head in the bathroom. It was different from insulin shock or identifiable dizziness. I held onto the door frame like I was in an earthquake, which made me think heart. Then I thought, Shoot! I ain't dying in the bathroom. That's ugly. I went sat on the couch. I thought if I die now I want to be in the living room. I hate fear worse than anything, so I decided to let the whole thought of dying that day go.

Printed in New England, from all over the land. I am an aberration, it might as well have said. Black people were ignored, even by Black doctors . . . Black cops harassed us just as well. I keep surviving sugar and a breaking heart. Black people shoulda been over with after slavery time, and we keep doing/ getting better, but the forces against our survival are the added too now, now all kinds of folks are niggarized, whether they want to say so or not. I'm talking more about health care and global warming even though (let me say this loud) THE DISPARITIES REMAIN! If the future is over, maybe we can finally learn from the past.

[*Light change as* ROBBIE *changes clothes and goes to podium right, reads and comments. She lectures, trying to keep control.*]

[*Improv rant*] Sugar was first used way-ay-ay-ay back and way far away from here, Southeast Asia [*walks about as if on map*] five-somethin' another B.C. and somehow or another it spread to India. This was cane sugar. They knew about bees, but this was the honey without! Bees, Um huh. They said Darius, a Persian king invaded India, found sugar and kept where it came from a secret but exported it for . . . you know what . . . starts with a *p*, which any good capitalist in the room knows about [*Holds out her hand and invites an answer, giving clues . . . such as*] . . . what Assata Shakur always said was more important than people when she compared slavery to the emerging prison industry before that became popular knowledge . . . an alliteration . . . a saying with the same letter at the beginning of several words. In this phrase two *p*'s! What is the anti-imperialist phrase . . .?

P [*mimes large pile of money*] is more important than people . . . [*She improvises until someone guesses . . .*] Profit. So way back then sugar was being exported for profit, which is how I got to Mick Jagger's song . . . 'cause though he's talking about cotton, he's also talking about the seduction and exploitation of black women, and everybody knows that sugar and slavery and liquor—the sensual, the seductive, the rot and ruin, the struggle for balance that's hooked up with diabetes so pervades European colonization/civilization which can be learned in school to fix it for the future. Our bodies objectified! Otherwise we stay with the seduction and rot of sugar instead how diabetics learn to live—just a little sweetness makes a balance of power!

[*Drops to floor. Light change.* ROBBIE *comes downstage center.*]

My greatest pleasure is talking. So you can imagine the frustration I suffer because of the open places in my teeth now. Gingivitis is a symptom of my chronic disease, so is bad breath. My next greatest pleasure used to be sex, but the symptoms fucked that up, 'scuse the bad pun. I understand the brother from Ohio! I learned way too late that once the vagina is affected by the infections caused by the symptoms, it can never get better. This was finally stated in a pamphlet put out by women. That was the end of a regular thrust. I think it's very nice to talk, to talk about creative sex lives like this, but diabetes makes you very tired. I wish there were something like an easy natural Viagra-type thing for older diabetic women. Shoot, I'm old, but [*to audience*] . . . I AIN'T DEAD!

Now I want to ask another question.

Please answer with one word,
without using the word "yes" or "no."

Is this art . . . ?

Anybody can discuss that among yourselves.

[*Lights dim and audience is invited to dance. Otis Redding's "(I Can't Get No) Satisfaction" plays.*]

INTERVIEW WITH ROBBIE MCCAULEY

E. Patrick Johnson

So the title of your play is *Sugar*. Talk a little bit about why you chose this title.

I chose *Sugar* for this piece because sugar is how diabetes is described in my community. What's surprising is that because the word "sugar" is often linked to sweet that the condition of diabetes is often dismissed. And so just that sense of the contradictions of sweetness and rot has tensed in a good way, I was wondering what more I can say. All of my work in performance has been based on a firsthand story, often my personal story. What I am relating is that my personal and family stories are a way of looking at the bigger story. And I have been thinking about how to talk about diabetes through storytelling. I am not an expert but I am connected to my life and the stuff around my life. Being African American, I am very much aware of racism in so many aspects of American culture, and am trying to give voice to that. And I always knew that health care for us was not as it should have been. It was much later, after having made references in other performances to this struggle to survive personally with this irritation. I was doing a piece called *Love and Race in the United States* and it was about the subject of love and miscegenation. Within that piece, I started thinking about the relationship of my body to romance and sex. One thing that a lot of people recognize in men is that diabetes affects sexual function, but it also affects sexual pleasure in women. So I was coming up with metaphors around the seduction and discomfort and somehow they related to sugar and I started thinking about how sugar was so basic to slavery. We think of cotton, but the money, the big money was made on sugar, it was the triangular slave trade based on sugar. Sugar was gold. That is what Columbus was looking for. So I just started thinking of these rants and by accident. It was the early 2000s and it must have been after 2007 that I accidentally—and I think accidents are wonderful for work—I accidentally found a journal, the *New England Journal of Medicine,* and I picked it up and there was a whole acknowledgment by several medical professionals on disparities in health care around African Americans and it was official. It stated information on how the medical profession had devalued African American people. And there the words were, in the official journal. And so I'm constantly looking at the working-class sensibility and then the official story on class and race in the country. I was shocked and delighted at the same time to have this information. It was from an old magazine. That study was done in 1997. And since then there have been article after article after article. I think it was 2005 that the *New York Times* ran a whole series on diabetes, the spread of diabetes itself as well as around disparities. So the information was all there. Diabetes is persistent and long term among African Americans. Yes it is in the larger population. Yes it is a silent disease. Yes there is much more awareness around health disparities. But it is not my job to get the facts and be done with it. My thought was, "You are not going to get away, world, without knowing the story." And that sounds really big. It makes the world that comes to the performance, and the work that many of us do is the work of giving voice to silent conditions and diabetes is often been minimized as a problem because it just related to sugar. I started to think about my story and having had it since I was a child, now knowing what the symptoms were and having had caring and loving family, tensions though there were, I got through those early years with symptoms like having to go to the bathroom all the time, symptoms of getting tired all the time, not playing outside as long as I wanted to, and different little things. And as my family would say about me, "being evil" so there were moods related to it that we don't even talk about so much in diabetes. And so then I didn't discover till much later how to talk about what it felt like. So the work is a storytelling and a bit of a rant with information. So that is a long answer for how the piece got to be called *Sugar*.

Did diabetes run in your family?

Diabetes did not run in my immediate family—neither my mother nor my father. My father had a heart condition and that was the main focus and toward the end all kinds of other things came but I don't think he had diabetes, so it was unusual. That is one of the ways it was missed by me later. But then I had a cousin who died and I talk about this in the piece. And then I discovered there is controversy over whether diabetes is inherited and how much of it is based on what you do to get it because many people feel like you should just stop eating sugar and you wouldn't have it. But it is clearly genetic in that it comes from your genes, whether or not it is inherited is another question. It is one of those things that gets picked up over the years, and it is amazing how little just that information is known about. In general, people are silently walking around with the condition . . . even now. So the whole care of diabetes has to do with accepting that it is a condition that we can live with and one must do whatever necessary for one's individual case. Some people can control it with diet. All has to do with diet in one way or another and the treatment for it has changed tremendously over the years. But there also is controversy and both ignorance and knowledge that affects the condition and these are stories I also tell. I talk about it in the piece. I have done groups of storytelling with people in both the African American and other communities. Because the Americas were where the sugar industry developed and so the Latino communities, Native Americans, as well as all the Americas are very much affected by the condition. And I want to get more of those stories and we know that the worse of the diabetic conditions turned up in skin problems, blindness, amputations, and sexual dysfunction and I think that people will want to know to try to control it. However, in my case and I am sure in many others, people were not given this. If you are not valued then you don't get the information. And so this is what has also been part of the process.

Do you think there is a connection between slavery and the history of diabetes among black people?

I can't say scientifically that there is a connection between slavery and bad health but I don't think it would take a genius to make that case. The stress around our conditions, the stress not only of slavery, but the trauma and stress of all the ramifications of slavery continue to affect our health, I'm sure. My father's condition was part of his childhood rheumatic fever, and yet the tensions and his unmitigated rage at the system and yet, he was a whole person so a good father, working man, good person but he had all of that tension and rage that I have seen throughout African American male culture. Men and women express it in different ways. These are aspects of the culture that we can't deny and I am sure it is related to our rage from generation to generation even as things are changing. Things are changing because the information is being put out. Thank goodness for these reports, thank goodness for the civil rights work, for the arts work in terms of telling it like it is, all continue to make good change.

Is humor a way to channel all of that rage?

I'm funny. To me the contradictions are hysterical and I think that is one of the ways we have survived, with a sense of fun and celebration. This is old news for us but thank goodness we can continue. We can tell the most horrible stories and be cracking up. A lot of times people just don't understand that we are just falling out on stuff that seems horrific. I put it in terms of the contradictions because the contradictions are absurd and that kind of absurdity is a part of what attracts people to the theater. We do work that ordinary people do not envy. We tell the stories of actual people's lives. I'm interested in the range of presence, of the emphasis of my work as a teacher, as well as in my acting. To me my work is a performance space for enacting and using metaphor for a range of experiences—to be present with others and to show the range of emotions that are possible.

How does the performance shift from audience to audience and how does that affect how you move in the space?

Well again it is the range. I think of the work like music. Like jazz. Like different voice and open space. These are all modes and ways of thinking that I call out. I want to talk about this, I say, how can I do it? Maybe it is more like a drawing or an aria. Sometimes it is unconscious that things will go into different modes. You may not know that I am switching modes, I am not a singer so I will not really do an aria but I will focus myself in that mode. And I think it is the actor's voice, the range of the actor's voice is related to the range of emotions. So I structure performance from the content. This is what I want to talk about and this is the story I want to tell. Where do I put it? Do I leave it in the space so I can connect it? It is a way of organizing the improvisation and a way of thinking about how to place bits; it is, of course, influenced by jazz, by hip-hop, by what is around us, by what we come from, as most contemporary artists are, whether we know it or not.

So you really draw on African American religious and cultural traditions—like call and response, the rituals?

You know, it is ritual. It is about what happens in the moment. I like using the method of talking to the audience. I like hoping and praying. Traditional theater for me is just fine. And I work within that frame often but breaking that frame and blurring lines in traditional theater attract me more in performance work because it helps people to transform. And people have their story and I figure, either they cut it off or they will drip. So hopefully you will get to uncover things sometimes with audiences and if people don't sometimes leave, if people don't get upset, I get nervous.

I heard that *Sugar* is part of a trilogy.

It is not a trilogy. It goes on and on but I've done several works. The earlier works had to do with my father and my grandfather and my father's stories: My father and the wars. He was from a military family and my grandfather was a soldier and the honor of that so again, the contradictions. I was coming into adulthood during the Vietnam War and I had all of these contradictions. I had to realize that I couldn't just go out there from an especially noble family that throughout history has been connected to the military. I was dealing with my feelings against war at that time. In dealing with it another thing you find working in theater is that what you think you think is not exactly what you think. So I had to realize that in true American culture the military and contradictions come up a lot?! After 9/11, for instance . . . And then I did *Sally's Rape* where I wanted to have black and white people have a discussion about rape. My great-great grandmother had the same first name as Thomas Jefferson's slave, Sally Hemings. Because she was a slave, it is called rape in the official sense, so that was a dialogue about rape. So *Sugar* is a part of that. Things come up and connect one way or another. I don't really tell Sally's story, but refer to it. I use it as a commentary on race mixing and social commentary in this country and how it is not even deep anymore, I mean I didn't find it all that deep in terms of resistance. I guess by facing the fact that I was married to someone who was white and what I found and wanted to tell was that the story was not about difference, it was about the history. It was about the fact that people carry the history in their bodies and those people resist those kinds of labels because how can you think of somebody as a history. But I think on that angle, I am one American willing and able to talk about race and those charged terms and issues. Theater work helps.

How do you see the relationship?

I think what I like is the work, whatever I am into and interested in at the moment but each person who does work brings his or her own look. When I do traditional work, I want to find things that relate to certain interests that I have. A group that I have been working with in Boston is a group of actors who are mixed racially, children, adults and older people. We switch roles around, not for blind casting but for conscious casting. For instance we did *A Streetcar Named Desire* with Stanley and his men friends as African American and Hispanic; the landlady was African American because the neighborhood that they lived in was very diverse. Tennessee Williams himself says he used the term "multicultural" way back when he was writing because that was what the neighborhood was and I said, "How did I miss this?" But I kept Blanche and Stella as white women and I looked at the whole subject of what he wrote about class and the coming down of class, about Blanche and how it was being acted out in this black community and you know Stan was Polish. We didn't change a word and we still used Polish and it became a joke on the stage. They weren't playing, it was perceived that they were using the word Polish for blackness and it became more of the found identity for the play. And so I am interested in that.

Do you think changing the setting is effective?

I like that changing setting but also I like folks to make changes. We have always made changes. It is a thing that we do know. In terms of survival, we have to be able to change. We examine our lives and make images. We have to look and find joy, comic and tragic stories—so we do this well. We also have been very well educated on how to change, so I learned very early that we were not lacking. We know about the self-esteem issues that have become aspects of slavery. Education and intellect is huge in our identity. As much as we don't say it enough and don't teach it, don't drill it enough in our children. It is our system that is way behind. We are—and when I say "we," the big group of African Americans—we are all connected to the slave trade throughout the world. Slavery was the biggest employer up to now which brings us back to sugar. So we are all part of the story, which is also about survival. We have sometimes taken it all in and made it big and untouchable but the artists have always been there. So when you talk about art and change and progress, I think much has been written off, especially in writing, not only writing but being seen as writers, with plays and the like, excellent work. Still again, changing. If one could imagine the kind of work, the kind of performance that could be present in this culture if people of color had more encouragement to make work. How many of us can afford the time and space to allow stories and images to emerge and to play them, to help shift visions for audiences? But we keep on . . .

Do you see yourself more as an actor or a writer?

I see myself as a theater person and I don't mind the work. I like artists so I like to see myself as a theater artist and therefore different aspects are seen as art. Certain things become art and in turns out that sometimes it is acting, sometimes it is writing.

When did you come to that realization for yourself?

Oh it was such a long time ago. I think students are smarter now because there is so much information and exposure. So many have a sense of the creative mode that the actor is sometimes the creator of the work. So in that way I think they are smarter and more willing to work. I think that what is lacking is the knowledge of knowing nothing. And that that younger people and many of us are not trusting that there is more work that is not guaranteed so you find these students wanting to know how to do it, rather than a space to explore what they don't know.

Where do you see *Sugar* going? Is it finished?

Well, it is still definitely a piece in progress, I use that word to say that it is about progress but it is also in progress. This piece is in progress so I have no idea if it should ever have a beginning, middle, and end. It is framed but it still changes. So what I have heard with people who talk back that people do get affected and people get information and they are entertained and that is not something that I always wanted to happen. I don't know why, I mean why wouldn't you want to be entertained but now I like the idea of entertainment and even critically, people who have written about it in small presses and colleges, it is respectable and recognizable as performance art.

Why do you continue to perform the piece?

Well, sometimes you just have to do it, because the time is right, and sometimes people give you money, so you make the time. It is being talked about at Emerson and about being developed as a faculty piece so that would be a finished piece.

Ultimately, what do you want this piece to say?

So many of us have diabetes and it is inconvenient to our lives. I hope to help myself and others live better with it. Doing this performance helps me face how hard it is, and to keep trying to live better. I hope such can happen for others, and that any people can have a good time at the theater.

You've been doing solo work for a while now, but you have also done ensemble work, even appearing in the original cast of Ntozake Shange's now-canonical *for colored girls who have considered suicide/when the rainbow is enuf.* **Say a little bit about your experience working with an ensemble and how that is different from your solo work. Which do you prefer? Do you gain something different in one genre or the other?**

I started, of course, with traditional plays, at Howard University, but I always felt there was something left unexpressed by concentrating on the character work. I love grappling with the art of acting. When I had the privilege of working with Gloria Foster in Adrienne Kennedy's *A Movie Star Has to Star in Black and White,* she used the word "substitution" in rehearsal talk about work. I'm not sure what she meant, but I felt a wide opening in that perception from such a master. The work I realized is always ensemble, including the audience. The actor is never alone. The crew, house manager, and ushers are part of it. People all have different roles, different costumes. I ask students whom I coach in solo work, "Who is with you . . .?" Whether in the room or not. In ensemble work I note that you are always alone with others onstage. How do you make with that? I love other people's stories. But who am *I* in *their* story?

What do you see as the biggest challenge to black women artists today? Do you think that they face the same challenges they did say, thirty years ago, or have things opened up for them?

I hope I'm wrong, but I think barely. We're still pretty much tokens in commercial, or even experimental, theater. Where are our stories, really? There's so much fear now around taking risks, so we fall back on the familiar. Racism is challenged by theater helping people shift views. I think the future lies in our taking the reins, being not afraid of not doing what's expected, making more work, recognizing that we need not draw lines between the disciplines of theater so much. Some of the most exciting work in theater now is coming from actors who write . . . like . . . well, like us.

"I'VE GOT THE SWEETEST HANGOVER": ROBBIE MCCAULEY'S *SUGAR*

Sandra L. Richards

In 1976 Diana Ross crooned about an obsessive love, claiming that even if there were a cure, she wanted no remedy because "[she had] the sweetest hangover." Many other singers have subsequently copied or sampled the song, proclaiming a pleasurable addiction to love, money, or sex. Performance artist, actor, and director Robbie McCauley directly addresses the allure of sugar, warning at the outset of her new work that "sugar is more than sweet." In fact, with her generous and courageous performance in which she reveals her own struggles with sugar—the black vernacular term for diabetes—this disease assumes a visibility and specificity that it may not have had for those untouched by the disease. Some of the physical ravages, shame, and silence it inflicts are named and disarmed, and audiences come face to face with the historical as well as contemporary connections between sugar, pleasure, slavery, sexuality, medicine, and profit. By play's end spectators are left with the challenge of deciding whether they choose, like Diana Ross, to continue a national love affair with a sugar that softens the perceived impact of racism or fight its discursive whiteness through active commitment to equality, wherein human needs are honored and kept in a dynamic, always-precarious balance.

In *Sugar,* McCauley interlaces personal stories of coping with diabetes, with memories and interviews of other diabetics, angry disquisitions about disparities in medical treatment, history of the discovery of sugar, and political analysis of connections between the intimately personal and the collective. As even this brief description suggests, McCauley does not pursue a conventional dramatic structure that organizes events and thoughts into a logical progression building toward a climatic, pivot point and conclusion. Rather, she pursues what scholar Omi Osun Joni L. Jones terms a theatrical jazz aesthetic. Deploying principles derived from jazz, this aesthetic views human experience as holistic, operating in multiple registers at the same time, such that socially authorized or conventional binarisms—material versus transcendent, logical progression versus intuitive leap, commodified versus innovative, or individuality versus group cohesion—are often dissolved or allowed to remain in seemingly competitive challenge. Several rhythms, voices, and narrative segments may sound simultaneously or engage in dialogue that may not result in closure but in an interlock of competing energies. The conventional temporalities of past, present, and future are often scrambled and syncopated. Mastery of form and tradition battle with improvisation and virtuosic discovery. The process of artistic creation and play becomes as important—if not more than—the product. Both process and product are "embedded" in the social such that the work pushes beyond the formal space of performance to challenge how artist and public live their lives and potentially move toward what Jones calls "everyday habitual acts of freedom" (Jones, *Experiments*, 9).

What does a theatrical jazz aesthetic mean for critical study of *Sugar*? An appropriate critical approach acknowledges the operative organizing principles while seeking to communicate clearly with affective force. As Craig Werner asserts in probing the jazz foundations of August Wilson's dramas:

> Because the concept of the organizing thesis derives primarily from European analytical traditions, criticism organized around a central proposition risks repressing the chaotic potential—and thereby subverting part of the functionality of polyrhythmic texts . . . As Benitez-Rojo observes, the point of polyrhythmic discourse is not to destroy or replace binary discourses but to understand them as part of a larger chaotic context in which other voices sound freely. This formulation suggests the appropriateness of an additional, not an alternative, critical methodology based on the polyrhythmic formal structures of the oral tradition. (Werner, "August Wilson's Burden," 38)

In this essay, I deploy both analytic traditions, offering first a more logically structured review of biographical intertexualities and medical information in order to orient the reader. Then, following the oral tradition in which an artist's call is met with an audience response, I forego "thematic consistency" (Werner, "August Wilson's Burden," 38) to point to several moments of high energy and challenge. Finally, as is true of all critical approaches to art but is emphasized more in jazz, where presence is privileged, I recognize that my analysis is contingent: presence at a McCauley performance will certainly add other layers of interpretation and likely, complication, but what any audience collectively and individually experiences is impacted by the specific moment in which the performance unfolds between McCauley and her engaged spectators.

"A PERSONAL/BIGGER": REPETITION WITH A CRITICAL DIFFERENCE

Like all other musicians, jazz practitioners are expected to learn the repertoires of the outstanding performers who have come before them.[1] But in jazz, the musician is also expected to perform the historical repertoire in a distinctive manner that displays his own understanding of that past in the present moment and possible future. As witness to the performance, the jazz aficionado must therefore recognize the salute to history as part of her evaluation. Relatedly, feminist critics have emphasized the importance of biography in criticism, because such knowledge allows one to perceive "authorship as multiple, involving culture, psyche, and intertextuality."[2] Thus, knowledge of McCauley's background helps us to appreciate how she deploys her past to create singular new works.

Asked in a 1993 interview about her practice of weaving personal biography with history, McCauley explained:

> If I'm being personal, it doesn't work—unless I connect with larger concerns. I'm not interested in just my biography. I'm very much interested in how what is personal to me connects to other people. That makes it strong for me. And I actually believe people connect that way. (Tillman, "Robbie McCauley")

Her stance toward those "larger concerns" was shaped during some of the major social and avant-garde movements of the 1960s. Having grown up in various parts of the segregated South, McCauley moved to New York City in 1965, "the year aspartame was discovered by accident by a chemist—aspartame—180 times sweeter than sugar and seemed to have no calories." That year and those that followed were also a period when blacks were openly challenging mainstream society through the civil rights and black power movements; the escalating war in Southeast

Asia provoked increased protest in the United States and overseas; college students were also challenging their education through calls for the establishment of black and ethnic studies programs; and women were rejecting traditional gender roles in what would later become known as "second-wave" feminism. In the arts world, groups like the Living Theatre and LeRoi Jones's BART/S used theater to protest the war or demand black liberation; performance art emerged, focusing on the body and its idiosyncrasies as a way of deconstructing the status of the art object; theater practitioners like Joseph Chaikin of the Open Theater encouraged scripts devised from a merger of the actors' personal experiences, current events, and canonical texts; Adrienne Kennedy's phantasmagorical plays (in which McCauley would act and later direct) with their blurring of fact, nightmare, history, and desire found productions; and other interdisciplinary, experimental artists of color like Laurie Carlos, Jessica Hagedorn, Dianne McIntyre, and Ntozake Shange began to gain performance opportunities (Willinger; Patraka, "Robbie McCauley," 31; Jones, "When the Ancestors Call"). Further, musicians like Edward Montgomery and the Sedition Ensemble, with whom McCauley collaborated, were exploring what they called "political jazz" or music that deployed the nonlinear structure, multiple temporalities, and together-and-apart playing, typical of jazz, for active critique of imperialism (Patraka, "Robbie McCauley," 37–38).

Not only do the form and ambition of Robbie McCauley's plays appropriate and revise these earlier experiences, but she also continues to seek connections between the personal and larger social. As she shares with the producer of one of her first performances of *Sugar:*

> Like most pieces I make, *Sugar* was started to articulate and transmit stuff from the energy of the scream. I see, think about, and feel oppression in my life that I know as connected to oppression in the world. (Jones et al., *Experiments,* 253)

Interestingly, though sugar diabetes lies at the center of her play, McCauley provides audiences with relatively few "facts" or medical data. Rather, at one point in the performance while waving a sheaf of papers at her audience, she instructs them to "look it up," and so I did. Given the epidemic proportions of people at risk and as McCauley so ably demonstrates in the play, the ignorance or denial surrounding symptoms and treatment, I suspect that a "detour" is in order, particularly for those of us who don't know someone wrestling with this disease. For others, a "skip" ahead to the section on "History/ies in the Blood" may be appropriate (see below).

"LOOK IT UP!": DIABETES FACTS

Formerly known as "juvenile diabetes," type 1 diabetes results when the body's immune system *attacks and destroys* its insulin-producing cells, while type 2 (formerly called adult-onset diabetes) occurs when the body either *does not make sufficient insulin or cannot use effectively* the insulin it does produce. Symptoms of both types include increased thirst and urination, persistent hunger, weight loss, extreme fatigue, blurred vision, and slowly healing wounds. People with type 1 must inject or pump insulin into the body, while those with type 2 can "manage" their illness through medication, healthy food, and exercise (National Diabetes Education Program, "The Diabetes Epidemic Among African Americans"). Type 2 accounts for about 90 to 95 percent of all cases in adults (National Diabetes Education Program, "The Diabetes Epidemic Among African Americans"). Furthermore, according to the U.S. Department of Health and Human Services's Diabetes Education Program (NDEP), approximately 40 percent of adults ages 40 to 74 (41 million people) "have prediabetes," a condition that raises the likelihood of developing type 2 diabetes, heart disease, or stroke. Of this population, African Americans are twice as likely as whites to develop diabetes (National Institute of Diabetes and Digestive and Kidney Diseases, "Millions of African Americans at Increased Risk for Type 2 Diabetes"). For reasons that are still unclear, "since the 1960s, the number of African Americans with diabetes has tripled, leading to a near-epidemic in a community already twice as likely than the general population to have the disease, according to the African American Community Health Advisory Committee ("African Americans and Diabetes"). One in four African American women over the age of fifty-five has diabetes (Office on Women's Health, U.S. Department of Health and Human Services, "Minority Women's Health"). Worse still, according to the Office of Minority Health in the U.S. Department of Health and Human Services, approximately four out of five African American women are overweight or obese, thus putting them at risk for developing diabetes, heart disease, stroke, and kidney failure (Office of Minority Health, "Obesity and African Americans"). Health care providers are also finding what appears to be increasing levels of diabetes type 2 among American children and adolescents,[3] and some claim that the majority of new pediatric type 2 diabetes is occurring in "African American, Mexican American, Native American, and Asian American children and young adults" (Kaufman, "Type 2 Diabetes in Children").

HISTORY/IES IN THE BLOOD

As scholar-performer Omi Osun Joni L. Jones has noted, because of an apprehension of the thick, dynamic dimensionality of human experience, within a theatrical jazz aesthetic, "many worlds swirl together. Just as one figment of a story trails to a close, another piece of memory or truth from a different time and place is taken up" ("When the Ancestors Call").[4] Such is the case in the opening moments of *Sugar* where the affective is conjured forth and later complicated by the analytic. Before Robbie McCauley is even onstage, hard-driving guitars and drums baptize the theater space, daring audience members to snap their fingers, move their shoulders, and tap their feet. The familiar sound of Mick Jagger and the Rolling Stones song "Brown Sugar" throws those of us who are McCauley's contemporaries in age back to memories of a youthful communality forged through joints, peace pipes and incense, rock concerts, protest rallies, and military drafts. It also entices younger spectators into the interpretive circle it is moving to create, for the overlay of up-tempo saxophones seemingly crowds in and complicates the melodic line, driving the energy even higher and overtaking lyrical content. Only the repeated refrain "Ah Brown Sugar how come you taste so good / Aha Brown Sugar just like a young girl should" is likely to be heard clearly and remembered. Perhaps later, when McCauley begins to speak of her own reservations, do we reflect upon the narrative advanced by these provocative rhythms.

This song, recorded in 1969 and released first in 1971, encapsulates the paradoxes of sugar: its pleasurable properties hit the body and sensations first; only subsequently is one challenged to confront the consequences of that pleasure. Reading the lyrics, one sees that McCauley has unwittingly been celebrating human degradation, for the song remembers the transatlantic slave trade in which young women (and men) were exported from the west coast of Africa—"Gold coast slave ship bound for cotton fields"—into the Americas to work the sugarcane and cotton fields. Selling his human chattel in slave markets like those in New Orleans, the old captain has no compunction about whipping the woman or young girl whom he also takes pleasure in raping.

> Scarred old slaver know he's doin' alright
> Hear him whip the women just around midnight
> Brown Sugar how come you taste so good.

White women and black men are also implicated in this violent scenario, for the allusive language of the next stanza with its unclear referents offers two different interpretations. The "lady of the house" may be wondering whether her planter husband will refrain from having sex with their slaves, or she may be attempting to resist her own physical temptations and racialized, sexual fantasies encoded in "Drums beating cold English blood runs hot." Similarly, the enslaved "houseboy" knows that he can take his own sexual pleasure with relative impunity, because any children from this "around midnight" liaison will simply add to the master's property. With the third stanza, history has moved "forward" into a period where slavery has ended, but the construction of black female sexuality as deviant and excessive has endured. Respectable women in the nineteenth century followed the dictates of the cult of true womanhood by remaining in the home where they transmitted society's cherished ideals to their children, but this young girl descends from a suspect lineage, for her mother spurns convention to dance in a touring show. She displays her body to earn money and the attention of multiple lovers. She is the brown sugar that the song's white male protagonist has tasted and celebrates in defiance of racial and sexual propriety.

Having inducted the audience into the energizing pleasures of this painful history, Robbie McCauley "switches" up her mode of address. She presents herself as professor about to deliver her "Lecture Thoughts": She will focus on the three *d*'s of diabetes—depression, denial, and drink—related to the politics of sugar that has "seduced" nations, thereby wedding chocolate, sugar, and sex to Africa, the Americas, and Europe. And she warns in a somewhat offhand, cryptic manner, "Life is bigger than biography / Sugar more than sweet . . ." (5). With the fading out of the music and a light change, McCauley seems to have shed the academic role to become a friend reminiscing about experiences some thirty years earlier when she and fellow performer Laurie Carlos frequented clubs on Manhattan's Lower East Side and debated the politics of the Stones's "Brown Sugar." In those heady days of free love and free speech, when the growing availability of oral contraceptives or the Pill substantially challenged taboos against interracial and premarital sex, they were happy to accept the Stones's apparent praise. Black women's sexuality was being celebrated rather than demonized, and they felt free to love whomever they chose. But as McCauley admits, their pleasure denied the downside of their choices. It would take Ntozake Shange's bold candor in her choreopoem *for colored girls who have considered suicide/when the rainbow is enuf* for them to acknowledge that some of these heady romances left women devastated;[5] it would require long conversations with black nationalist and black arts proponents for them to recognize the implications of the triangular slave trade that the song unabashedly trumpets. Running parallel with memories of her past is a quarrel with herself in the present about the appropriateness of opening her performance with such a problematic song. McCauley honestly claims what she implies is less than a politically astute past, even while she makes space for other memories of this period, when she explains that "upsouth" in a northern United States segregated by habit, the coterie of black poets debated the worth of "Brown Sugar," while in the violently desegregating "downsouth" black folk proclaimed, along with singer Otis Redding, that they couldn't "get no satisfaction" no matter how hard they tried. As will be discussed later, this second Rolling Stones song also presents contradictions: though in his cover version, Redding bemoans both useless advertising and the lack of sexual activity, the frenetic musical pace, coupled with his large smile and breaks into "twist" and "mashed potato" dance moves assert an exuberant determination to persevere (Redding, "Satisfaction").

Changing the topic of conversation yet again, McCauley next asks for audience participation in an exercise whose ground rules she has not yet stipulated. With such a move she tests the trust her audience is willing to grant her; furthermore, by telling volunteers that they must respond with the emotional truth lodged in their guts, she is not only indirectly commenting on the fluid interplay between spectators and actor essential for performance but also rendering them performers, vulnerable to their own imaginations and the expectations of others. Surprisingly, because of its seeming irrelevance to all that has just transpired, the question McCauley poses concerns the audience's evaluation of the U.S.-Iraqi War. At the 2011 Northwestern University performance, various spectators proposed adjectives like "mortifying," "shameful," "indecent," "contrived," and "pitiful." McCauley declined to comment, saying simply, "I don't need to add to that." As the performance proceeded, it became apparent that these adjectives could also be applied to the diabetes that McCauley was discussing, because the three diabetes coping strategies that she posited at the outset constitute familiar mechanisms, on both the individual and group levels, for responding to painful knowledge and minimizing social responsibility. Having launched the interpretive strategies that she and spectators will deploy in a call-and-response fashion, this jazz playwright is now ready to offer narrative variations on a melodic base line.

And riff McCauley does, mixing stories of early, intoxicating yet destructive romances in New York, with tales of insulin shocks in Minnesota and Canada, public health statistics and loose associations between Columbus, Ohio, with its high rates of diabetes among black residents and Columbus, Georgia, where her own juvenile diabetes and that of her cousin went unaddressed for a long time. If we as spectators or readers are willing to relax our anxiety or desire for logical, linear development, if we begin to listen fully—with head, imagination, heart, and muscles— we begin to realize that some stories interrupt other stories, tales nestle within other narratives; they dialogue with each other, echo, reverse, and expand upon other narratives. We begin to apprehend that McCauley is proceeding via a stunning set of analogies that link diabetic experiences and shame to racism, struggle, and surviving with "a breaking heart." Consider, for example, the instance wherein McCauley reenacts the pained rage of a man who charges that diabetes repeatedly attacks his body, ravaging his sex life and his spirit, despite all his attempts to follow medical advice and thereby manage the disease. The man admits that exhausted by this struggle, he was preparing to commit suicide but stops only because there will be no one to care for his dog. Link that story of temporary truce to the sketches of her father who, despite the memory of siblings who died of medical neglect, takes Robbie to the hospital at a moment of crisis, yet vehemently denies that she has diabetes and forbids her involvement in socialist causes. Add to those, perhaps, the vision of Robbie's mother who seemingly smothers her own grief at her brother's death in concern for the nurse tasked with informing the family. And then there is the bigger history that McCauley researches concerning doctors who historically prescribed pills to black patients rather than insulin because they believed blacks should not have access to hypodermic needles; there are the studies and charts that McCauley displays documenting egregious health disparities between white, middle-class, and poor populations of color. There is the history of sugarcane that has fueled a drive for "profits over people" since its discovery in India two millennia ago.

Throughout these meandering, layered stories McCauley cares for herself. Crawling across the floor while narrating a near-diabetic coma, she drinks orange juice; at another moment, she checks her blood sugar and shoots up insulin; and later, she eats avocados and bread. In so doing, she brings out into the open the daily battles diabetics wage. But these are not necessarily instances of "art imitating life." Rather, before our eyes is a woman struggling to remain alive and in balance. This is life and its constant companion, possible death. This is a woman whose fierce honesty propels her beyond the fixed categories of art or activism into "everyday habitual acts of freedom" (Jones, *Experiments*, 9). From this space of vulnerability and independence, McCauley offers her most potent analogy: racism is like sugar. It offers a Faustian bargain of pleasurable consumption in exchange for a diminished humanity that we embrace for ourselves and inflict upon others. Lulled by its comforts, like addicts we seek more and more sweetness, ignoring the rot of our decisions. But McCauley proposes that we can also choose to live like diabetics. We can acknowledge the constantly changing forms that racism adopts and fight to remain in balance, honoring life.

> It's all about balance . . . balance, the way we think about race.
> I know they're getting ready to call this a post-racial society.
> What? . . . post-racial racism? It seems so much easier to keep
> at it, to try and find the balance, 'cause they're gonna keep on
> . . . change the medicine again and again. Keep the metaphor
> of finding balance with sugar as long as you can?[6]

But the playwright isn't content to allow audiences to rest with this arresting metaphor; instead, she offers one more call, calculating that our responses will germinate long after the performance has ended. Referring to all that has just transpired, she asks: "Is this art?" One possible answer fills the performance space with Otis Redding's voice singing the Rolling Stones's song "(I Can't Get No) Satisfaction." He too complains of advertising that manufactures desire and distorts one's generative capacities. But though he proclaims that he's unable to get satisfaction no matter how hard he tries, he exudes life in response to the music's rapid pace and invitation to improvise new dance steps. Responding to the music's and artist's exuberance, McCauley dances too, gifting spectators with a parting vision of the bodily joy of perseverance in the face of the depredations of sugar/racism. "Is this art?" Is this how we might live, balancing art and politics, creativity and struggle? Or, might we continue with the "sweetest hangover"? Robbie McCauley's work here is finished. Ours is just beginning.

NOTES

1. The term "personal/bigger" in the section title of this essay appears in an interview that Elin Diamond conducted with McCauley. While the term "repetition with a singular difference" appears in Henry Louis Gates's work, many scholars and practitioners of African American cultural production use a similar formulation. See, for example, introductory notes to Suzan-Lori Parks's plays where she offers the shorthand "rep and rev."

2. Here, Ellen Gainor is quoting Cheryl Walker's articulation of "persona criticism" (Gainor, *Susan Glaspell in Context*, 4).

3. Though according to the Centers for Disease Control and Prevention website updated May 2011, a statistically significant increase has been found only in American Indian children and adolescents; see "Children and Diabetes—More Information," http://www.cdc.gov/diabetes/projects/cda2.htm. But earlier in 2002, the president of the American Diabetic Association, Francine Ratner Kaufman, located the rise in pediatric type 2 in minority populations. Kaufman, "Type 2 Diabetes in Children and Young Adults: A 'New Epidemic,'" *Clinical Diabetes* 20, no. 4 (October 2002): http://clinical.diabetesjournals.org/content/20/4/217.full.

4. This quotation comes from a longer, unpublished version of the essay "When the Ancestors Call" that performance artist Sharon Bridgforth generously shared with me.

5. *for colored girls* was first produced in neighborhood bars and cafés in California's San Francisco–Bay Area and then in New York City before garnering off-Broadway

and Broadway productions beginning in 1976. Laurie Carlos joined the cast in 1975 and played the Lady in Blue in both the off-Broadway and Broadway casts. See Shange's 1977 introduction to the play for a production history that conveys the exciting creativity of a multicultural, feminist community that nurtured the talent of many emerging artists who would have substantial impact on late twentieth-century theater and dance in the United States.

6. These lines are from the slightly altered version of the script that McCauley performed at Northwestern University.

WORKS CITED

African American Community Health Advisory Committee. "African Americans and Diabetes." http://www.aachac.org/healthfactsheets/diabetes.html.

Centers for Disease Control and Prevention. "Children and Diabetes—More Information." http://www.cdc.gov/diabetes/projects/cda2.htm.

Diamond, Elin. "We Keep Living," *Theatre Journal* 62, no. 4 (2010): 521–27.

Gainor, Ellen. *Susan Glaspell in Context: American Theater, Culture, and Politics, 1915–48.* Ann Arbor: University of Michigan Press, 2001.

Gates, Henry Louis, Jr. *The Signifying Monkey: A Theory of African American Literary Criticism.* New York: Oxford University Press, 1989.

Jones, Omi Osun Joni L. "When the Ancestors Call." http://sharonbridgforth.com/content/wp-content/uploads/2009/02/when-the-ancestors-call.pdf.

Jones, Omi Osun Joni L., Lisa L. Moore, and Sharon Bridgforth, eds. *Experiments in a Jazz Aesthetic: Art, Activism, Academia, and the Austin Project.* Austin: University of Texas Press, 2010.

Kaufman, Francine Ratner. "Type 2 Diabetes in Children and Young Adults: A 'New Epidemic.'" *Clinical Diabetes* 20, no. 4 (October 2002). http://clinical.diabetesjournals.org/content/20/4/217.full.

National Diabetes Education Program. "The Diabetes Epidemic Among African Americans." http://ndep.nih.gov/media/fs_africanam.pdf.

National Institute of Diabetes and Digestive and Kidney Diseases. "Millions of African Americans at Increased Risk for Type 2 Diabetes." http://www2.niddk.nih.gov/News/SearchNews/07_19_2004.htm.

Office of Minority Health, U.S. Department of Health and Human Services. "Obesity and African Americans." http://minorityhealth.hhs.gov/templates/content.aspx?ID=6456.

Office on Women's Health, U.S. Department of Health and Human Services. "Minority Women's Health." http://womenshealth.gov/minority-health/african-americans/diabetes.cfm.

Parks, Suzan-Lori. *The America Play and Other Works.* New York: Theatre Communications Group, 1995.

Patraka, Vicki. "Robbie McCauley: Obsessing in Public, an Interview." *TDR: The Drama Review* 37, no. 2 (Summer 1993): 25–55.

Redding, Otis. "(I Can't Get No) Satisfaction," 1966. http://www.youtube.com/watch?v=A3wJM3OtIhA.

Shange, Ntozake. *for colored girls who have considered suicide/when the rainbow is enuf: a choreopoem.* New York: Macmillan, 1977.

Tillman, Lynne. "Robbie McCauley." *BOMB* 41 (Fall 1992). http://bombsite.com/issues/41/articles/1595.

Werner, Craig. "August Wilson's Burden: The Function of Neoclassical Jazz." In *May All Your Fences Have Gates: Essays on the Drama of August Wilson,* ed. Alan Nadel, 21–50. Iowa City: University of Iowa Press, 1994.

Willinger, David. "Developing a Concert for the Spoken Voice: *Solo Voyages* and an Interview with Robbie McCauley." In *Intersecting Boundaries: The Theatre of Adrienne Kennedy,* eds., Paul K. Bryant-Jackson and Lois More Overbeck, 224–30. Minneapolis: University of Minnesota Press, 1992.

BIG-BUTT GIRLS, HARD-HEADED WOMEN

Rhodessa Jones

PRODUCTION HISTORY

Big-Butt Girls, Hard-Headed Women premiered at the Women's Theater Festival in Boston, Massachusetts, in September 1989. The musical accompaniment and stage direction was performed by Idris Ackamoor. The original development and production were made possible in part by support from the National Endowment for the Arts, Grants for the Arts of the San Francisco Hotel Tax Fund, The San Francisco Foundation, The Grousbeck Family Foundation, The Zellerbach Foundation, The San Francisco Art Commission, and The William and Flora Hewlett Foundation.

CHARACTERS

[*all played by the same woman*]
Artist, African American, any age
girlchild, African American, preteen/teen
Mama Pearl, African American, about seventy
Lena Sorrentina, Italian American, about thirty, muscular build, former ballet dancer
Doris, African American, about nineteen
Regina Brown, African American, about thirty

STAGING

Center stage is a platform that serves as an aerobics platform. Upstage right is a set of stairs placed against the stage wall that serves as "The Hole." Downstage right, one chair in a pool of blue light; this is the visiting room. Downstage center is washed in stark, harsh light; this is the day room. Center stage left is an altar that depicts various shrines from many cultures: it is a mixture of candles, fruit, found objects, dolls, milk bottles, an African fertility goddess, huge bouquet of fresh flowers; everywhere there are dried flowers, spices, and Hershey's chocolate kisses.

[*Lights go down to come up accompanied by offstage singing "The Blue Valentine" by Tom Waits. The* ARTIST *continues singing as she enters the stage.*]

. . .

[*The* ARTIST *finishes the song in the altar space; removes her gold robe and hangs it on the altar, and the robe becomes part of the altar. Sound cue "Forest in the Ghetto," a musical collage that depicts monstrous urban reality: horns blowing, tires screeching, babies crying, cat calls, sirens, et cetera. The* ARTIST *portrays a sound and movement solo, juxtaposed to the sound track. She will take us from the innocence of an African American* GIRLCHILD *to the all too frequent situation/existence of prostitution that results in incarceration.*]

NARRATOR [*in the voice of the* GIRLCHILD]: Milk shake, milk shake, cream of tartar

Tell me the name of her sweethearter

[*à là Aretha Franklin*] *What you want*

Somebody got

What you need

You know I got it

[*She dances suggestively—hands on hips.*]

I got it. I got it. I got it.

Git it, girl! Gon girl!

[*She freezes into a position of fatherly authority and speaks.*]

Git in the house! Git yo' big butt in the house!!!

[*The* GIRLCHILD *whines.*]

But I wasn't doin' nothin' . . . nothin', nothin'. I ain't nothin'.

[*She freezes, then speaks, assuming the attitude and posture of an adolescent girl, trying to be a grown woman.*]

Hey, Tony! Hey, Jerry! [*Over her shoulder, conspiratorially*] Girl, that looks like Tony and Jerry. Let's go to the sto'.

[*She circles downstage, with her back to the audience. She mimes necking, petting, fondling, heavy breathing, lustful panting, childish groping.*]

I love you. Nobody does it like you do. Just kiss me.

[*She speaks in a masculine voice.*]

Is it good? Tell me that it's good.

[*This scenario evolves from passion to labor to childbirth ending with the* GIRLCHILD *facing the audience holding a baby. She freezes into a position of motherly authority.*]

Git in the house. Git yo' big butt in the house. Don't be so hard-headed. Haven't you done enough?!

[*She whines.*]

But I wasn't doin' nothing' . . . nothin', nothin'. I ain't nothin'.

[*She moves into a frenzied dance of self-defense . . . Warding off blows while holding the baby.*]

You better stop, Jerry. I'ma tell my daddy. Stop!

[*She mimes being punched in the stomach, knocked to the ground, and she's sexually assaulted ending with her legs opened facing downstage. She rolls to her side and assumes the voice of authority.*]

Git in the house. Git yo' big butt in the house. A hardhead makes a soft ass.

[*She is rising from the floor. It is painful. It is a struggle.*]

But I wasn't doin' nothin' . . .

[*Sound of a car horn. She beckons in a pleading voice.*]

Hey, you! You wanna kiss me? Yeah, kiss me, kiss me.

[*The sound of sirens, and suddenly she's handcuffed and struggling, caught.*]

Motherfucker, take yo' hands off me. I wasn't doin' nothin'. Regina, call my mother. Tell her they takin' me to jail, girl. Lena they got me on a humbug. Motherfucker, take yo' hands offa me! Doris, tell my grandmama they takin' me to jail, girl, and I wasn't doin' nothin'.

[She struggles as though she's being arrested with handcuffs, the lights change simultaneously with a musical interlude of Marvin Gaye's "What's Goin' On." In the back light we see her change into blue prison coveralls. After changing she steps across the aerobics platform and comes center stage.]

ARTIST: Good morning. I am Rhodessa Jones from the California Arts Council. I will be teaching aerobics here every Wednesday morning at 9:00 A.M. My pass is newly issued. I have clearance for all the jails. You got to run a check? Look, Sergeant, why would I want to break into jail, most folks I know want to break out? Whoa—It's not that I'm trying to be a wiseass. I just have no great need to sneak into jail, first thing on a Wednesday morning! Oh this? This is my beat box. These are my tapes. Here. What does NWA stand for? "Niggas With Attitudes." They advocate what? Cop killing! Look, well, I don't know about all that. The women in my class like and requested this music. I'd love to discuss it with you, but I've got a class to teach. I beg your pardon? Read my lips: I have far better thangs to do with my time than sneaking into jail first thing in the morning. Could I have my pass please?!

[Light change. She is on the aerobics platform, overly enthusiastic.]

Good morning, Ladies. We're going to begin with some windmills. Now everybody smile and one . . . two . . . three . . . four . . . C'mon Latoya, you too. Alright good . . . Good. And now for all you big butt girls, it's time to get another booty for your body. That's right, we gon do some booty building this morning! What's the use of having a big ol' butt that you can't use. You know, to express yo' self. You know, a butt that commands attention . . . One that stands alone. Let's begin by tightening up with some lunges and press one . . . two . . . three . . . four . . .

[She freezes. Lights change with a musical interlude. She steps down from the platform to downstage center. Addressing the audience:]

In jail. A black woman artist, working in jail. I look out at all those faces. There's my mother's face, my sister's face, and my daughter's face. And I'm wondering how in the *hell* did they get here in the first place. And I realize that it is but for a flip of fate that it could be me in here and she out there.

[*Lights change with musical interlude. The Falling Woman Dance: She moves as though she's catching bodies falling from the air. It is sporadic, and she calls out simultaneously.*]

Vanessa! Jeanita! Paula! Beverly!

[*She stops and spouts statistics.*]

Eighty-five percent of all women incarcerated in U.S. penal institutions are women of color.

Donna! Naomi! Paulette! Jessica!

Fifty percent are African American women.

It is a revolving door.

[*Music . . . She sings, softly, lullaby-like. The Falling Women's Dance continues throughout the song.*]

Can a body, catch a body?
Can a body, catch a body?
Can a body, catch a body?

[*She addresses the audience.*]

And how can I, as one woman artist, make a difference, provide a supportive environment in the face of women who know that it's so god damn hard to live anyway. Women with no jobs, who've lost their children. How do we counter life-threatening situations such as alcoholism, drug addictions, sexual abuse. How do we discuss and explore the reality of AIDS, coming to grips with the fact that screams, "Women die far faster from it."

[*Lights change. She returns to aerobics platform.*]

Today we're going to work with the mask—in theater your face is the mask. Let's begin by stretching the face. Big face. Little face. C'mon—it is an anti-aging device. Now, use the tongue. Stretch to the side . . . To the top . . . To the other side . . . All you working girls, pay attention.

[*Lights and music change.*]

So many faces . . . So many masks . . . So many stories . . . So many songs.

[*Public Enemy's "Terminator" is heard. As the music plays the* ARTIST *portrays glimpses of many different women. As the music crescendos, the* ARTIST *assumes the character of* REGINA BROWN, *who is having sex with two other women.* REGINA *is an African American woman of about thirty. She is strong and aggressive and appears taller than she is.*]

Fuck a bitch. Hit me! Bigger and better bitches than you have hit me. Just because I let you smell my pussy, don't make it your pussy. It's still my pussy. Everybody and anybody will use you so you best get to using first. I learned early, a man or a woman ain't nothin' but a plaything. I tell them all, "It's like the lotto, baby. You got to be in it to win it." Later for all that "Ooh, baby" this and "Ooh, baby" that. I believe in action, so you best get on with the A team. Like Tyrone, he's in love with me, always has been, and I can understand that. But I told him, "I was born a full-grown woman, and it ain't about 'my woman this' and 'my woman that.' I'm my own woman." But, like a lot of men, he don't want to listen. Wanted to control me . . . Thought he was my daddy. My daddy is dead, baby. And my mama raised me to be strong and on my own. He got all mad, 'cause he wasn't ready for the real deal. Brought some other girl, some Lily Lunchmeat lookin' bitch I don't know, home! I told him, "Hey, if sister girl can hang, it's all in the family." Thought he was gonna work my nerves with that shit. And now, who's crying? Tyrone. Because I'm carrying another man's baby. And that man ain't even important. The reality check has to do with me, my baby, and my baby's staying with Gerber's. I am a prostitute, straight up. I decided a long time ago, wasn't no man gonna tell me what to do. I'm a full-grown woman, straight up and down. Or my name ain't Regina Brown. WORD! Hit me bitch . . .

[*She rolls forward with a slap. The* ARTIST *returns to the aerobics platform and addresses her class again.*]

Down on our backs . . . OK, we're going to stretch up and down through the hands and feet. Now take the feet back over your head. Breathe and stretch. This will make you very popular. You can go home and scare him to death. He'll say, "Damn, baby, I thought you was in the joint." Then you say, "No, baby, I've been at a health spa." Breathe. Work the body, ladies, work the body. You can't sell chicken if it looks like Jell-O . . . Now because everyone's been working so well we're going to end with some hand dancing.

[*She addresses the audience.*]

That means you've got to say what I say and do what I do. And I know what you're all thinking, "She's from California, anything can happen."

[*The* ARTIST *demonstrates the American Sign Language movements for the following words, as the audience mimics.*]

Dancing is defined as any movement of the feet with the body in a standing position. Dance officials will issue a warning if two women are not dancing . . . Are not dancing.

[*"As Time Goes By" is played on a saxophone. The* ARTIST *addresses the character of* MAMA PEARL.]

Hey, Mama Pearl, I missed you in class today.

[*The* ARTIST *becomes* MAMA PEARL, *an African American woman who appears to be about seventy, though she could be younger. She is a sage, a crone, and she speaks with the voice that a velvet rock would have, if a rock could speak.*]

MAMA PEARL: Well, I can't always be coming to class now. They done made me a trustee, you know. That means I get to move around—to work.

ARTIST [*addressing* MAMA PEARL]: You look great. I like your hair. But then, Mama Pearl, you always look spiffy, sharp.

MAMA PEARL: Baby, that's why they made me the trustee. I take pride in my appearance. They know they can send me all over this place. Yeah, I can come and go instead of sitting in that day room with all that noise and these bitches smoking. Somebody always cussin', clownin' or fightin'. But I'm glad you're here, and if you don't do nothing else teach them how to have enough self-respect to wash they funky asses. Here my hand to god, some of them so young they don't know how to use a Tampax. I've been in and out of the joint since 1965 and I ain't never seen it as bad as it is now. The young women coming and going in this day and time don't have no sense of theyself. I got three daughters. My older daughter was born deaf and dumb. She's the reason I went to jail in the first place.

[*She pauses and looks around before continuing in a more secretive tone.*]

You see, I embezzled some money from the company that I was working at so my daughter could get special training so that she could take care of herself, despite her handicap.

These girls need somebody to help them understand that you ain't got to be in and out of jail to feel important. They got to find a reason to let go of that crack and cut loose these men that pimp them for drugs, money, cars, even a leather coat. Look at them. Most of them not even twenty-five yet and have the nerve to be pregnant up in here. Like I told you, I got three daughters and I'd rather see these bitches flush these babies down the toilet than grunt them into the world and treat them the way they do. How? The way they will sell them, lease them to the dope man for some rock. They're flesh and blood, honey. Then the dope man, he gon get busted, and then the baby is lost to child protective services. And these bitches want to cry about they babies. This ain't something I heard; I seen this with my own eyes. You know what I tell 'em? "Take that whining and complaining someplace else coz when you was out there fucking and sucking, high out of your mind, I did not get one nut. I did not experience one thrill behind your bullshit. So take all that drama somewhere else."

[*She pauses and addresses the audience.*]

Here my hand to god, please, I know that it's a hard line, but in this life I've learned you better come with something if you wanna get something.

[*Lights change.*]

ARTIST [*addresses* MAMA PEARL]: I'll see you next week, Mama Pearl.

[*The* ARTIST *returns to the aerobics platform and performs the following lines while doing handstands.*]

The last session of today will be taking the weight. Learning to carry your own weight. So let us begin by pressing up. It's good for you to go upside down. It's good detox measure. It puts fresh blood in the brain. Come on LaWanda. Get with the program. I wish Sorrentina was here. She'd be right up here doing all this stuff. But then she's gone home; she's out of here. What did you say? No, she ain't. Are we talking about the same person? A short little Italian sister? Another bitch in the hole? Since when? She's only been gone two weeks. OK everybody, that's the end of the session for today. I've gotta check on Lena.

[*Lights change. The* ARTIST *moves from the aerobics platform to "The Hole." She becomes* LENA SORRENTINA, *a diminutive Italian American woman of about thirty.* LENA *has the tight muscular build of a former ballerina. She is detoxing and climbing the walls.*]

LENA: Hail Mary, full of grace.
The Lord be with thee.
Blessed are the fruit of thy womb.
Jesus.
Holy Mary, mother of God.
Pay for us sinners now, and in the hour of our death.

I'm so damned tired. I'm tired of being sick and tired. She's fucking dog meat, man. Just one little shot. This bitch snitches at Work Furlough. She was getting stoned too. Piss in a cup. Piss on your family, OK. Fuck you. Count time, my ass. When will this shit end? This is the longest nightmare I have ever had.

[*She begins a hallucination, addressing an invisible audience of classmates. She is very perky in this address.*]

As valedictorian of the class of '82 I just want to say thanks to my Pop. Daddy. Daddy. We did it Daddy!

[*She jumps, waving the diploma.*]

To my guidance counselor, Mr. Carter. Yo! Mr. Carter, I'm up in here. It's me Lena Sorrentina. I'm up in here. To my dance teacher, Mrs. B. who was always sayin', "Lena Sorrentina, dance witcha hands, you gotta dance witcha hands." Well I'm doin' it Mrs. B. I'm dancin'.

[*She goes into a balletic extension, attempts a relevé, and breaks her foot.*]

No. No. Dr. Karea. I gotta dance it. I been workin' four years for this part. I gotta . . .

[*Frantically.*]

Mama, Mama, tell him I gotta dance it. Dr. Karea, gimme a shot like they do in sports. Just one shot.

[*She returns to valedictory speech.*]

I say to you today, class of '82, when we leave these halls this afternoon we are gone forever. I want you to go out into the world and grab it by the collar and give it a big ole' shake. Because we've earned it. We deserve it.

[*She makes a farewell gesture.*]

Good-bye. Good luck. And God bless you one and all. Remember, this is Lena Sorrentina, and I'll see you all on Broadway. I'll see you all on the big boards.

[*She falls back into withdrawal; slapping her arm to find a vein she picks up the needle. Just as she finishes shooting up she looks up and sees her father.*]

Pop, forgive me Daddy. I'm so sorry. My friends . . . Pop, you don't understand. It's not my friends.

[*She becomes incredulous.*]

Move?! Outta your house. Well fuck you, man. I'm outta your house.

[*This propels her back into "The Hole."*]

I choose my friends. I choose my friends. Oh, God, please give me one more shot.

[*Coming out of a dream.*]

Let me go. Let me go.

[*She opens her eyes and seeing the audience, cries a silent scream. She climbs the walls, sobbing.*]

Let me outta here. I was clean for two whole weeks. I feel like a
fucking fish on the line. They give you a little slack and then, no,
no, no . . . And now they're reeling me back in again. The pigs have
me again. Get me outta here. Somebody help me. Let me go. I'm so
tired—so damn tired. I'm tired of being sick and tired. Somebody
help me please.

[*The lights go down and come up on the character of* DORIS, *an African American woman of about nineteen. The classic girl child with a child of her own,*
DORIS *sucks her thumb as she speaks.*]

DORIS: Hey, Mama. Hey, Mama. Hey, Brittney. It's Mommy. Hi, Baby.
Now don't cry. Mama's gonna be home real soon. I promise. Stay
with Grandma and be a good girl. Mama, what did Mr. Sullivan say
about when I can get out of here? Ain't that some stuff. He know we
ain't got no property. Collateral my butt. And anyway, I wasn't doin'
nothin'. Resisting arrest?! Mama, I wasn't resisting arrest. I was with
Big Willie, and we was on our way to his sister's house, when the
police stopped Big Willie, ran a check on him, came back to the car
and asked for some I.D. I asked why. They said I was in the company
of a known felon. I said, felon or not, this is my baby's daddy. Then the
white police say, "Then your baby must be a felon, too." I say, "Your
mama is a felon." Then the black police gets all up in my face and calls
me a dope man's bitch. I told him he was the dope, and he could kiss
this bitch's butt. Then he gonna try to snatch me out of the car. So
by that time you know Big Willie was all over him. So the next thing
we know, we down here in jail. Mama, don't worry. Did my job call?
This morning? See, that's dumb shit. I'm gonna lose my job behind
this mess. And I wasn't doin' nothin'. Mama, call Mrs. Ryan. Tell
her I got to reschedule my GED test. Don't cry. I'm a little worried
about Mr. Sullivan. He's from the Public Defender's Office. So he's
gonna make one move for me and two for the state. Mama, how are
you feeling? Now, Mama, listen. Don't cry. Remind Aunt Ossie to
call social services. Tell them that she will keep the kids while you in
the hospital, 'cause these people ain't seen no criminal activity until
some of them try to take my babies and put them in a home. I love my
kids. I love you too, Mama. Don't worry. Pray. Pray for Big Willie.
Bye Brittney. Mommy loves you. And you give little Willie a kiss for

Mommy. Be a big girl, you hear? Take care of Grandma. Don't cry. I love you. Bye, Mama. Bye, Mama. Bye.

[DORIS *walks down over to the day room and proceeds to watch TV with* REGINA *and* MAMA PEARL.]

DORIS: Regina, don't turn that. That's my favorite soap. Can't you see I was watching it?

REGINA: Well you ain't watching it now. Who gives a fuck about the days of *our* lives.

MAMA PEARL: Regina, why can't you have respect for other people sometimes? "All My Children" is coming on next and I fully intend to watch it. I need something to calm my nerves after all that excitement we done had around here this morning.

DORIS: Yeah, ya do. Did that lady really kill her baby, and because of some crack. I just don't understand that.

REGINA: She did it. Trust me. But it wasn't because of no crack. It was because of that man of hers.

MAMA PEARL: Yes, if the truth be told, she smothered that baby to get even with him for leaving her.

REGINA: This is what I heard. Check it out.

"Bitch, we through, 'cause you finished. You to the curb. You ass out. You ain't nothin' but a dope fiend and all I care about and want is my baby out of this motherfucker, because you a dope fiend."

She da dope fiend, after he brought the shit in the house in the first place.

DORIS: You mean they was tweakin'?

MAMA PEARL: Yeah, that's the sin of it. They all out of they minds on cocaine . . . When he decides to leave her, poor thing. I hear she loved him with a hungry love.

REGINA: Deborah ain't no stupid woman. She got a degree from Berkeley, had a good job. They used to be happy until they started foolin' around with that shit.

DORIS: That's why I don't do no dope. I really love my kids, No man could ever make me do something like that for all the love in the world.

MAMA PEARL: Doris, don't ever be sayin' what you won't do. You just keep your eyes open. Keep on livin' darlin'.

REGINA: Yeah, 'cause I seen some motherfuckers do some strange things in the name of love. Fuck love. Love kills.

[*She punches the television.*]

And it's too bad this shit had to happen, ain't it? Love is the motherfucker.

[*She pounds television.*]

I WANT MY MTV!

[*Lights change and music goes up. The* ARTIST *addresses the audience.*]

ARTIST: Who are these women? And what are they to you, and you, and you.

[*She points to the audience as she speaks the last line. She sings the chorus from Bernice Reagon's "Joanne Little."*]

She's our mama.
She's yo' lover.
That woman,
The woman who's going to carry your child.

They wear my mother's face, my sister, my daughter. And now, if I'm to believe statistics, my granddaughter? You know, working in the jails, I don't delude myself and pretend that the time I spend with these people is gonna make a whole lot of difference.

[*She mimes struggling under weight.*]

Their problems are too great. Too immense. Benign neglect. Alienation. Isolation. Blind rage. Living in some township just outside of Amerika.

[*She poses beatifically, with hands joined as in prayer.*]

But I was raised in a family by a mother and a father who taught me that when you're called to something too great, too immense, you can always take it to God. Now the African in my American teaches me to take it to the Ancestors.

[*The* ARTIST *begins an incantation, "Take It to the Ancestors," building a dance with a chant and a chorus.*]

ARTIST: Take it to the Ancestors.
  Build spirit catchers.
  This is a spirit catcher for one
  Regina Brown, age twenty-seven.

REGINA: Daughter, Sister, Lover, Mama.

ARTIST: Regina Brown, murdered in the
  Winter of 1989, after her second
  Release from jail.

REGINA: Daughter, Sister, Lover, Mama.

ARTIST: Regina Brown, mother of two children,
  Left here howling on the ground. A boy
  And a girl, left to make it in this hard luck
  Place called the world.

REGINA: Daughter, Sister, Lover, Mama.

ARTIST: Regina Brown, whore with a heart of gold.

REGINA: Daughter, Sister, Lover, Mama.

ARTIST: Regina Brown, who, with a little direction,
  Could have been running the world.

REGINA: Daughter, Sister, Lover, Mama.

ARTIST: Regina Brown, one of my best drama students.

[*The dance ends with the* ARTIST *next to the altar with the spirit catcher. She picks up a brass owl from the altar, and addresses the audience.*]

I'd like to ask you here tonight to help me complete the spirit catcher with sound.

[*She reaches into the bowl and begins sprinkling water on the audience through-out the following history.*]

This is a bowl of sterilized water. Because I was raised in the house of one Estella Jones, my mother, who taught me that if we kept a bowl of sterilized water in all the cupboards, and under all the beds, we could drown sorrow . . . We could read the weather . . . So right now I'm asking you to participate in a lullaby written by one Harriet Schiffer. It is a call and response. It goes like this.

[*The* ARTIST *and audience sing together with musical accompaniment.*]

All women love babies.
    All women love babies.
All women love,
All women love,
All women love babies.
    All women love babies.

REGINA: Daughter, Sister, Lover, Mama.

[*Again, addressing the audience:*]

ARTIST: Thank you very much, it's a California thing.

Before I go I'd like to ask you a few questions. Please speak right up. You can talk to me. You'd be amazed at what people have said to me, so speak right up. How many people have ever been mugged? Show of hands, please. Let's keep it simple. Had your bike stolen? Apartment broken into? Car broken into? And in that car was your favorite camera with the best film you ever shot in your life? Had your credit cards misused and abused? Been raped? Know somebody, who knows somebody, who knows somebody, who knows somebody, who knows somebody who's killed somebody.

My point is, we're all involved here. My point is this ain't no time to be buying dogs and locking doors 'cause you see "them" comin'. 'Cause "they" could be "us" and you may wake up and find that you've locked yourself in and they're sitting at your breakfast table.

Let us not forget to remember that the struggle continues for all of us.

And, you know, when I first made this piece it was for the Women in Theatre Festival in Boston. On returning back home I was approached by the San Francisco Sheriff's Department Work Furlough Program. They asked me to do the work as a way to introduce my workshop "Living on the Outside." And I said fine, I'll do it, but you've got to remember, this is a feminist theater piece. And they brought me seventy men. The men liked the work and encouraged me to continue speaking on the lives of these women. Soon after I received my first contract to do a run in San Francisco, and it made me nervous, feeling that this was a piece for a particular population. And in my mailbox that day was also this letter from my nephew.

[*She moves back toward "The Hole."*]

My nephew is twenty-five now. He has been serving ten to fifteen years in the State Penitentiary in northern California for manslaughter. I love him very much. He writes . . .

[*She reads excerpts from the letter.*]

Hi Aunt Rho, I was glad you wrote. How is everyone? (I hope things are well, I haven't heard anything from anyone in my immediate family. I wrote Dad a while back and he send me a song that he had written, but other than that I haven't heard from anyone.) I hope that my brother is OK. I was shocked when I found out he had a baby, it made me think once again about how much things will have changed once I get out. Everyone is growing and changing, and so is the world; places that were there when I came in will no longer be there when I get out, and so many other things. On the one hand, it's kind of depressing, but on the other hand it is very exciting, the idea of being set free in an old world that's new to me seems appealing. I guess I just like the challenge some things offer. This may sound strange, but a great deal of the time that I am in here I am happy in my own little way. Don't get me wrong, I'll jump at the first chance I get to be free, but I am very content now. I am learning a lot. My music is coming along very well. The truth is, I feel as though a person coming out of the pen should have a better chance at making it than the average person on the streets, but I guess that only applies if the person has used his time wisely while incarcerated. This place can really be a great place to get your mind together. Even the violence and games that people play help you learn and grow, and this place in all reality is just a microcosm of the outside world. So I guess it's up to the individual to use this time the way he or she feels will best benefit her or him. I love you Aunt Rhodessa. Thank you for sticking by me through these times, god's peace be on you.

Strawberry thoughts

&

chocolate dreams

forever,

love

god

[*After reading the letter the* ARTIST *performs a reprise of The Dance of the Falling Woman.*]

Vanessa! Jeanita! Paula! Beverly!

INTERVIEW WITH RHODESSA JONES

E. Patrick Johnson

The title of the piece, *Big-Butt Girls, Hard-Headed Women*. Now I know in the black community people know what that is. Talk a bit about that title.

My father used to always admonish us. "Sit your big butt down. Don't be so hardheaded." This was like his way of pulling rank when things just got out of control. Then when I started working in the city jail here, one of my earliest memories and experiences of coming face to face with that population was this woman named Deborah. Deborah could easily have been six feet tall, and just a warrior queen, in some other life—Concord grape, colored woman. Not fat, but big, strong. And she's in chains. And I'm sitting there waiting to be allowed to go in and gather the women from my aerobics class and Deborah walks by in chains with these men and they are taking her off to one of the prisons in California. And she was just so fabulous-looking and at the same time I want to be supportive. So as she comes up to me, gets ready to pass me, I say, "Take care of yourself. Good luck." And she walks past, and she just turns slowly and looks at me, and she says, "Oh girl, don't worry about it." And marches off. She's taller than all four of these men that are with her. And she walks off, and it was like her butt was an army coming up behind her. And immediately my father's words came into my head: "Sit your big butt down, don't be so hardheaded." And at the same time, I took a breath. I thought, "I am glad I was raised in that house, so that it's not me." And then Bill T. Jones, my brother, says, to name things is the intention to make things. So I wrote down, "Big-Butt Girls, Hard-Headed Women." So I thought *Big-Butt Girls, Hard-Headed Women* was just this caption and things started coming into play after that.

So you came up with that title even before you knew it was going to be a piece.

Yes, exactly. Because they were everywhere. You know as an African American, my mother used to say, "You know, you better listen to me. You are going to have it hard if you don't listen to me." And that was one of the things when I first started working in the jails. All these sisters. All of them. I'm like, how does this happen? You know? And then again my family, my own instruction in the world would always come into play. Where yeah I'm thinking, "Thank God, I'm glad I have those parents. I'm glad I listened. I'm glad I grew up on a farm away from the city." So they were everywhere. Some of them were giving those guards as good as they caught. Just cussing everybody out.

When you went into the jails and prisons, were you afraid?

No. I was more afraid of the police, the guns, you know? That's always been. For me, I had a brother who was at Attica. When Attica went down, my brother was there. And then that same brother had been on the chain gang when he was sixteen, seventeen, he went on the chain gang. He was just rowdy, out of control, my brother Boot, Richard. So no the police scared me. There was just guns everywhere. And as the years went by, I was in Susanville, California, about seven or eight years after I became established as an artist in corrections. And I was up there performing. And Susanville is like on the moon. And at the same time it's a maximum-security prison that sits out in the middle of nowhere. And you go inside and there's a catwalk with all the guns. And I am thinking are these people trained to handle an emergency where if something goes down, I am inside, I am in the middle of this prison. And I am thinking, we can all be like fish in a bowl. And these cats with the guns—all of them were black and brown—they decide if trouble's happening, how are they going to know that I should be somebody to be saved? But to answer your question, No. I was not afraid of the people. The clanging of the doors is nerve-wracking. And that whole idea if something goes down. Are they going to let me out? I found out with 9/11 there really aren't exits for prisoners. There are ways that the walls will go down. The walls will go down and create a metal fortress if something happens. And the authorities will get to go out under the facilities. But the prisoners, there's no outlet for prisoners. And I work belly to belly with prisoners. And I love that stuff. I love it. I really do.

So you started this work in the mid-1980s, is that right?

Yes, 1989 is when I got the call to come in and do it. But I was already an artist with the California Arts Council working in communities. I was working in grade schools before this. And then they called me and asked me would I be interested in coming in and replacing the belly dancer. I'm fascinated like, what? And they said, "Well you know you can teach aerobics." And I'm like, "I'm not an aerobics teacher. I don't even think of myself as a dancer. I'm an aerialist and all this, but fine, I'm in. Sign me up." And that was how it all began.

What are some of the changes you've seen from when you first started doing this work to now?

Well. Inside San Francisco, bless its heart, has the Five Key School, that's come about over the years. The Five Key School is actually a public school inside the prisons, inside the city jail where you can get your GED. See that wasn't happening when I first started. There were classes—writing classes—and I was a part of the art program. And we have a wonderful sheriff, Sheriff Hennessey, who has just retired this past year and he really believed that art can change lives. Maybe its educational reform across the country where it's back to the basics, you know: writing, reading, and arithmetic, that kind of thing. So they created the Five Keys inside of the jails, and that was amazing. The sad thing about it was that it usurped us as artists, there wasn't much room for us to go in and do our work. But that was one of the major changes. And my Medea Project I've done across the country has always been about education, about writing, and about reasoning. Being a part of the global cultural conversations. Can you talk about who you are? Can you talk about why you think you are in jail? And they always wrote. And that tripped people out inside because they just assume that these people don't have it together. And then for me, I started saying, "Why don't you write a rap about it." And everybody thinks they know what rap is. Or the Latina girls are fabulous letter writers as far as love. And they would always do that for all the inmates. If you can write, you can get somebody—you used to be able to give them a pack of cigarettes, and they would write you a love letter or write you a good-bye letter or . . . So all this was going on because I was belly to belly. I saw it all. But that was the major change for me, because I was happy that they had a school and they had a bank of all these computers and all these rooms. And they got certified teachers to come in and work. But, like I said, it took away from the space that we used to have to go in every night and build a work. And I see that more and more, women are still going to jail. The jails are filling up with women. And they are getting younger. And that is different than it was back in the day. Back in the day, it was the old dope fiends. The young women—at least they keep their nose clean. They'd be on the street for a minute. And now it's like, they are just in it. And I think what's happening was their grandmothers and their mothers were going to jail and they were just kind of left on their own. Your grandmother used to be able to bring you to the jail to see your mom, but then it's like, well you know. And then if your mother is doing hard time, you just want to be in there with her. Whatever it takes to be in there with her.

A lot of these women were doing hard time. How do you see the work that you do with them as being rehabilitative? Because in some ways they are not going to get to see the outside anymore. So what is the work that they are doing, doing for them?

I think it's an affirmation of their womanism, their humanity. My way of teaching, sharing is that we make a circle and it's all about what's going on. What's happening? And nobody asks them that. You know? Don't give me the line on how you were railroaded. But tell me what's happened. I tell them, "I can look at your chart. I know how long you're doing. I know how much time you're doing. How did it get to this place? And what are we going to do about our children? What do we tell our children?" And also it's not ya'll versus me, but *us*. I think that there is a sisterhood. And that's just my own cultural training in this society where I came into the arts when the feminization of women, the womanization of women was really happening. We were trying to find a common ground for us as a group—females. And I take that into the prisons and I think it educates them that this is not only happening to you. In *Big-Butt Girls*, when I do the sign language "dancing is defined," that came out of trying to find a device to make it fun, but also impress upon these people that we all are a community. Whatever you do is going to affect a lot of people. I think I even say that in the show. When I was working in the jails I thought, how do I have this moment where we all come together and we are thinking as one? And we started to learn the sign language, and to learn it as a chorus. And you saw the leaders. You saw the people who remembered that they were more than a number, more than a ho', more than a crackhead. And they would take it upon themselves to work with people who were having a hard time. And it was also a way to say to people, "It's OK if you don't know. The sin is if you are going to stand back and pretend that this is beneath you, when it's really that you don't know. You're scared. It's not a sin not to know how to read, because I got a team here. We're here to help with all of these things. So let's just open up, and let's get real, and because we are all in captivity right now, there are no secrets." Back to your question, I think it's just opening the heart, you know? And I think we as people all need that. We just need to be. 'Cause you meet a lot of people incarcerated who will say, "Yeah, I did that." I mean you meet a lot of people who are not guilty. But you meet a lot of people who say, "Well, I did that." And then they want to just cave in. I don't see them as victims. The resignation is resounding of that, "Well, I'm a bad person." "No you are not, you are a full person." There's the good and evil and let's examine both. And the artist invites them to participate in that. And that resonates long after I'm gone, how they treat each other. Sean Reynolds, who has been my social worker partner in crime, would always remind me. She said, "Girl, the thing I love about incarcerated women is that they have great generous, sometimes whack humor." And we laughed a lot. And these women were surprised that it wasn't going to be. Because they are dealing with psychotherapists; they are dealing with therapists; they are dealing with lawyers. And they got that line down, because they are bullshit artists. We were all sitting and kicking it. And it takes us back to a whole other place. Or for some of the women, they have never had this with other women. They've never had this kind of camaraderie. So when we laughed a lot, this woman said, "That got me through. It would get me through." Sometimes I would just sit there and say, "What would Miss Jones be doing right now? What would she have us doing?" And she said, "I did exercises, I did my hand-stands." You know, and I'm just like, "Thank you God." You know. She said "It got me through, the workshop I did with you at the gym."

Moving to the piece itself, but related to what you were just talking about: one's impulse as an artist would be to make these women saints. You don't do that in the show. You present a really complicated portrait of them. Was that a deliberate choice on your part? Because another motivation of your doing this is a kind of advocacy on the one hand, too. One might think, "I can't show the ugly side of these women. I only got

to show that they are human." But you go there in the show. Talk about that a little bit.

Anna Deavere Smith, her pieces where she takes on all these characters and all this kind of stuff. Cecil Taylor says that multiculturalism is always the next breath. Whatever is going down is like the wave amongst artists that we are all kind of feeling. That's one thing. Secondly, it was such a gift to be in there with them. I love them. Regina Brown alone was magnificent. She was just magnificent. You think about actors. And I thought, "How Hollywood, television, can they deal with this?" You know that everybody ain't a ho or a junkie. They're complicated. And I wanted to do them, you see. I wanted to put them on. And they were fascinated that I wanted to do them. So no it was a deliberate choice but I couldn't imagine doing anything else because on a certain level *I'm* a bad girl. I just didn't get caught. [*Laughs.*] And I had to go up against a couple of them in there where I had to put on my niggatude. You know, "No no no no no I ain't the one." And you have to get ugly and say, "They pay me to be here and what's your problem." And the other women would say to the prisoner who is trying to get me: "Girl, sit down. Miss Jones done told you. Can we get on with the workshop?" So I felt I had entrée. It was rites of passage. And then I started to say to them, "Show me how Mama Pearl moves. Show me how Regina moves." And I had had a wonderful director when I was living in Scandinavia years before. I was working for the Theater of the Blue Horse. A director, Alexander. And he said, "Rhodessa, you have the ability to be ten, fifteen feet onstage. Find it. Find it." And those kinds of things were what interested me. Because I wanted to come charging in with these incarcerated women. With *Big-Butt Girls* I wanted to just come charging into the communities and say, "No you don't have any idea about what's going on here." And I'm a physical artist. And when I made the piece I was on top of my physical game—that was twenty-five years ago now. And I knew it was sacred. I knew it was divine. I had been handed all of this real information. It was like going into the land of the dead. I feel like I would be dropped into these amazing places and my job was to get out alive. I felt like Indiana Jones. I was like, "I'm going in." And they would just be like, "Who is this bitch?" They'll just talk about you when you are right there. I got to be a bitch. "My name's Rhodessa, what's your name?" And they were like, "Oh, oh, oh." You know, I'd say, "Come on ya'll. Let us be as sisterly as possible." "Sisterly, hm?" "Yeah, that's what we got. I can walk in here and tell all of ya'll I got cramps. I got my period and people are going to feel for me, aren't you?" And they were like, "That's true. That's true." It was as basic as that. So in a lot of ways yes it was a choice, but then I had no other choice, as an artist given the mix that I was in. You got to keep it real.

In the piece ritual is very important. You begin with an altar. Talk about how ritual plays a role in the piece and why it's important for you.

Each one of us deserves to die some sort of natural death. Ritual is made for all the people who did not make it. There were a lot of people, when I started out working in the jail cells that didn't live to make it. They overdosed. They were murdered. Disappeared. So that was one of the reasons. And this theater is holy. For me, I feel like the theater is its own kind of temple. Coming of age in the '70s and '80s. Winston Tong, who used to say to me, "If you can get an audience to listen. If you can get people to gather, and you say, 'over here, over here, I got something to say.' You damn well better have something to say." And we are moving out of the whole thing of art for art's sake. And also the entrance of others, of us, diversity. So the altar did all of that for me, as well as it was a way to take a very simple space and just like put this thing with light and candles and light and shining masks. We made the masks out of Regina Brown. Regina was murdered and before I made the piece she was brutally murdered at McLaren Park in San Francisco. At that time I was doing co-ed classes out at the county jail with men and women when we got the word she had been murdered. And I said, "Well, as a group, if we had all had some sign or portents that the last time we were in her company that would be the last time, what would we have said to her? So the mask that hangs over the very top is made up of things that people wrote to say to her. Good-byes. Warnings. So that is what that is. It's all papier-mâché, but it's also handwritten messages. That's what that mask is. It's a very simple way to do a set, that's effective. Because it is the Misadventures of an Aerobics Teacher. I was thinking about all that as I was putting the piece together. I wanted the platform to be very real. The altar was this place I could come and go from. And as I said, it is my own kind of religiosity. I really did tell people that I am a theater goddess. And I am. An actress, yeah sure. But you got to be able to stir up the molecules. I am blessed with that. And then doing *Big-Butt Girls* at the National Black Theater Festival. And it's all these old ladies—I mean our grandmothers show up and I'm like, "Oh my God." And it's like you know, Ms. Who, Ms. What, Ms. Was. This summer they got pastel hats on and they're like "humph." And *Big-Butt Girls,* the title, drew all kinds of people because, as we began earlier, we all know it on some level. And after the show, there was one lady in blue. Chocolate lady. Big bosom. She had her program like a bible. And her friends were just looking at me. And I also make the altar a place to stand so people share amazing things with me after the show. People will admit they've been incarcerated. That used to be where my talk back was, just standing there talking to people. So she's waiting, her friends are thinking she ain't got time. They are sort of looking at me. They're close to me now. And my hair is short. I'm probably cussing. I had a cigarette so I'm reeking of tobacco, whatever. She is like, "No, no, no, uh-huh." She climbed up the stairs. And she got her turn and she grabbed my hand. And she said, "Honey, this ain't theater. This is a ministry. That's what you're doing." And that was such an affirmation for me. Particularly, *Big-Butt Girls* was divine. It was like I was sent to present that piece. And then to have a mother, one of our grandmothers, tell me this ain't theater. *Big-Butt Girls* was designed as an opening. It was designed to let the public into the life of the incarcerated woman. Something that is so private, even we don't talk about it. I mean I had a woman come to me, a sister fabulous black woman. Well paid, Gucci shoes, whole thing. And she came to me at the National Black Theater Festival. And said, at first she was all light. She said, "Girl, we know the brothers in jail, but girl." And I said, "Come on now. Don't we all have a Lucy, a cousin, or a Margaret or a Millie that we have been told not to hang around with because she's a bad girl?" I said, "Come on now. We all got somebody. We got women in jail." And she's like "yeah." And then her eyes filled up with water. And I said, "What is it?" And she said, "You know my twin sister. My twin sister is in jail in Arizona forever and ever. And we were so tight, so close. And at fifteen, she went one way and I went the other way. I came here because I heard about it. I heard about the piece." And she said, "I am going to call my sister. I haven't seen my sister. I haven't seen my sister in ten years. I just don't go visit her. I don't do jail." I said, "I know. That's my moniker too,

I don't do jail." And she said, "That's my twin sister." I said, "Go see your sister. And you can afford it!" Because she was like laid. And she started laughing.

Why was it important for you that this be a solo piece? Why not have an ensemble?

Because I didn't think people were ready. I didn't think that people were ready to take up this burden. 'Cause it's a lot, you know. It's a lot to bring it, to keep it intact. And I didn't want—I have to admit—I didn't want the input. I didn't want all these other people worrying about maybe it's too hard because I got a lot of that anyway. And then Idris Ackamoor. He has always been my partner and my friend. We even were a couple for a long time. I brought him my notebooks, because I was just hearing these women all talk. I was just writing, because I wasn't allowed to record. I was just writing down their language. And I said, "You know, I think I want to do something." And he was the other person who said, "Yeah." Between Idris and me, see, we used to say, you got to be able to make theater in a living room. You got to be able to perform in a living room and have it resonate, powerfully. And he was just the person to have me do it. And like I said, I just didn't want the other people worrying, I didn't want people worrying me. You think all this. No, I'm going to do this. I'm going to do this, this way now.

There's a moment in the show that stands out to me the most near the end where you are catching—

The falling women.

The falling women. Talk about that moment. How did you come up with that image for the show? Because again that's the one I remember the most.

"Can a body catch a body?" Well, you know "Catcher in the Rye" was a children's game. But what was happening all around me was that people were really dying. In the jail, I'd come and they'd say, "You heard?" And I'd say, "You heard what?" "Well so and so she got out but they say somebody shot her." And then inside catching those women who was telling me these stories. How do I help them? Because they would find me. "Miss Jones, you heard?" They'd be like [*huffing*]. And I'm like, "No, what's happened." I was honored and burdened that they could tell me. And fast forward to Africa. Oh my God, last time I was in Africa the stories of domestic violence where women have killed men. And these women say you got to tell Miss Jones. Tell Miss Jones. So catching the bodies. And the other heavy thing was bodies are falling everywhere. There's a war on women. Women are at war with each other. And all of that came into play. And also I would go to the museums with my brother, Bill. He was living in New York many years ago, and that would be a date for us. We'd go sit in a museum and look at paintings. And all of this came into play when we were looking at this painting. What would it look like to have women falling? So all of this stuff became a part of making it, making this section. I thought, "Can I make the audience believe I am really catching people? Where is it going to work better? Is it going to work when they are settled down, they're broken? Do I have to pretend they are marionettes and I have to set them up?" I think painterly a lot. What kind of pictures am I making—stage pictures? I write the same kind of way, you know, making word pictures. And *Big-Butt Girls* was this amazing opportunity because it expands. You know Idris and I started in his living room working on this piece. And then we got space to like open it up. But like every juncture I had to figure out what can I work on if I only got a room this big? What can I do? Do I just work on language, learning language? Making sure I have inflections? Making sure that it resonates with me and then I can work to make sure it resonates with you? Or in big spaces as a dancer, as a physical theater person, catching the bodies was a hoot. To be like, "OK, where are the bodies falling from? Are they being thrown out of things? Are women just jumping out of buildings?" I played with all these images. And how many of them can I catch? And how I was like feeling, even at the end of that piece, if you may remember, that I can't catch them all. And the ones I talk about, Regina. I didn't catch her. I saw her falling and I didn't catch her. I couldn't catch her.

If you were to update this piece today, how would it change?

I think I would do a total remix and I would put it on my company. I think I could really direct it on my company. I could rock it on my company. And that's just the rage right now. I'm getting ready to do *Blessing the Boats* in New York. I am going to remix that. Sekou [Sundiata]'s piece. But that's what I would do. There's this data that I'd update more. Mama Pearl, I think, would have a much more central role. I think the aerobics teacher would have to stay in there. Or maybe she'd become a yoga teacher. I think that's happening now in the prisons. I am thinking about putting it on my company just to see what it would look like with more voices than mine. Maybe expanding monologues. And the altar, I would have the altar built throughout the show. By the end of the show the altar would be finished. But that would be an action people would be doing. Because so many people are interested in the altar. I sort of assume that we all sort of got it, which I think basically we do, but I think that it would be wonderful that out of their monologues comes another piece. And I would try to incorporate the art-making in jail. The visual arts, the writing. I'd want to figure out how to do that so the audience could see all the workings behind the damn thing because sometimes it all becomes part of the altar.

IN THE SPACE BETWEEN LIVING AND DYING: RHODESSA JONES'S *BIG-BUTT GIRLS, HARD-HEADED WOMEN*

Lisa Biggs

> Charlie, I'm pregnant.
> Living on 9th Street
> Right above a dirty bookstore off Euclid Avenue.
> I stopped taking dope.
> I stopped drinkin' whisky.
> My ol' man plays the trombone . . .
> And he says that he loves me
> Even though it's not his baby . . .
> —Tom Waits, "Christmas Card from a Hooker in Minneapolis"

Big-Butt Girls, Hard-Headed Women opens with music, invoking characters that are at once shabby, chic, shameful, and utterly fantastic. Actress and playwright Rhodessa Jones appears wearing a long, sparkling, red cape. She holds a small candle aloft in one hand. As she places the candle on a large altar built upstage left, she summons the Tom Waits song "Christmas Card from a Hooker in Minneapolis." Shimmering in the light, Jones unfurls the tragic ramblings of a slightly sleazy working girl, who, we come to realize, has a heart of gold and some beautiful dreams despite her troubles. Waits's song weaves the woman's fictions and truths, lies, aspirations, and failures in a lilting, loving, bluesy style that Jones delivers with reverence and joy.

At a time when poor black women were represented in the popular media and in American political discourse as incorrigible, hypersexual, parasitic, "welfare queens," "bitches," and "crack ho's" incapable and undesiring of anything other than a life of crime (Escobar, "No One Is Criminal"; Collins, *Black Feminist Thought;* Mauer, *Race to Incarcerate;* Roberts, *Killing the Black Body*), Jones birthed *Big-Butt Girls, Hard-Headed Women* to encourage and represent the incarcerated women she came to know while working at San Bruno, the San Francisco county jail. With a critical, loving playfulness, Jones uses her solo performance to reanimate their journeys to jail and their collective lives behind bars (hers and the prisoners'), answering fundamental questions about how they all came to be there, and how they did their time.[1] But unlike other arts initiatives that arose in the fiery aftermath of the 1971 Attica Uprising, Jones's performance piece was not designed as a rehabilitative tool to fix prisoners (Balfour, *Theatre in Prison;* Hart, "Historical and Social Role"; Thompson, *Prison Theatre*). Rather, she describes *Big-Butt Girls* as an exercise in "personal transformation" as well as a "place of concrete memory." She hoped that the piece would demonstrate to the women inside that they could personally transform, but by the time Jones completed it, one—Regina—was dead and the others had moved on. Instead, for the last twenty years this solo work has memorialized a moment and staged a series of critical interventions in dominant discourse about crime, criminality, and justice for other audiences of men and women, incarcerated and free.

Harry Elam Jr. theorizes that solo performance can be utilized by black performers to "explore, expose, and even explode" concepts of race, in particular how blackness is "conceived and performed both on stage and in life" (Elam, "Black Performer," 288–89). Solo performance is an effective tool for this because audiences understand the theatrical event as an opportunity for performers to take on or play other roles than they would in everyday life. For black performers who don black characters, the performance provides an opportunity for them to mine the differences between social constructions of blackness embedded in the performance text, audience perceptions and misperceptions of black people, and their own personal experiences. The performance event facilitates the juxtaposition of multiple registers of blackness, and enables the solo performer to demonstrate that blackness ought not to be reduced or represented as a singular, monolithic, reductive entity. Playing the alternative or "excess" blacknesses allows them to critique, "transcend and even subvert" the known "socially patrolled boundaries of race," in particular the popular "political constructions and violent manifestations" that circulate at all levels of our society (Elam, "Black Performer," 289). Rhodessa Jones uses *Big-Butt Girls, Hard-Headed Women* not only to challenge racist thinking about black people, but to critique, "transcend and even subvert" reductive depictions of the criminalized, with a particular emphasis on representations of women offenders who, for the first time, were being sentenced to prison and jail in substantial numbers, and whose real-life experiences were most often erased or ignored in discussions of law enforcement. Her nuanced portraits demonstrate that there is more to being a criminal than simply being black, and more to humanity than what power and authority allow.

CONTEXT

Jones is the daughter of African American migrant farm laborers from Florida. She gave birth to her only child, a daughter, at age sixteen. Popular wisdom predicted that as an unwed teen mother she would go nowhere fast, but theater "saved" her life. By the 1980s, she was supporting herself and her daughter as a working actress and a dancer with the Tumbleweed modern dance ensemble in San Francisco. The California Arts Council recruited her to work at San Bruno, but jail administrators prohibited her from offering theater workshops due to concerns raised about her predecessor, Jaime, whose belly dance classes they disparaged as "stripper training." The 1960s "war on poverty" had morphed into the "war on drugs," a resurgent attack on the very same poor black, red, and brown people that twenty years prior had been recognized as standing in the greatest need of positive governmental support (Alexander, *New Jim Crow;* Davis, *Are Prisons Obsolete?;* Garland, *Culture of Control*). The "culture of control" that prevailed instead insisted on "the essential 'otherness' of the criminal," and equated poverty, especially the poverty of people of color, with criminality (Bumiller, *In an Abusive State,* 6; Garland, *Culture of Control,* 184). Criminologists such as James Q. Wilson and George L. Kelling encouraged the dismantling of government-funded, public and privately run social welfare programs in favor of more aggressive policing. At a time when the labor market was shrinking, these actions left the most vulnerable members of society with limited or no access to essential resources such as basic housing, medical care, and food. Under the guise of "law and order" and "self-help," the changes—initiated under Richard Nixon and extended by Ronald Reagan, George H. W. Bush, and Bill Clinton—enabled the nation "to mask its responsibility for creating and maintaining the sub-par living conditions of marginal groups" (Cohen, *Boundaries of Blackness,* 82–83). Unfounded fears that a new class of "super-predators" born of drug-addicted, African American welfare mothers would soon terrorize the nation reframed the public welfare debate, until "non-punitive government action on behalf of black and brown poor people" was dismissed as "ineffective and impolitic, if not misguided" (Adolph Reed quoted in Cohen, *Boundaries of Blackness*, 83). Instead, millions entered into the prison system.

The fastest-growing segment of the imprisoned population was women; their numbers skyrocketed 700 percent from 1980 to 2000, from 13,000 in all the local, state, and federal facilities combined, to nearly 92,000 (Johnson, *Inner Lives*, 34–37; Bureau of Justice Statistics, *Bulletin*, 2001). This shift was not the result of an increase in the crime rate, but was due to changes in legislation and law enforcement, especially a new emphasis on policing nonviolent women addicts, sex workers, and shoplifters (Bumiller, *In an Abusive State*).[2] Building upon a long history of discrimination, poor women of color received the most severe sentences (Flavin, "Of Punishment and Parenthood," 628). By 1990, the overwhelming majority of people arrested nationwide were white, but the majority of women behind bars were single, poor but working, of black and brown mothers between eighteen and thirty-five years old, more than 60 percent reported being survivors of prior physical and/or sexual abuse (Bureau of Justice Statistics, *Special Report*, 1999). As their numbers ballooned, jail administrators faced enormous pressure to respond.[3] Those that believed people could change, and had enough resources to offer rehabilitative, educational, or vocational programs, looked for courses to offer.

At San Bruno, Sheriff Michael Hennessey and his Assistant Sheriff Michael Marcum, himself a former "juvenile offender," facilitated Jones's entry (Warner, "Restorytive Justice," 237). Jane Fonda's trendsetting aerobics videos had launched a nationwide exercise craze bent on molding every woman's body into a new, slender ideal (Lloyd, "Feminism, Aerobics"). Marcum and Hennessey wanted to offer their women prisoners the most innovative, gender-appropriate, feminine physical exercise program possible. Jones had no experience teaching aerobics, was critical of the thin but physically weak body Fonda was selling, and had no desire to go to jail, but she decided to make it work. *Big-Butt Girls* is a chronicle of her early experiences behind bars and a record of the life stories of the women she encountered there. Her full and complex portraits destabilize popular representations of imprisoned women and men as deviant "superpredators" or "non-human others." By educating audiences about who is really behind bars and what their journey to jail entailed, *Big-Butt Girls* weakens the authority of the tellers of the popular, reductive tales about the criminalized, and the procedures and technologies that have been imposed to redress conflicts between people. Performances of *Big-Butt Girls* subvert penal authority by challenging the fundamental logics of the "culture of control." It establishes a community space for audiences to critique the everyday performance of law enforcement and transcend the norm to imagine other outcomes.

I WASN'T BORN A BITCH, A LOT OF SHIT HAPPENED

The process of undermining the "culture of control" begins with the opening Tom Waits song. The script indicates the protagonist is a hooker, but audiences encounter her without the designation of her criminality. Instead, Jones evokes her vocally as she stands, still, downstage. The lyrics reveal her to be living in difficult circumstances, "above the dirty bookstore on Euclid Avenue," with a good man who loves her and the child she carries "even tho' it's not his baby." Her tender reminiscences about the listener's greasy hair and the people they both have known present her to us as a sympathetic, engaging woman who has known troubles but is not without joy. Because Jones stands still onstage and delivers the song with little noticeable physical characterization, we are left to imagine what she must be like. Thick, thin, short, tall, pockmarked, elegant or shabby chic? White? Black? Native? Latina? Asian? Which Asian? Red hair? No hair? Something else? We conjure her in our minds individually and we like her. Her story makes us laugh, but in the last stanza our images are challenged by a series of revelations. She admits there is no man, there is no money, she is in jail and needs money for a lawyer. The woman we thought we knew has been replaced by this complicated, distant, criminal figure asking for our help. Her parole date on "Valentine's Day" hangs like a bittersweet promise as the last notes fade away. What are we going to do about it?

Dispossessed by legal and civil society, prisoners occupy a liminal, "provisional existence" in the popular imagination, one marked by multiple losses—of family, coworkers, support networks, morality, dignity, and time. They are figuratively suspended in a state of backward-looking, paying penance for past wrongdoings, and divorced from the "prospect of a different future" (Kanter, *Performing Loss*, 148–49). To compensate the state and other victims for their losses and suffering, the prisoners' future is imagined as being painfully "stripped away" from them, with prisons and jails the sites where both the removal and transference of time occurs (Moses, "Time and Punishment," 71). As imprisonment strips the prisoner's body of the capability to advance through space or time under its own propulsion, it diminishes or dehumanizes the prisoner into "a thing that is held, observed and controlled" (Leder, "Imprisoned Bodies," 64). People become their mistakes. Using song and a series of vignettes centered on the character girlchild, *Big-Butt Girls* restages this accepted narrative with a critical difference.

Following the opening song, Jones transitions into girlchild, a mythical every-black-girl-who-grew-up-in-the-hood. Girlchild appears as the last notes of "Christmas Card" fade away. The montage that follows tells the all too typical story of her "decline" into prostitution. At first, she appears vibrant, surrounded by girlfriends with whom she confidently and happily sings and dances. Her original rendition of Queen of Soul Aretha Franklin's "Respect"—"What you want, somebody got . . . What you need, you know I got it"—builds into a celebratory but "suggestive" dance with the other girls, demonstrated by Jones twisting her hips as she cheers herself on with "I got it. I got it. I got it . . . Git it, girl! Gon girl!" At the swirling and chanting crescendo, girlchild garners attention from unseen forces and there is a sudden change. Jones interrupts girlchild's play, dropping her voice and raising her hand to manifest a parental authority figure.[4] Girlchild is in trouble now. The parent orders girlchild to "Git in the house! Git yo' big butt in the house!!" Girlchild whines in response, "But I wasn't doing nothin!" to no avail. Dejected, she turns upstage toward the house, complaining, "I gotta get in the house? But I wasn't doin' nothin'."

As those words reverberate, Jones advances girlchild into her teen years. Hand on hip, she spots a couple of neighborhood boys and hails them. Imaginary girlfriend(s) in tow, she sashays over to meet Tony and Jerry at the corner store. There, an enthusiastic make-out session with Jerry ensues. Alternating vocally between Jerry's deep register and girlchild's high, thin voice, Jones enacts their love talk. Jerry begins, "You love me, baby?" and girlchild coos back, "I love you . . ." The scene continues with Jones's back turned to the audience, her hands caressing her own shoulders like young lovers do. Her voices shifts back and forth from

Jerry to girlchild: "Is it good? Tell me that it's good . . . It's good . . . You like it baby? . . . I like it." Almost as quickly as these lines are delivered, however, the make-out session escalates into a whirlwind movement sequence in which girlchild gets pregnant, goes into labor, and delivers a newborn baby girl.

The arrival of the baby signals the transition into the next confrontation with authority. A stunned girlchild holds the baby in her arms for only a moment before her parent(s) literally knock her off her feet. Angry entreaties to "Git in the house. Git yo' big butt in the house. Don't be so hardheaded. Haven't you done enough?" are accompanied by open-handed slaps to her head and body. Dodging the blows, girlchild dances the "frenzy of self-defense," crying out, "Mama, don't hit me! Daddy, don't hit me!" The attack dissipates, but parental disapproval, it turns out, is not the only obstacle she faces. When her mother and father fade away, Jerry lashes out like a tornado. Girlchild can hardly get a word out of her mouth when his assault begins. Jerry echoes the words and actions of her parents, but rains fury down at an unprecedented level. He curses and knocks her to the ground. When girlchild defends herself, he berates her. When she tries to rise and return to the house as ordered, he beats her harder. She repeats her earlier protestation, "Stop! I didn't do nothin'!" until the incantation grinds down to the realization that it does not matter. Nothing she says or does matters. Everyone that is supposed to love and value her believes instead that she "ain't nothin'." Alone, abandoned to the streets, and in despair, she takes her first drink. Trembling hands search the ground for drugs and find them. She touches a crack pipe, lights it, and inhales. Her mind and body deteriorate. When girlchild finally does stand again, she sways under the lights. Girlchild has been transformed into another worthless junkie, another "nothin'" black woman.

The final moment of girlchild's story depicts the last step of her journey to jail. As she struggles to stand, there is the sound of a car horn. Girlchild solicits kisses and caresses—any kind of affection—from the invisible driver. Before we hear their response, Jones turns away from the audience and thrusts her hands behind her back signaling the imposition of handcuffs. Girlchild has been arrested. She struggles against the police pleading, "I wasn't doin' nothin'." But as before, her cries fall on deaf ears, and this time, Jones does not bother to stage their reaction. Girlchild has become a person whose story is not worth hearing much less believing. Girlchild resists this devaluation and the arrest, calling out to other women—other prostitutes perhaps—who we now learn are nearby. She demands that they contact her family, and that they acknowledge the police have got her on "a humbug," on manufactured charges. Her denial of criminal wrongdoing echoes her previous encounters with authority figures, but now, her credibility has been damaged. Did we not just see her prostituting herself? Do we not recognize this story?

Only the last authority figure, the police officer, has the power to encase her behind bars. Jones's staging ensures that the officer's designation of girlchild's activities as criminal emerges from a continuum of confrontations with other authority figures—mother, father, boyfriend—that have marked her as offensive long before the cuffs come out. Girlchild's act of prostitution may have been illegal, but in performance, Jones does not focus on her actions alone, but instead enacts a pervasive "culture of control" that devalues girlchild everywhere she ventures, from home to street to store to corner and courthouse, and around again. The people who inhabit these places contribute to girlchild's criminality by labeling and treating her like "nothin'," like a deviant, monstrous, nonhuman "other" whose presence and actions are always so offensive they demand isolation ("Git in the house!") and corporal punishment. Girlchild may be bad, Jones seems to say, but she is not bad all by herself. Her criminality is not innate or endemic; society has identified certain behaviors as inappropriate or criminal and she is their target.[5]

Having established that criminality is not inherent to a degenerate class of criminals, but rather the product of interlocking social processes that accumulate and evolve over time, Jones advances through a series of monologues set inside the jail. She weaves glimpses of herself as an enthusiastic aerobics instructor in between monologues told by the four other main characters—Regina, Mama Pearl, Doris, and Lena. The monologues reveal details about each woman's journey to the jail, beginning with Jones's own. Each story, each woman, differs from stereotype. The contrast between the women's life stories and the popular myths reveal the myths for what they are—stories about women behind bars rather than stories of or by women who have been in those circumstances. By juxtaposing the popular myths with the text of their life stories and the embodied performance, Jones reveals the limitations of the popular representations, and destabilizes the authority of the tellers of those tales.

TROUBLE INSIDE

We enter San Bruno with Jones as herself, the enthusiastic aerobics instructor. As the chorus to Public Enemy's "Terminator X" fades in the background, Jones introduces herself to an imaginary officer on duty in the visitor's lobby. They immediately challenge her right to be there, deciding to "run a check" on her despite her "newly issued pass."

"You got to run a check?" she quips in response. "Look Sergeant, why would I want to break into jail, most folks I know want to break out? . . . Whoa, I'm not trying to be a wiseass. I just have no great need to sneak into jail first thing on a Wednesday morning!"

We laugh at Jones's humorous, yet direct, challenge to the officer's authority. It demonstrates that her character will occupy the jail space in surprising ways that exceed our expectations. Jones will joke inside; she will question officers; she will not be intimidated; and, we later learn, she will not be afraid of the prisoners. Unlike girlchild, she will be seen, and heard, and taken seriously. In the visitors' lobby, her resistance works and Jones is allowed to pass without further confrontation. She carries a perspective of critical playfulness inside with her.

A unique kind of aerobics class ensues, one that is light on lunges and heavy on offers of support without castigation or preaching. Jones engages the imprisoned women like girlfriends.[6] She cajoles them into doing face stretches by appealing to their (everybody's) vanity—these are "anti-aging devices." She rotates her tongue "to the side . . . the top . . . the other side . . ." and around, in a gesture that she acknowledges evokes sexual activity. Jones recognizes it and jokingly entreats all the "working girls" to "pay attention." She encourages them to continue to work other parts of the body, in particular the butt and legs, to improve their health and their livelihood. "You can't sell chicken if it looks like Jell-O," she remarks, and you cannot run from the pimp, the trick, or the police in high heels unless your legs are strong. Jones represents an approach to working with these stigmatized people which stands in sharp contrast to the agonistic perspective that characterized previous "authority figures" in the show, and which habitually frames discussions of crime and its perpetrators in everyday life (Lugones, "Playfulness"). Instead of enacting or enforcing distinctions between herself and the prisoners, she sees similarities. In a moment of soliloquy between exercises, Jones reflects on how familiar the women look: "I look out at all those faces. There's my mother's face, my sister's face, and my daughter's face . . . It could have been me in here and she out there." She blurs the lines further between the criminal and the supposedly law-abiding and innocent rest of us when she has audience members join the imaginary exercise class in the "Hand Dance."

Subsequent monologues by Regina, Mama Pearl, Doris, and Lena explode the boundaries between criminals and the innocent rest of us. The women's stories reveal them to be complicated figures, but never lazy, self-indulgent bitches as the "welfare queen" lore insists. Each acknowledges they have engaged in objectionable behavior, but their stories also offer pointed critiques of mainstream values that resulted in their imprisonment. For Regina, sex work enables her to achieve and maintain independence: "I am a prostitute, straight up. I decided a long time ago, wasn't no man gonna tell me what to do." If Mama Pearl had been able to access appropriate care for her disabled daughter in the 1960s, would she be sitting behind bars? If Lena could have gotten adequate treatment services when she injured her foot as a dancer would she be detoxing in the hole? Finally, Doris's case reveals how random police power can be and how imprisonment can destroy families despite the efforts of single mothers—which most women behind bars are—to keep multiple generations whole and together.

The culminating conversation between Regina, Mama Pearl, and Doris puts all the issues each individual character raises about crime and punishment onstage at once. Rather than a single, monolithic, fixed image of women behind bars, the audience must drink in a multitude of characterizations with Jones always at the root. Her performance in this scene achieves her stated goal of demonstrating that transformation is possible, as she moves her voice and her body from one characterization to the next with clarity, ease, and grace. The dialogue provides outsiders with a glimpse of how incarcerated women—a population that we never hear from—think, talk, and feel about crime. It is through their dialogue that we are introduced to Deborah, a woman who killed her baby, and therefore epitomizes society's worst fears about women, that they will refuse or fail to be good mothers. Mama Pearl, Regina, and Doris, like the audience, do not know what happened between Deborah and her man, the baby's father, but Jones stages how they contend with the rumors, critiquing what they have heard from the wellspring of their personal experiences.

It begins with Doris, who caught that Deborah killed the baby "because of some crack," but Regina counters, "It wasn't because of no crack . . . It was because of that man of hers." Regina continues that once Deborah got hooked on dope, he threw her out. The irony is that "she da dope fiend, after he brought the shit in the house in the first place." For Mama Pearl, the problem began when the baby died because they were both "tweakin' . . . out of they minds on cocaine." The tragedy happened, though, "when he decides to leave her, poor thing . . . I hear she loved him with a hungry love." Doris dismisses their compassion for Deborah, saying no man "could ever make me do something like that for all the love in the world," leading the others to challenge her conclusions. Mama Pearl admonishes her, "Doris, don't ever be sayin' what you won't do. You just keep your eyes open." Regina's last words, "Yeah, 'cause I seen some motherfuckers do some strange things in the name of love. Fuck love. Love kills," go to the heart of it all. These three women behind bars know that human beings do things that may not be right or acceptable, and that we even go so far as to destroy one another. Human beings do this, they say, and we do it all the time.

When Jones returns as her narrator self, she poses the meta-question to us all—"Who are these women? And what are they to you, and you, and you?" Her reply, which draws us to the final moments of the performance, begins with the song "Joanne Little" by famed civil rights chanteuse Bernice Johnson Reagon.[7] The lyrics, "She's our mama, she's yo' lover . . . that woman, the woman who's going to carry your child," tie Doris, Lena, Regina, Mama Pearl, and Deborah to the larger struggle for black liberation as gendered subjects. In 1974 Little, a twenty-year-old imprisoned black woman, went to trial on murder charges for killing her jailer, Clarence Alligood, a white man forty years her senior and known racist, who had entered her jail cell with sandwiches and an ice pick to rape her. When the jury found her innocent of the murder, for the first time in U.S. history, the courts sanctioned black women's right to defend themselves using deadly force against a white man's sexual assault and other bodily incursions. The Little case set a legal precedent that recognized black women "deserve justice," regardless of other people's racial bigotry and sexism, and despite the victim's at times less than "respectable" past (McGuire, *At the Dark End of the Street*, 225). The defense's successful argument that the jailer had abused his power and acted with "lawlessness and indifference toward black women's humanity" was a watershed moment in the long black liberation struggle, as well as for women's rights, prisoner rights, and antirape organizing (McGuire, 224). The song "Joanne Little" was their battle cry. In performing this archive Jones places the prisoners' stories in a context that frames their criminality as having roots that reach back through generations of inequality perpetrated by other authority figures, as well as in inequalities in operation now. The women reappear then as both victims and perpetrators of wrongdoing, not as one or the other as dominant discourse would suggest, but as both, and more.

The question of what to do about them—the women, the inequalities, the injustices—will take more than aerobics class or a theatrical event, but she begins an answer in the final moments back at the altar.[8] Her decision to bring the issues "to the ancestors" shifts us outside of the punitive trajectory of law enforcement into the realm of spiritual possibility. We participate in finding an ending to the performance, and with it a solution to the bigger issues that the piece grapples with. In the ritual she conducts, by raising our hands we acknowledge we have known crime from both sides of the fence—we know victims and we know perpetrators (we may even have been both at various times). Our participation evidences that there are no real boundaries between the criminal and the rest of us. Criminality, like race, is a performative, a framework we utilize to inhabit, make sense of, and navigate the world. The altar becomes a place in which to lay our fears of criminals and of crime aside. Where penal institutions are designed to commemorate past wrongdoing by placing perpetrators in a painful state of perpetual backward-looking, the altar enacts a practice of commemoration that memorializes the past but enables us to grow toward a future as new tokens of our experiences are placed upon it. Altar practice connects us to the past, the dead, even the dying, while working to enact change for the living, the present, the future.

In the final moments of *Big-Butt Girls* Jones enacts a vision for the future. She unfolds and reads a yellowed letter from a nephew serving time for murder. Taking it from the altar, she shares with us his dreams for the future as well as his sorrows. The dreams, given new life by her reading, point to the possibility of futurity for people locked in steel and concrete cages. Not only will what he wrote be remembered, but in her performance of his text Jones reenacts the moment of dreaming. As she reads, we travel with them, and we know how very close, very real, very human, very vulnerable we all are. Our act of collective witnessing affirms one of Jones's closing statements: "We're all involved here . . . this ain't no time to be buying dogs and locking doors because you see 'them' coming. 'Cause they could be us and you may wake up and find that you've locked yourself in and they're sitting at your breakfast table." Because she has shown us who we/the criminals are, these final words land without evoking fear. Her arms outstretched, dancing, calling to catch imaginary women falling all around her as evidence that the struggle continues, and that we need not be still or silent in it.[9]

To rehumanize the criminalized means to do more than just release the incarcerated body from the confines of the penal institution, but to free it so it may enjoy the rich sociocultural practices of human life. In the words of Holocaust survivor Primo Levi, not only must the material body be valorized by such acts of liberation, but "the culturally inscribed human practices which animate" human beings as people must be enacted over and over again; all our humanity depends upon it (Ross, *Primo Levi's Narrative of Embodiment*, 10).

NOTES

1. I use the terms "prisoners," "incarcerated women or men," "men or women prisoners," and "imprisoned women or men" interchangeably in this paper to refer to those study participants who are under some measure of penal supervision, whether they be physically in prison or jail, on probation, or on parole. I utilize this terminology rather than refer to them as "female convicts" or "inmates" to continually evoke the participants' political relationship to the state as gendered—as well as racialized and classed—subjects. As Megan Sweeney argues, the terms "convict," "inmate," and "prisoner" are used widely, interchangeably by prison professionals and the general public. However, each signifies "different political charges" (*Reading Is My Window*, 271). The term "prisoners" encompasses all persons *deprived of liberty*, a key concept in the development of American judicial and penal practices that specifically evokes the image of a person "held against [their] will" (Willie London quoted in Sabo et al., *Prison Masculinities*, 9). "Imprisoned" and "incarcerated" highlight the penal institutions' "act[s] of 'enclosure'" and the "process of cancellation" that moving from a state of *citizenship* to the status of a *prisoner* confers (Billone, "Performing Civil Death," 263). While I recognize that prisoners and officers prefer "inmate," for this study I utilize the alternatives so that I might continually highlight the incarcerated people's gendered "status" while I "denote their physical confinement

without conferring on them an existential or fixed identity as criminals" (Sweeney, *Reading Is My Window*, 271).

2. Under the guise of pursuing fair, gender-neutral justice, in the late 1980s police officers nationwide implemented a policy of "dual arrests" in domestic violence calls. This led to the heightened persecution of women as offenders, many of whom were actually victims of abuse who had injured their attackers while protecting themselves. For many poor women and racial minorities, the changes led to increased "involvement with officials" who, once they arrived on the scene, inquired about unrelated issues such as their immigration status or parenting ability. These "unwanted interventions by the state" placed already marginalized women in still more vulnerable positions vis-à-vis their abusive partners and the government (Bumiller, *In an Abusive State*, 11).

3. Jails hold three primary categories of prisoners—those who have been convicted of crime and sentenced to serve up to one year behind bars (prisons are for those sentenced to one year or more time); those that have been accused of crimes and are awaiting trial behind bars because they have been denied bail by the court; and those who are awaiting trial, but cannot afford their bail. The latter are the majority of people confined to U.S. jails.

4. The script indicates this parental authority is a father, but in the Northwestern performance Jones conjured the mother instead. Over twenty years Jones has made many new discoveries in performing *Big-Butt Girls.* Many of these discoveries have been incorporated into the performance, but they remain unscripted. My discussion of Jones's work utilizes the published script as a foundation, but relies heavily upon my own experiences seeing the show and video documentation of the performance at Northwestern University in May 2011.

5. Simply put, during Prohibition the sale and consumption of alcohol was illegal, making a host of brewers, merchants, and drinkers criminals. As soon as Prohibition was lifted, this class of criminals disappeared.

6. Jones never stages stereotypical jail scenes or stereotypical people. We never see the prisoners in those spaces you would expect, such as immobilized in a jail cell or lounging around an outdoor exercise yard. Her performance intervenes in common perceptions about the internal architecture of jail spaces as well as prisoners' uses of them.

7. Though spelled Joan, Little's first name was pronounced Joanne.

8. Installation artist Amalia Mesa-Bains was another inspiration for Jones's performance and her inclusion of the altar. Mesa-Bains describes her altar practice as a repository for the past and an enactment of healing. Altars are sites of women's specific memory-making in domestic spaces. The accumulation of objects upon their surfaces mark singular moments in the life of the women who erect them, but taken as a whole, the altar serves as an indicator of the passage of time. For Mesa-Bains, altars stand at the intersection of the past, the present, and the future, what she calls "the space between living and dying" (Munro, "Moving, Personal Works").

9. This choreography also references the Progressive Era notion that white women who were engaged in crime had "fallen" from their original, god-given state as virtuous "true women." Because women of color were never granted such esteem, Jones's efforts to catch them as they fall stages an important intervention in penal discourse by confronting the raced as well as gendered practices of law enforcement (Rafter, *Creating Born Criminals;* Freedman, *Their Sisters' Keepers*).

WORKS CITED

Alexander, Michelle. *The New Jim Crow: Mass Incarceration in the Age of Colorblindness.* New York: New, 2010.

Balfour, Michael, and NetLibrary Inc. *Theatre in Prison: Theory and Practice.* Electronic Resource ed. Bristol, Eng.: Intellect, 2004.

Billone, Nina. "Performing Civil Death: The Medea Project and Theater for Incarcerated Women." *Text and Performance Quarterly* 29, no. 3 (July 2009): 260–75.

Bumiller, Kristin. *In an Abusive State: How Neoliberalism Appropriated the Feminist Movement Against Sexual Violence.* Durham, N.C.: Duke University Press, 2008.

Bureau of Justice Statistics. *Bulletin: Prison and Jail Inmates at Midyear 2000,* no. NCJ 185989 (2001). Washington, D.C.: U.S. Department of Justice.

———. *Special Report: Women Offenders,* no. NCJ 175688 (1999). Washington, D.C.: U.S. Department of Justice.

Cohen, Cathy J. *The Boundaries of Blackness: AIDS and the Breakdown of Black Politics.* Chicago: University of Chicago Press, 1999.

Collins, Patricia Hill. *Black Feminist Thought: Knowledge, Consciousness, and the Politics of Empowerment.* New York: Routledge, 1999.

Davis, Angela Y. *Are Prisons Obsolete?* New York: Seven Stories, 2003.

Elam, Harry J., Jr. "The Black Performer and the Performance of Blackness: The Escape; or, Leap to Freedom by William Wells Brown and No Place to Be Somebody by Charles Gordone." In *African-American Performance and Theater: A Critical Reader,* ed. Harry J. Elam and David Krasner, 288–305. Oxford: Oxford University Press, 2001.

Escobar, Maria. "No One Is Criminal." In *Abolition Now! Ten Years of Strategy and Struggle Against the Prison Industrial Complex.* Ed. CR10 Publications Collective. Oakland, Calif.: AK, 2008:

Flavin, Jeanne. "Of Punishment and Parenthood: Family-Based Social Control and the Sentencing of Black Drug Offenders." *Gender and Society* 15, no. 4 (August 2001): 611–33.

Freedman, Estelle B. *Their Sisters' Keepers: Women's Prison Reform in America, 1830–1930.* Ann Arbor: University of Michigan Press, 1981.

Garland, David. *The Culture of Control: Crime and Social Order in Contemporary Society.* Chicago: University of Chicago Press, 2001.

Hart, Steven. "The Historical and Social Role of the Arts in Prison." *Prison Journal* 66, no. 11 (1986): 11–25.

Johnson, Paula. *Inner Lives: Voices of African American Women in Prison*. New York: New York University Press, 2004.

Kanter, Jodi. *Performing Loss: Rebuilding Community Through Theater and Writing*. Carbondale: Southern Illinois University Press, 2007.

Leder, Drew. "Imprisoned Bodies: The Life-World of the Incarcerated." In *Prisons and Punishment: Reconsidering Global Penality*, ed. Mechthild Nagel and Seth N. Asumah, 55–69. Trenton, N.J.: Africa World, 2007.

Lloyd, Moya. "Feminism, Aerobics, and the Politics of the Body." *Body & Society* 2, no. 2 (June 1996): 79–98.

Lugones, Maria. "Playfulness, 'World'-Travelling, and Loving Perception." *Hypatia* 2, no. 2 (Summer 1987): 3–19.

Mauer, Marc. *Race to Incarcerate*. New York: New Press; W.W. Norton, 1999.

McGuire, Danielle L. *At the Dark End of the Street: Black Women, Rape and Resistance—A New History of the Civil Rights Movement from Rosa Parks to the Rise of Black Power*. New York: Alfred A. Knopf, 2010.

Moses, Greg. "Time and Punishment in an Anesthetic World Order." In *Prisons and Punishment: Reconsidering Global Penality*, ed. Mechthild Nagel and Seth N. Asumah, 71–75. Trenton, N.J.: Africa World, 2007.

Munro, David. "Moving, Personal Works at Fresno Art Museum." *Fresno Bee*, August 18, 2011.

Rafter, Nicole. *Creating Born Criminals*. Urbana: University of Illinois Press, 1997.

Roberts, Dorothy E. *Killing the Black Body: Race, Reproduction and the Meaning of Liberty*. New York: Pantheon Books, 1997.

Ross, Charlotte. *Primo Levi's Narrative of Embodiment: Containing the Human*. New York: Routledge, 2011.

Sabo, Don, with Terry A. Kupers and Willie London, eds. *Prison Masculinities*. Philadelphia: Temple University Press, 2001.

Sweeney, Megan. *Reading Is My Window: Books and the Art of Reading in Women's Prisons*. Chapel Hill: University of North Carolina Press, 2010.

Thompson, James. *Prison Theatre: Perspectives and Practices. Forensic Focus*, vol. 4. London: Jessica Kingsley, 1998.

Waits, Tom. "Christmas Card from a Hooker in Minneapolis." *Blue Valentine*. Asylum Records, 1978.

Warner, Sara. "Restorytive Justice: Theater as a Redressive Mechanism for Incarcerated Women." In *Razor Wire Women: Prisoners, Activists, Scholars, and Artists*, ed. Jodi Michelle Lawston and Ashley E. Lucas, 229–46. Albany: State University of New York Press, 2011.

PASSING SOLO

Based on the Novella by Nella Larsen

Adapted by Nancy Cheryll Davis-Bellamy

PRODUCTION HISTORY

Passing Solo was originally performed in October 2007 at the Black Middle Class Performances Conference at the University of Iowa. It was directed by Nancy Renee and Tony Robinson, with lighting provided by Nathaniel Bellamy and Tony Robinson, and sound by Nathaniel Bellamy. The production stage manager for this performance was Sarah Allyn Bauer.

CHARACTERS

[*both played by the same woman*]
Irene Westover, light-skinned African American, twenties or thirties
Clare Kendry Bellew, light-skinned African American, twenties or thirties

[*Two chairs with a small table between them appear on center stage front. A beating heart can be heard, which transitions to music.* IRENE *enters as music starts. Slides appear on a screen at the back of the stage. The words "RACE," "GENDER," "MEMORIES," "PASSING," and finally "Passing Solo" appear in succession. After the slide show ends,* IRENE *crosses center with letters in hand. Another picture comes up.*]

IRENE: Purple Ink. Trouble. Clare Kendry, an old girlfriend from child-hood. She was famous for getting me into awful scrapes. She always courted disaster and the moment it appeared, Clare jumped in head *first.*

[*The music of a harp lasts for a twenty-second interlude.*]

We were constant companions, Clare and I. More by circumstance than by choice. Caught between two worlds, one opened, one closed, we existed the only way we knew how—depending on each other for survival. Her beauty was breathtaking, even at an early age, but underneath there was a coldness that no one could penetrate, not even me, and she held no allegiance beyond her own immediate desires. She was selfish, cold and hard. And yet she had too, a strange capacity of transforming warmth and passion. Catlike. That was the best way to describe Clare. Like a cat she sometimes appeared to have no feel-ings at all, and the next moment she could be extremely affectionate and impulsive. And she could never understand how we could look so much alike we could be sisters, but what was it about her, and not me, that scared people so? I would never have imagined the situations she got us into—yet I have to admit, there was always a sense of danger and excitement and . . . I enjoyed it.

There was that time with Knickerbocker, the school headmaster—who we called "Knickerbutt"—and his precious record collection, which no one was supposed to touch. I knew better than to go along with her scheme, and that we were to steer clear of the gramophone.

CLARE: Come on Rene, we have to practice for the dance and Knicker-butt is hoarding this gramophone and will be in hot water himself if the board ever finds out. And how are we going to beat Ophelia and Gertrude for best dancers if we don't practice. Come on Rene, she begged . . . don't be a 'fraidy cat.

[*Music plays as the performer acts out* IRENE *and* CLARE *dancing.*]

IRENE: Of course, we were caught and punished, first by Knickerbutt and later by my father. Her father, the school janitor, was a mystery to us all—he had been a classmate of my father but had fallen on hard times—Father used to say Poor Bob Kendry—what a terrible end he came to, losing his wife so early and all . . . Clare paid dearly for her father's mishaps and bad fortunes—and was constantly teased at school . . .

[*The audience hears a mocking chant: "Old Man Kendry uses his mop to sop his whiskey slop. Old man Kendry uses his mop to sop his whiskey slop."*]

CLARE: SHUT UP! Shut up all of you!

IRENE: She fought back though, for when driven to anger, she was capable of scratching and very effectively too—how savagely she clawed those boys that day—"like an alley cat, my mother used to say—"most unladylike." But still I stood by her, even during the worst of it. There was that time at Sears and Roebuck—we would get dressed up and shop as "ladies"—which really was nothing more than shop looking. One of our schoolmates, Albert Brickhouse, worked there as an elevator operator—he and Clare were constantly fighting but I think he really wanted to be her beau—but she wouldn't give him the time of day:

CLARE: There is nothing a poor colored boy could ever do for me and as far as I can see, Albert Brickhouse, you are always going to be poor and you are always going to be colored.

ALBERT'*s voice*: You need to come down off your high horse, girl. You daddy be doing the soft shine cross the barroom floor and you got the nerve to be looking down at somebody.

CLARE: Excuse me, Miss, but the colored boy insulted us, and perhaps, he should be dismissed?

IRENE: Which he was . . . immediately. I, on the other hand, was never so embarrassed in my life. But for reasons I can't explain, even now, I defended her to the last. The others didn't know how hard her life was and that she really could be very sweet and had such a "having" way about her . . . When we were teens, her father was killed. Right after the burial, within days, Clare was gone. For twenty years *I did not see or think of her.*

[*Piano music plays, as in a fancy restaurant. The volume decreases.*]

The Drayton is "Whites Only." But sometimes—depending on how much sun catches me, I sport a touch of something exotic, a bit of Portuguese or a little Italian perhaps. They're never really certain, but still it's passable. And while I usually live quite happily in my Negro world, on occasion, passing permits me some segregated comforts that should rightfully be mine anyway. The maître d' assumes this well-off white lady will leave a nice tip, so he graciously seats me and takes my order. The maître d' assumed correctly. I am a good tipper. But then I assumed that everyone else would assume as he had assumed . . . and that I would be fine. [IRENE *sees* CLARE—*bends down to get scarf.*]

CLARE: Pardon me, but I think I know you. Certainly we have met before. Don't tell me you're not Irene Westover, or should I say Rene? Rene, it's me, Clare. For the last few weeks I've had the feeling that something amazing and truly wonderful was going to happen. Dear Sweet Rene, I'm not a ghost. I'm real. Touch me. I've thought of you each and every day since we were last together. Yes, last month was twenty years since my father died, how sweet of you to remember. I wanted to say good-bye to you, but as soon as they buried him, I was whisked away to Boston—an old spinster aunt from my mother's side took me in. I never knew she existed until I was sent to her. It was a cold barren life. No visitors were allowed and we did not visit. As soon as I was able, I left and did not look back.

[*The audience hears the sounds of an ocean and an ocean liner.*]

CLARE: I'm sorry but I don't hold conversations with strange men. It's not proper. Pleased to meet you, Mr. Bellew. Yes, Clare, Clare Kendry. Yes . . . the ocean is very relaxing. Watching since we left port? I'm not sure whether I should be flattered or frightened by that. [*A giggle turns into a cough.*] Oh please don't put the cigar out on my account—I love the smell of a good cigar. My own father—God rest his soul—he loved them dearly. He fell ill a few weeks after we arrived in England

and I just buried him in his family burial ground near his grandparents. My mother died when I was just a month old and there were no brothers or sisters. Yes, I am all alone. Well, thank you Mr. Bellew, you are very charming—very charming indeed. So tell me, what brings you on this winter cruise? Oh, you're looking for a wife and you thought you might find one on a cruise. How quaint! Perhaps you'll meet a passing mermaid . . . dinner? I'd love to.

[*The restaurant music plays as she crosses.*]

CLARE: Dearest Rene, so many times I wrote you, but tore up the letter before post time. It was so odd to go from sharing everything with you, until quite suddenly nothing . . . I've lost count of how many lifetimes ago it was when we were such passionate little girls . . . don't you ever think about them? No? Those schoolgirl imaginings were my light in the darkest of times. Do you ever wonder why more people like us don't pass? It's such a frightfully easy thing to do. You must come to my house for tea—*I insist!*

[*Light changes.*]

IRENE [*reading letter*]: "For I am lonely, so lonely . . . I cannot help longing to be with you again, as I have never longed for anything before. It's like an ache, a pain that never ceases . . . and it's your fault Rene dear. At least partly. For I wouldn't now, perhaps, have this terrible, this wild desire if I hadn't seen you that time at the Drayton . . .

[*A telephone rings, and* BRIAN'*s voice calls.*]: Ready dear?

IRENE: I'm almost ready to go Brian, I just want to make sure I have everything—I need to go to the printing office on 116th Street to see about some handbills and more tickets for the dance. Yes, everything is all set—the boxes are sold and nearly the first batch of tickets—then there's all that cake to sell—it's a terrible lot of work . . . you're a dear to wait for me.

[*Phone rings.*]

Yes, I'm sure that's her again—she's been calling all day—Of course you're right, its best to head these things off at the start—but you just don't understand—Clare is not an easy person to ignore—

[*Phone rings.*]

I'll answer it this time Zulena—Hello? Clare—yes Zulena gave me your messages—so sorry I haven't called—we just got back from Idlewild—Brian and I and the boys went to Gertrude's family cabin for the weekend—yes—it's quite the thing you know . . . Tomorrow? I'll have to see—may I call you back? What was it about Clare's voice that was so appealing, so seductive . . .?

BRIAN's *voice*: Irene . . .

IRENE: Coming Brian.

[*Light changes as* IRENE *puts letter in mailbox.*]

[*Doorbell rings once.*]

CLARE: Thank you Edward, that will be all—Please show Mrs. Redfield into the drawing room.

Rene, I'm so glad you changed your mind about visiting me. I know you can't stay long, and that you must get back to your boys, but it's so good to see you again. Ironic, isn't it? You with two boys, and me with a girl. I know I said I would never have any, but I had to produce an heir for Jack. My God, the whole experience from beginning to end was terrifying. No, I don't mean the pain—I was more concerned about what color the child would be. We both know Negro children can be born pale, but the complications show up a few days later when they start to get a little color. Thank goodness, Margery looks exactly like Jack, same coloring, facial features. Everything. She's a homely little thing, but I thank God for that every day. And he brags about her all the time. Her teachers say she's a natural linguist—fluent in five languages and German. She's been away at school since she was six, but she comes home for long holidays. I rarely see her—but in the end my distance will most likely save her. And I've provided Jack with what he wanted most—a nice, respectable family portrait.

[*Fast white flash of light to simulate a photographer's flash.*]

Mostly he fulfills his needs with other women, and everyone is *happy* . . . But enough about me. Tell me about your Brian.

IRENE: He's a doctor, and a wonderful father. He has gotten a bit restless these days with his practice, which I suppose is to be expected with any profession—after all he doesn't always see the good he does . . . No, Brian doesn't care for ladies, especially the sick ones. I sometimes wish he did.

[BRIAN'S *voice*:] How I hate sick people and their stupid meddling families in smelly dirty rooms—climbing filthy steps in dark hallways to reach them.

IRENE: It's South America that attracts him. His dream is to study plants in the Brazilian jungle. Sometimes he includes me and the boys, but mostly it's just him in a pith helmet foraging. Clare, I don't mean to be rude but I am curious, how did you convince Mr. Bellew not to try for a son?

CLARE: He hasn't completely given up on the idea. However, I will never have another child. Now we know what my reasons are. On the other hand, you have no such constraints. You could have something as dark as the ace of spades and all would be well. No little girl to complete the painting? I see—well Brian must know a few tricks, being a doctor and all. I had no such expectations with Jack. On our wedding night, he lumbered over me dripping sweat on my face. The best part is it never takes him long . . . yes, he still wants a boy, a girl can't carry on his name and all, but I will never risk that again, never . . . [*walking down hall, clearing throat*] Jack meet my forever first friend—Irene Redfield.

IRENE: Charmed to meet you, Mr. Bellew. Oh the old days—I'm sorry—I can't share more stories about Clare with you—I must confess memories fade with age . . . Excuse me, I don't think I heard you correctly. Did you say "Little Nig"? Oh—a nickname, how charming. She was as white as a lily, but is getting darker and darker all the time and you're afraid she'll wake up one day and turn into what? You don't like Negroes, Mr. Bellew? Have you ever known any? [*puts on gloves*]—Ahh, yes, well all that robbing and killing all the time and worse would be a deterrent. I'm sorry, look at the time—I really must get back to my boys.

[*As she crosses stage left, she says*] It was just like her not *to warn me.*

[*Door slamming—raise volume in slamming.*]

IRENE: She led me into a trap without the slightest bit of concern for me. He despises Negroes! She could have warned me. [*Picks up letter from basket.*] She actually expects me to forgive her for subjecting me to her ogre of a husband.

[*Reading letter*] "Rene Dear—how do I thank you for your visit? I know how you are feeling under the circumstances, that I ought not to have asked you to come or rather insisted. But if you could know how happy, how excited I was to meet you again and how I ached to see more of you, you would understand me wanting to see you again, and maybe forgive me a little. My love to you dear Rene, and as always, my poor thanks. And as a postscript, I must add, dear Rene, it may just be, that after all, your way may be the wiser and infinitely happier one. I'm not so sure just now. At least not as sure as I have been" . . .

[*The lights change. The audience hears the sound of chimes and the voice of* ZULENA]: Mrs. Bellew is here to see you Mrs. Redfield.

CLARE: Dear Sweet Rene, how are you? Thank you for seeing me without notice . . . I understand you've been busy, but didn't you mean to answer my letters? Every day I went to that nasty little post office, expecting something to be there and every day there was nothing. I'm sure they were all beginning to think I was carrying on an illicit love affair. And now, please tell me quite frankly why you didn't answer my letters.

IRENE: Clare, I apologize for not answering your calls and letters. I've been frightfully busy and knowing you I thought it *better to be in touch.*

[*Phone rings twice.*]

IRENE: . . . Once I wasn't so busy. [*Picks up phone.*] Thank you, Zulena, I have it. Hello? Hugh—[*to* CLARE—"Hugh Wentworth!"]—Oh quite, and you? I'm sorry every single thing's gone—yes I suppose you could. Not very pleasant though—Wait, I've got it, I'll change mine with whoever's next to you, and you can have that. You're welcome—See you then—good-bye. The NWL Dance. Negro Welfare League . . .

I'm on the ticket committee, or rather I am the committee. Thank heavens it comes off tomorrow and doesn't happen for another year. I am about crazy and now I've got to persuade someone to exchange boxes with me. Yes—THE Hugh Wentworth is coming to our dance. Do you know him? It's 1927 in the City of New York—hundreds of white people come to Harlem all the time—Brian says:

[*Voice-over by* BRIAN]: Pretty soon the colored people won't be able to get in at all or will have to sit in Jim Crow sections.

IRENE: What do they come for?—Same reason as you, to see Negroes.— Various motives. A few purely and frankly to enjoy themselves. Others to get material to turn into shekels. More, to gaze on those great and near great while THEY gaze on the Negroes.

CLARE: It all sounds terribly interesting and amusing. Rene—suppose I come too? In a crowd of that kind I shan't be noticed at all and I don't think we have to worry about any of Jack's friends going to the Negro Welfare League Dance. I'll take my chances on getting by. Not a good idea? Such games, Rene. First you ignore me until I take matters into my own hands and arrive unannounced. Now this. I understand you're angry with me about that afternoon with Jack, and I must say you behaved beautifully. And don't you understand Rene—it was that partly that has made me want to see other people. It just swooped down and changed everything. If it hadn't been for that, I'd have gone to the end—never seeing any of you. But that did something to me and I've been so lonely ever since. You can't know what's like. Never anyone to really talk to. Not close to a single soul.

[*Voice-over by* BRIAN]: Irene?

IRENE: I'll be right there Brian, just looking for an earring. Clare is downstairs?! She's early, right just excited. What's she wearing? Red of course. She's extraordinarily beautiful, isn't she? Oh Brian, you're trying to protect my feelings. Don't worry. The one thing I've never tried to deny is how beautiful Clare is . . . I've just one thing left to do and will be right there—do be a dear and entertain her a little longer won't you?

[*Party music*]

[*Voice-over by* HUGH]: Rich man, poor man, beggar man, thief, doctor, lawyer, Indian chief . . .

IRENE: Yes, that's it Hugh. They all seem to be here with a few more that can't be labeled—it's quite a collection of specimens, I agree. I sold a good number of tickets by simply mentioning the fact that the Hugh Wentworth would honor our humble little dance with his presence. The beauty in red out of the fairy tale? That's my friend, Clare Kendry Bellew. She wanted especially to meet you. No, she has not stopped dancing all night. I'm sure she'll dance with you, all you have to do is ask her. Well, you have to admit that the average colored man is a better dancer than the average white man—that is, if the celebrities and butter and egg men who find their way up here are fair specimens of white Terpsichorean art. Beg your pardon Hugh? Oh, you are so clever, you usually know everything. Even how to tell the sheep from the goats. What do you think, is she? Don't let it worry you. Nobody can, not by looking. I'm afraid I can't explain it clearly. It's easy for a Negro to pass for white. But I don't think it would be so simple for a white person to pass for colored. No, of course you wouldn't think of that, why would you? There Clare is again, dancing again with Brian. Yes, they do make a stunning pair, don't they? . . . Hugh, would you excuse me for one minute, I see someone who can't seem to find their box . . .

[*Lights and music change.*]

CLARE: It's so lovely out here on the balcony. Thank you Brian for the punch. You must be very proud of Irene. It's quite an event she's put together. She's always been like that—perfectly organized and dependable. If you moved her to South America, she would organize something like this in the middle of the jungle in no time at all. So what's down there in those jungles? Ah, Mysteries—many and mighty hidden in the saps of nameless plants. Oh, aren't there enough mysteries closer to home? Well, perhaps you're seeing too many of the same ones . . .

[*Traffic sounds.*]

IRENE: I'm so glad you had a good time Clare. And you were right, no one recognized you or suspected anything, not even the perceptive Hugh

Wentworth—he wasn't sure and even if he were, he would never cause any trouble of that sort. Yes, Brian is a gentleman and it's awfully nice of him to offer to run you downtown—Good night Clare—Brian—goodnight . . . [*Reaching out to touch her, crosses to center.*]

And that began my new friendship with Clare Kendry. She came frequently after that, yet I could never tell if her comings were a joy or vexation. Certainly she was no trouble, she didn't have to be entertained or even noticed, as if anyone could ever avoid noticing Clare. So on it went, she came with us to parties and dances, and as time went on even I ceased to be perturbed about the possibility of Clare's husband *stumbling on her racial identity.*

[*Park sounds.*]

CLARE: Hugh Wentworth?! Of course I remember you . . . Allow me to introduce you to my husband, Jack Bellew. Jack Bellew—Hugh Wentworth. Hugh is a famous writer, Jack. I was introduced to him by Irene Redfield. You remember her, don't you? It's good to see you Hugh—Jack would you hail us a cab? I'm sorry, I'm not feeling well—drinks another time perhaps [*coughs*]. Jack doesn't know it yet, but we're planning on staying in New York permanently—I promise him he won't regret it. I'll explain about the dance in the cab dear—Again, it's good seeing you Hugh.

[*Laughter; lights change.*]

IRENE: Clare? What a surprise—you're early—I wasn't expecting you for a few more hours—Brian?—I thought you had an appointment. Canceled again? I see. I've got just a few things to do and will be right down—you two don't mind do you? Brian, may I speak to you for a minute? I'm not blind Brian! I don't blame you. I know how cunning she can be. She seduced you. I am not being absurd! I have watched her with you!

How dare she return to do this to me. I won't be bullied any longer. Yes Operator, I'd like the number for a Mr. Jack Bellew. Mr. Bellew please. Yes, this is, this is, Irene Westover Redfield. I am a Negro. Your wife is also a Negro and she is having an affair with my Negro husband. That would just about kill him on all fronts, wouldn't it?

[*Blackout. Tango music.*]

CLARE: Rene, Jack wants to have you and Brian over for dinner. I'm supposed to arrange something before we leave to see Margery. Of course you can't have dinner with him, silly, we know that! Right now he thinks you're out of town. When you get back, I'll go on vacation. When I return he'll be busy and around and around it will go. Where it ends no one knows! There isn't any chance of you two running into each other, Rene—you don't travel in the same circles. And I won't leave you again, no matter what.

IRENE: You must be insane—the risk is too great. Clare, I want you to leave New York immediately. Have you ever seriously considered what it would mean if he were to find you out?

But just as she had done when we were children, she forged ahead—not thinking of anyone but herself. Clare's permanency in New York weakened me in many ways—I found myself wanting to take risks with her, and knowing it would not be the right thing to do, I would back out at the last minute . . . but the straw that broke the camel's back was the day I ran into *Jack Bellew myself.*

[*Calliope music.*]

IRENE: I was in Central Park with my boys—Albert Brickhouse—I haven't seen you in ages. Yes, these are my boys—Junior and Ralph—yes, quite a handful. He's a doctor—Harlem. As a matter of fact Clare and I have been in touch recently—yes, she's still passing—in fact she married a white man . . . [*sees Jack*] He saw me and he knew.

[*Laughter.*]

CLARE: Surprise Rene! Brian says I picked the most perfect day to pop over for a visit. He's invited me to Hugh's party—you don't mind do you?

IRENE: The cat had my tongue. What I wanted to say was—Something awful happened today. Jack Bellew saw me in the park. He knows I'm a Negro. But instead I said . . . I only need to freshen up and then I'll be ready.

[IRENE *crosses to the table. There are continuous sounds of traffic, a party, ringing doorbell, music, and ticker tape.*]

Hugh lives in a type of a building called a skyscraper. He waited five years for the top floor. The "Penthouse" they call it. The view alone is worth it. We sometimes lean out of the window and look down on all of New York. I can't—I don't—I never clearly remembered what happened that night at Hugh's party. Clare and I were at the window—smoking cigarettes and—someone turned on the gramophone—or was it the radio? The talking—the laughter—never for a minute ceased. Everything was confusion. The doorbell rang. I heard Jack Bellew's voice above the rest. He came rushing toward us—I put my hand on Clare's arm . . . One moment she was standing there—the next she was gone.

[IRENE *turns back to audience—takes off gloves.*]

RADIO ANNOUNCER: Clare Kendry Bellew—wealthy wife to businessman Jack Bellew—fell twenty stories to her death from the downtown penthouse apartment of the famous writer Hugh Wentworth.

IRENE: We were constant companions, Clare and I . . .

[IRENE *closes lipstick. Wah-wah music plays. The slide show comes up after the wah-wah music fades.*]

INTERVIEW WITH NANCY CHERYLL DAVIS-BELLAMY

Jennifer Devere Brody

Let's just start with the question about how you came to do the play *Passing*?

I was given the book *Passing* by Nella Larsen when I was twenty-two by an acting mentor as a suggestion that it would be a good book for me to look at in terms of material for myself as an actor. I read it and fell in love with it, I mean fell in love with it. And I was determined to make it into a movie at the time. This was 1979. I carried the book around with me, I would tell everyone I knew about the story, wouldn't it make a great movie? I was in San Francisco at the time, studying acting at the American Conservatory Theater. Then when I moved to Los Angeles about two years later, various people I met and told about the book would also get excited by it. I wasn't a writer so I knew I needed a screenwriter. I had all these dreams of you know, Lonette McKee would play Irene, I would play Clare, Denzel would play Brian. In 1987 I met an actress, Nancy Renee, who later became one of my cofounders at Towne Street Theatre. At the time she and I were acting together in the "Scottish" play, I guess I should say it like that, even though we aren't in a theater. We were the witches, two of the three witches rather. Anyway, so she and I had formed a production company, at that time it was called A 2N Production. We met a writer and she wrote a screenplay that we liked. But it needed something else. It didn't have enough spice to it. Because I think the novel has a lot of spice to it. Anyway, so then we put together a whole package. Now this was in the days before digital, so making a movie was a big thing. You couldn't do it unless you had some real money because it was film. We put together a package, we had a proposal, a budget. Suffice to say that part didn't happen. And so it kind of sat on the shelf for a little bit. But I still had this in my head to do. Then in '93 we cofounded the Towne Street Theatre along with my husband, artist Nathaniel Bellamy. I asked another friend of ours who was a screenwriter to look at the piece because I was still determined to make this movie. And he looked at it, and he suggested that it would make a good play.

And I had never thought of it as being a play, I had always thought of it as a film. Anyway, and so I said, really? And he said, yeah, I really think it would make a great play. So I went back looking at it. Anyway, then we got a grant from the LA County Arts Commission. We were able to hire a writer-for-hire, Sheri Bailey, who came aboard to flesh it out, and we did a reading of it and the response was amazing. We said, oh, we have something here. At this point, we have our own theater. By this time it's '96. We've got our own theater and we said, you know what, we can do this. Then we got another grant from the LA Cultural Affairs Department. And we put the first version of it on in 1997.

I was fortunate enough to have seen that 1997 production in Los Angeles. It had a complete cast and marvelous costumes and set. You have since had a revival of that production and it's won a lot of awards—including a Best Actress Award for you! What for you are the dramatic elements of the novel, which is presented in three parts, Encounter, Recounter, and Finale? I am curious about this because I kept the advertising postcard for your show and you billed it as a tale of love, lies, deceit, and passion. But for you, what details comprise the inherent drama of the story?

I think it is the friendship of those two women. Obviously the element of passing for white during a time when it was a dangerous thing to do, it was really a life-or-death situation. I don't think people today can understand that if you did that you didn't come back. If you lived with a racist like Clare did, it was a dangerous thing because her life was at stake. And the possibility of the triangle between Clare and Irene and Brian, which is not actually set completely in the book. The thing about the book is that it leaves itself open for a lot of interpretation. Of course there has been a lot of discussion and writing about what did Nella Larsen really mean, did she mean this, did she mean that, did she not mean any of it, is it just a story, you know. But the themes of friendship, the themes of how far do you go for your friends, and what friendship means, and how it changes relationships, what you really feel about something are there. Those kinds of things, it just has so many elements to it.

I agree! I wanted to ask you a question about the various dramatic translations you have done. The versions make such an interesting produc-

tion history. For example, I know you have been the artistic producer, as well as an actress playing the lead, and in this production, *Passing Solo,* playing both Irene and Clare. But it started out as an ensemble piece. Now it has become *Passing Solo* and there were some other strategic changes you made. Can you talk about some of the specific translations you made before we go back to talking about passing as a social and political phenomenon?

I played Clare in the original version. We did it in '97, and again in '98 because people wanted to see this play. So anyway, I played Clare in both of those versions. Then in '99, I wanted to see it, I wanted to step out and see it. What is the audience seeing? I'm in it so I can't see it in that context. So at that point Nancy Renee and I codirected it and we cast other actors in the roles, and it was fascinating to codirect it. And then we put it away for a while, still thinking of this film element. And then . . . because we had the theater, there were different plays in between, but people would ask us about this play—it was amazing—when are you doing the play again, when are you doing the play again? We had a lot of people who had come to Towne Street Theatre and this was their initial view, their initial introduction to us, and they are still coming to our shows because of that play. Anyway, so, in '04, by this time we had moved out of the original Towne Street Theatre downtown and we are in residence at Stella Adler Theatre in Hollywood. And so we decided to bring it back. And what was wonderful was the actor who originated the character of Brian Redfield, Brian Everet Chandler, a wonderful actor who did it in '97 (he received a Best Supporting Actor nomination from the NAACP in 1997), was able to reprise his role. We had a different Irene, a company member, a wonderful girl, Lira Angel. And Nancy Renee, and Sy Richardson, who was the original director of the first two productions, they codirected it. And this time we expanded it. We had seven characters originally, I think the next time we had ten, and then by this time we expanded it to fourteen, so that you had many more people in the dance scenes, some were background, there weren't any really critical characters, in terms of expanding those roles. It was still just about Irene and Clare, and Brian of course. And then when we did it in '04, it was still this thing of, going to make it into a film, and now it's becoming easier to do so, and that's still in our heads. In '07, Vershawn

Young from the University of Iowa, who had become a member of our company, went back to Iowa. He was doing a symposium there, and he asked me to come be a part of it, and present a paper on *Passing,* and then a few weeks later he called and said, instead of a paper, can you do a solo show, and I thought, Sure, I can do that. Fourteen characters to one, two. Anyway, I remember saying yes and then not thinking about it for about a month . . . I would think about it, you know, it would sort of twirl in my head . . . How am I going to do this? Just really trying to figure out how to conceive it. Anyway, then I went back to the book. I went to the book, I went to our script, and started really thinking how to do this for one person, and what comes out is . . . like the book and like the play . . . it's about those two women. It's about Clare and Irene. Everybody else is around them, revolving around them. They're incidental to their story. And so then, through that process I adapted it, using bits from the book, using stuff from the play, putting original things in there.

Can you talk about some of those original changes that you made? Maybe things such as the lighting cues, were they in the original script?

The lighting, no, the lighting is all different. Some of the sound is from the original play, like the park sounds, when they're at the Drayton hotel is similar, some of the music that we used. And we incorporated voice-over after Iowa and the projections were added before coming back to Northwestern. So, it continues to grow. Every time we do it, it continues to grow. We look at other places, in terms of opening it up and making it fuller, even though it is a solo show, to still give that illusion that all these other things are going on. But the lighting, very different, obviously, because it's just one person.

I love your choice of bathing Clare's character in red light because that also comes from the book where the "scarlet" character is indexed by red accessories—a dress, a metaphoric spear, et cetera.

And you know that actually was Tony Robinson, who came on as co-director for *Passing Solo,* with Nancy Renee, she was the obvious choice to direct it, being as she had started this journey early on with me. And when she had to go out of town, I still needed to work on the show, and I asked him to join us. He's a wonderful director, a member of our company as well, and it was his concept for the red lighting to be Clare.

And which character do you enjoy playing more?

[*Laughs*] It's interesting, because I did play Clare in the stage productions, the full productions of it I should say, she was easier for me. There's elements of her that are sort of elements of my personality, just a little bit more vivacious, and flirtatious, shall we say, and Irene was more of a challenge because she is much more conservative, much more repressed, and that's why I really worked very hard to distinguish the two of them, because I was concerned that I didn't want to make Irene too much like Clare. Could I really make the difference in the two of them in one hour? So that's why I used the technique of the voices, because to me Irene's voice should be much lower and calmer. The rhythm of it is very different. And Clare's is very light and airy and a little more breathy. So, it was a challenge to get to Irene, it really was. As in the book, as in the original versions of the play, she's I think the harder character to play for a lot of the actors we found, even over the years, because there's a lot of subtlety to her. And there are a lot of things that are underneath her, but you have to be able to see it. It can't be so subtle you can't see it.

So are there gestural things in addition to the voice that you had to work on?

Yes. The way that Irene sits is very different than the way Clare sits. Irene always sits very upright; she crosses her ankles. She would never cross her legs . . . of course, in the twenties, you know, crossing your legs was a pretty advanced thing to do. Of course, Clare is very animated, she uses her hands a lot. She crosses her legs. The way she sits in the chair is definitely much more suggestive. She's more comfortable in her skin. Irene represents, to me, the way a woman was supposed to be, in that box in the twenties. She's very concerned about what she looks like and how she behaves.

You got an award for Best Costumes. Will you share your sense of why the clothes matter so much in this production?

Best Costumes in '97, and when we did it in '04, we also got Best Costumes Award from the NAACP. The clothes are just to die for. Just stunning. We had Joan Francis, our costume designer in both cases. Beautiful clothes, you know, the feathers, the boas, the silks, the wools, the . . .

brocades, you know, just all of that. All of those very rich elements were part of the appeal of the play. But I remember one of the actresses who played Irene said, "Oh, you know, her clothes are so muted." They were muted, obviously, because that represented who she was. "And Clare has all the real fancy stuff." It's because that's who she is, she is the wife of someone who is very rich. Very, very rich. And of course, Irene is the wife of a doctor, there's a whole different look that one has. The costumes also help with getting into the character. It sounds so corny to say this, but it's like an out-of-body experience. But it really is, just closing my eyes and becoming those people. I think because I am so connected to this book and to this piece, it may be easier in some ways, but whenever I step away from it, I have to go back to the book and read it. It really helps connect me with them. I read the play somewhat, but it's mainly the book I go back to. And remembering who those women were of that time. It is a conscious effort for me also in terms of the physicality of them, and like you said the way they sit, the way they move, the dresses, the heels, putting those heels on, putting on the hats, the gloves, that helps connect me to the characters, the physical elements of it as well as remembering mentally who these people are.

Did you think more about some of the class issues in casting, for example with the character Zulena the maid? I am thinking here of the stereotype, represented problematically in the book, of the black maid. How do you think about such challenges as an actress? Or Albert, the elevator operator?

It's interesting, the actors that have played them through the years and what they have brought to the roles. Zulena (who is in the book) at first was very subtle, very much in the background, and the thought of black people having a maid is an interesting way of looking at class. We think, well, white people have maids that are black people, but black people had and have help too. You know, nowadays, of course, that's not so much a thing, but in that time period it was a very big thing, and what those characters represented in terms of class differences. Zulena evolved over the years depending on the actor that played her. The first actor, I think, she had the right tone. Some of the other actors, they sort of pushed it a little bit more, which made her, in some ways, a little more comical, which was not the intention of that character at all. It's not written like that at all. We expanded her role somewhat to have more of a confrontation between Zulena and Clare, so that you have this person who is of a lower class, but she knows exactly what Clare is doing, and, you know, doesn't call her on it, per se, but she really lets her know that she knows what's happening. And then, with Albert (who was added to the play and is not in the book)—he represents a working-class black man versus Brian's professional aspects of being a doctor. In the solo piece we reworked Albert again, I added the line about, he's done well for himself. To let people know that even though Clare thought he would be nothing but a poor colored boy that would never have anything, indeed he was able to make something of himself.

Can you talk a little bit about the phenomenon of passing as a social act, to return to an earlier moment in our discussion? I'd love to hear your thoughts about connections, if any, to your own life, or your thinking about issues such as cross-casting? And then I have a question about humor.

Yeah. Being very fair, fair enough to pass for white myself, has always been a part of my makeup. It's not something I ever did. I thought about it. You think about these things in terms of, oh, what if I were to be somebody else, or pretend to be somebody else, how could that benefit my career? I mean, that's where I would think of it—how it would/could affect my acting career.

Of course, I, too, think about passing—for white, for straight—every day. In fact, the first article I ever published was on the novel which I read my last day in college where I spotted the hardcover book at a secondhand book sale. The spine of the Arno Press edition was literally black and white. Something about the graphic caught my eye and when I opened the book, I was hooked. I was thinking here, though, about how cross-casting can intervene in how audiences understand the play. More specifically, in Lydia Diamond's play *Harriet Jacobs*, about fair-skinned slave Harriet Jacobs, she stipulates in the script that what we presume are phenotypically black actors play the white characters as well—all without any makeup or masks. There are many, many contradictions involved in playing race (as well as gender and sexuality) onstage.

Right, right, because as a fair-skinned actor, not so much now, it's opened up somewhat for the younger actresses, but when I began, it was very difficult. I mean, I would be told point-blank, you know, we love you, but you look white. We need somebody who looks black. I lost so many roles to that point—not on talent because I would be in the running, but on skin color. And I grew up in a town where I was probably the fairest person there. There weren't many fair-skinned people in my town in River Rouge, Michigan. But I always wanted to be black. That was my thing. I never wanted to be white. I thought being white was actually bad because growing up I was ostracized for it. And in my own family, everybody looks like something else. They don't all look traditionally, or not traditionally, what is classified as an African American person. My oldest brother, who is very fair-skinned, blue eyes, blonde hair, he actually made the choice to pass and actually has lived his life for the last, I don't know how many years, he's sixty-something now, but he actually stepped out of the family. So that is an element in my own family. Needless to say, that's why I identify with it. People always mention that they find Clare much more sympathetic than they imagine they would, and it's because there's a reason people pass. It's not necessarily just to have a better life. There is that. But there's also the element of being in a place where you feel like you belong because it's a strange thing to look like another ethnicity and be of a different ethnicity. The identity aspect. I remember it wasn't till, maybe I was eighteen or so, and I met this young man, and he was fair-skinned, and he came from this whole fair-skinned family, and they were very much into class and color. And I remember the mother making a comment about lighter folks being better then darker-skinned people. In my family it was never like that. Even though people were fair-skinned, there were also those who are brown-skinned . . . one of my sisters, she is browner than the rest of us, as it is in African American families, the colors shift. My nieces are brown, you know, so there's that whole rainbow element. But I remember going to this guy's house, this mother making this comment, and I'm like, "What is she talking about?" Anyway, they lived on the northwest side of Detroit, which had a large class of lighter-skinned African Americans. I remember going to Boston in 1978 and experiencing the same thing, and going "Wow," because honest to God, I did not know that there were all these people that looked like me that were out there and in these circles of people, but it was never a circle that I was in. I was sort of in the other circle. So, choosing to be-come an actor, I remember a guy telling me I was absolutely insane. He said, "You'll never work." He said "You look white, what are you talking about? Nobody's gonna believe you." And my response was, what dif-ference does it make? I'm an actor. So that was maybe the naïveté that I started out with, but I was determined that it doesn't matter what I look like and it mattered to a point, but the fact that I was able to work, to be hired in film and television and stage, and also to create my own work, sort of proved them all wrong—I've been thinking about that, and you know, that's pretty good for a girl from a small factory town.

Can you talk about the brilliant use of humor in *Passing Solo*? Because I don't know if there's as much humor in the book.

And it's interesting how some of it wasn't really intentional, but when people laugh at certain things, sometimes we wonder, "Are they laugh-ing because they're uncomfortable? Or are they laughing because they actually find it humorous?" Clare is very honest about, for example, what her daughter looks like, which I'm sure happens with people who have children that they think are going to look a certain way, particularly if the woman is very attractive, and they think they're going to have a very attractive child and the child is not, as in this case with Margery. People find that very humorous, the fact that she would admit that the child is homely, but it's a good thing, because then, by her being homely, she won't be noticed as much as if she were beautiful, per se. The whole bit with Albert, again, he was not a part of the book, he was a creation for the play. And he was added as a bit of humor. Not intentional humor, but how it comes out, but he was added more of a definition, of defining the classes, actually thinking back. But some of the scenes with him are very humorous because it's just the way the lines are delivered, it's his sassiness, I guess, with Clare, his forthrightness with her, in saying what he thinks and calling her on the carpet, and that has, I think, a lot of wittiness in it.

And with the voice-over?

The voice-over. You know, those voice-overs, it was so funny because I don't think any of us were there directing . . . We asked some of our com-pany members, who was it? Forrest Gardner, Robin Ray Eller, and Mick

Harrity, I think it was just the three of them. So it was their take on it. And at first, we thought, "This is over the top. This will never work. They're way over the top." But then we listened to it again and the thing that I'm finding out in solo performance is some of the stuff needs to be over the top, whereas if someone was actually delivering that line and it wasn't a voice-over, it may appear to be over the top, but I think that it works in the context of the solo part of it.

That's fascinating. Why do you think that's so?

Because sometimes I think it needs to be bigger than life. And that the subtlety doesn't work as well if you don't have the visual to go along with it sometimes. And that's what I found out in my performing it, was this subtlety thing that I would normally do in an ensemble piece and Tony, who is a comedian, really helped me with bringing out the aspects of being bigger than life, and playing it much broader in some cases than I would ever do. I remember thinking, "Are you sure? It just doesn't feel right. You know, I'm very organic, like oh my God I don't want to feel like I'm acting, what do you mean?" And he said, "No, it works because it is based in the context of it but because you're just one person, it has to be bigger." Which was a difficult adjustment for me to make as an actor, it was a challenge, I should say, not difficult, but it was a challenge to work in that context.

I know you do tremendous work with younger audiences and reach out to young folks through various community programs. Passing seemed to be the buzzword of the 1990s, how do you think it plays today, particularly with the next generation, or this post-Obama generation if you will? Or do you have a perspective on that?

Actually I do. My nephew, one of my nephews, is twenty-five, just graduated from Howard, he's working in a corporate environment, the whole bit. And one time he asked "Why does it say 'Towne Street Theater, LA's Premiere African American Theater Company'?" He said, "Why does it say African American? Why do you have to say that?" And I said, "Because that's what it is. And we want to define it as such." When I was in Virginia working, I ran into a young lady, very beautiful, very dark-skinned, ebony colored, smart, bright, et cetera, and she was telling me about the issues she was having with people because she was so dark.

And I was actually surprised by it. I was really surprised by it. I was like "What? Is that still going on? Are you kidding me?" My niece who lives in Los Angeles, went to a Catholic school, and has more Hispanic people in her upbringing and social circle, but it's an issue in that community as well, this thing of wanting to look white. It may not be called passing, but I think it's still there. That is the representation of what is acceptable and attractive around the world still. The blonde hair, the straight hair, the blue, green, gray eyes, nowadays you can have any color eyes you want.

Even passing for straight, in the novel, in terms of sexuality, which is another issue. One that I think you implicate in your versions of the play as well.

Right. Exactly.

Or in the military.

So it's still relevant. And I would actually like to do it, I haven't done it yet, for some high school students, but that is a path that we want to put the show on because I was advised that it would be good to show them this, that you need to be comfortable in your own skin because we all pass, and we all pass all the time on different levels. I did just get a booking to perform it at high school so it will be interesting to note their reactions to the piece. Regarding the issue of sexuality in the book, that has always been a question for a lot of people, is it there, isn't it there? That is something we created, it's not so much in the solo show as it was in the full productions, or I don't know if it comes out. In the original productions, it's definitely there without question. And we were called on it by some people who were upset by that because they felt the book didn't really say that because . . . of the way Nella Larsen wrote it—it leaves it open to interpretation—Is it just a friendship? Is it something more? But when I first read the book, I thought for sure they were more or had been at one point, more than just friends. Was it just a childhood dalliance for Irene perhaps and Clare looked at it a different way? But then when Clare comes back into Irene's life, she cannot escape her and whatever feelings she may have suppressed come back into play. It also made for a more dramatic arc in terms of it being a play to have them be lovers.

She's clearly obsessed with her, and so I think there are multiple ways you can read it.

Right, exactly. It was suggested to me to bring that out more in the solo piece. I don't know if that's necessary because again, it's about interpretation and some see it in the solo show and some don't, but the play is still evolving, that's the beauty of the piece is that twenty years later, it's still evolving.

Let's hope we see the screenplay one day. I know a young Spelman graduate who did do a film version as a school project. I could really see it as a major film . . .

Ah yes, we're working on that.

Anything we didn't cover that you want to say about the piece?

Just that it has been, and continues to be, a wonderful artistic journey for me. I am fortunate to work with such a talented group of artists—Nathaniel's brilliant set, lighting and sound designs, Nancy Renee, Tony (and Sy's) insightful direction, and all the people who have contributed to the piece over the years. It also speaks to Nella Larsen's legacy, which I think is really important for people to have, and probably she would never have known that her book has affected so many people in so many ways. I'm always amazed by how many people have read the book and how they've been affected by it. I love the new people I get to meet through productions of *Passing Solo* and that get to experience it and want to read the book if they haven't already, because of the show. Again, it speaks to the power of literature, what reading can do. How reading one book can literally change your life.

PERFORMING *PASSING* AND *PASSING* AS PERFORMANCE: ON NANCY CHERYLL DAVIS-BELLAMY'S *PASSING SOLO* BASED ON NELLA LARSEN'S NOVELLA *PASSING*

Bryant Keith Alexander

The novella *Passing* by Nella Larsen is a stirring case study that focuses on blacks seemingly unmarked by racial signifiers who are thus able to assume an identity of whiteness, to pass as white.[1] But what makes passing possible? I suggest that short of the materiality of bodies passing is a *psychology of performance*—the things that motivate how people think and how their cosmologies of knowing inform their behaviors; the choices they make, and thus how they live with the consequences and challenges of their actions in everyday life. In passing, this would fixate in their operations between black and white social realities. A psychology of performance is also about how people engage in the management of mental investments (a complicated sense of the self in racial terms) and how those psychic realities manifest in embodied displays as they connect and contact with others.

I am suggesting that while whiteness or lightness of skin might facilitate the accomplishment of passing, the true accomplishment is motivated by an intense desire to escape the presumed constraints of blackness, particularly in the novella, as these are constructed as social derision and restrictive mobility, fortified by an intense desire to market the potential of the light skin one lives in, for personal gains that transcend racial categories reductively marked by skin color. Hence, passing becomes performance, embodied engagement with intent.

Under this construction passing is then engaged through manipulative behaviors; a series of subtle tactical maneuvers, an argument of actions that are dialogically negotiated between the one passing and those who would accept or deny, support or sanction the accomplishment. Not the accomplishment of passing, but the presumption of the real (a socially constructed performance of whiteness), which results in the success of passing for white and socially becomes white—which is not exclusively about the color of skin, but what is presumed to be white. Each party in the performance of passing (for example, the one passing and the audi-

ence to that performance) must buy into a prescription of racialized identity giving way to a set of social and performative executions of identity
that maintain (for example, a set of performative embodiments—walk,
talk, manner, tone, inflection, language use—a performed set of politics
of racial orientation, of the presumed attendants of class and privilege, of
race and difference) a farce in human social relations—the real and the
presumed to be real as it relates to the ubiquitous construction of race.

Passing is a reflection of one's psychology—a sensed manifestation of
one's orientation to self and society; be it race, culture, gender, or sexuality
made manifest in performance. It is an acting and reacting, the assuming
of otherness and a confirmed acceptance by others—hence the psychology
of passing—both on the part of those who would engage in passing, as well
as those who would accept the performance of passing. Yet, the existential
accomplishment of passing always resides in liminality—not the process
of becoming but the state of being betwixt and between two performance
communities, with the performative expectations of both communities
serving as mediators in a tensive feud (or maybe a fraud) of identity—
acceptance and denial, the knowledge of which concentratedly resides
in the psyche of the one passing. So, as the characters in Nella Larsen's
novella might attest, while passing is an adaptive tactic it is also one that
is filled with an anxiety of engagement and the fear of discovery.

STAGING *PASSING SOLO*

Nancy Cheryll Davis-Bellamy's performance of *Passing Solo* is for me
stunning as a theatrical (one-woman show) experience that takes the audience into the world of the literary text and the lives of the characters
therein. What the performance does is illuminate the politics of Nella
Larsen's novella, allowing the audience to enter the psychology of the
characters. Based on the previous discussion linking the notion of psychology to the particular "performance of passing"—what *Passing Solo*
does is to dramaturgically foreground the mental processes of the characters of Clare and Irene (for example, who is thinking what, why, and
how, in social and physical relations of time and space). The novella by
Nella Larsen is brilliant in describing the thought processes and logic-
making mechanisms of each character. It provides the reader a kind of
omniscient access to the motivations of action, furthering what is already

the psychological experience of reading a novel, and it invokes imagination and forces a particular psychic connection with the characters, who swirl in the mind of the person reading the text. In the performance of *Passing Solo* Davis-Bellamy embodies the psychology of that narrative and the two primary characters of Irene and Clare.

While the simple set of the traveling show (for example, a small round table, two chairs, and a side table) helps to establish context as do the meaning-making signifiers of any theatrical space,[2] the performance gains its force not in the accoutrement of the stage set, but in the magic of embodied performance. The embodiment of each character is accentuated through a series of subtle shifts in voice, facial expression, and mannerisms along with strategic blocking, tight circular turns that in each bow distinguish the characters from and onto each other—along with visual prop signifiers such as a scarf, cigarette holder, gloves, and hats; these along with a few music cues that establish mood and context, as well as recorded voice-overs of more articulated mind thoughts, particularly of Irene. Davis-Bellamy makes visual the psychology of the characters so that the audience can see the shifty mind play of passing in the complicated relational dynamic of the two primary characters. Maybe Davis-Bellamy also provides the audience with a performative script of the manifestations of passing.

Drawing from the logics and traditions of the oral interpretation of literature, that for me always dovetails with *systems of rehearsal* in acting,[3] "perhaps we could say that the physical techniques, such as inflections of voice, qualities of voice, stresses of voice; and action such as gestures and posture" serve as the anatomy of Davis-Bellamy's performance of this literary text; "while psychical techniques, such as processes of imagination, reasoning, memory, emotion, are the" organic components of the performance drawn from some deep connection that the actor has with the characters and the politics of the engagement giving life to the text.[4] And maybe this is the complicated beauty and brilliance of this performance; a performance that invites the audience to revel in both its art and artifice, an expression of a particular truth and the constructedness of performance that illuminates a reality both on and off the stage.

In this strategic process of staging the critical interactions of the novel, particularly the relationship between Irene and Clare, what Davis-Bellamy also does is reveal a psychology of the performance itself. Davis-

Bellamy's interpretation of the text becomes evident to the audience as she translates and makes that manifest in her performance. In the performance, the audience sees Davis-Bellamy's attraction to both of the women that she portrays in a kind of intimate sensuous play with both, the constrained control of Irene and the carefree danger of Clare—which also alludes to the lesbianic overtones often read between the two women in the novel. Davis-Bellamy's performance is itself a story that she is telling; the narratives of both the literary text and the particular story that she is telling in *Passing Solo*, which is and is not exclusively the novel written by Larsen, "key both to the events in which they are told and to the events that they recount, toward narrative events and narrated events."[5] The characterization of Irene and Clare is sutured not just to the actualization of how Larsen wrote the characters, but they are animated in this performance only through Davis-Bellamy's portrayal of them in performance—each perhaps taking on qualities of her own identity and life challenges as a light-skinned woman of African American descent. Davis-Bellamy herself alludes to this challenge in postproduction talk-backs, noting that she had to make strategic choices about her own negotiation of identity politics, as well as the promises and pitfalls of passing; or at least the social and racialized politics of walking through the world in the skin that she lives in.

In terms of the mechanisms of this performance, the show is an interesting exemplar that sits at the intersection of several traditions of staging narrative texts in Chamber Theatre and Readers Theatre,[6] but as a solo performance not as group activity. It is evident through the promotion of *Passing Solo* that the theatrical production is based on the novella. The performance achieves a close fidelity by not rewriting the text, but suturing critical lines from the novella into a performance script that condenses the novella into a 45-minute performance, highlighting the moments of dialogue between the two main characters—thereby exploiting the dramatic medium of the novella in the theatrical presentation. But Davis-Bellamy also maintains significant narrative and descriptive components of the novella that provide spatial and locational context, and, more importantly, illuminates the operations of the mind, particularly of Irene—as the primary character through which the reader and audience experience the happening of the story. It is this delicate balance of the dramatic enactment and what is almost a readerly presence of the novella (though the physical text is not present in the performance)—that gives the overall performance a level of authenticity as it pays a respectful homage to the original text. In *Passing Solo,* Davis-Bellamy bleeds the borders of multiple theatrical and staging histories to provide the audience with a theatrical experience that signals to the importance of the literary text from which it is drawn. The performance is as much an exercise in literary study as a unique theatrical experience that stands alongside the novella.

COMPLEXITIES OF *PASSING SOLO*

In brief, allow me to further elucidate on three additional complex issues that are particularly compelling and important about Nancy Cheryll Davis-Bellamy's performance of *Passing Solo.* The first is the concentrated manner in which the performance at large focuses our attention on what is (are) the most important relationship(s) of the novel. This construction of relationship(s) is both singular and plural. There are a series of relational dynamics at play in the novella that are clearly alluded to and made clear in the performance: the relationship between Irene and her husband, a dark-skinned African American man; the relationship between Irene and her dark-skinned male children; the relationship between Clare and her white husband; the relationship between Clare and her singularly referenced light-skinned female daughter who unknowingly passes as white; the relationship between the materially marked difference of race—black and white; and the relationship between the performance of racialized identity and the social construction of beauty, desire, acceptability, and privilege. Nonetheless, the key relationship is between Irene and Clare—which in and of itself is complex, pivoting on and around all other relational dynamics of the novella.

In *Passing Solo* Davis-Bellamy operates in the middle ground of these competing yet informing relational dynamics. The script of the performance is really an exemplar of script construction from a narrative text, foregrounding the complexity of the Irene and Clare relationship. Two women who could be sisters, but speculatively could be lovers, and rivals—tied together not simply by the light-skinned materiality of their bodies and the politics of possibility available to them through performance (nay passing), but also by their potential desire and disdain—for each other;

and how they play with issues of race and identity in ways that are both fixed and fluid throughout the novella; each serving as a psychological doppelgänger of the other.

What Davis-Bellamy does with this dynamic is to show the power of performance that passing invokes and engages, passing as a strategic engagement of *faking and making*,[7] of becoming and the limits of racial biological determinisms. More importantly, *Passing Solo* foregrounds performance as a process of making real one's intention through the strategic crafting of material and social culture, the embodiment of being, and the social constructions of acceptable (or expected) behaviors. Through a very strategic set of choices, *Passing Solo* foregrounds the politics of performance practice as a site of opposition and that "performance practice has, for African Americans, been central to the process of decolonization. . . . Performance [is] important because it create[s] a cultural context where [black people] could transgress the boundaries of accept[ability] in relationship to the dominant White culture, and to the decorum of African American cultural mores."[8]

In this sense, the performance that Davis-Bellamy offers uses theatrical staged techniques to foreground performance in everyday life, forcing the audience to see the entanglements of each as strategies of being and doing—hence foregrounding the dramaturgical and performative nature of cultural and racial performance in everyday life. In other words, as in the traditions of performance studies, this particular performance helps the audience in "comprehending how human beings fundamentally make culture, affect power, and reinvent their ways of being in the world" in and through performance.[9] This is particularly true as the audience follows the trajectory of performative deceit in the character of Clare. In this sense, Davis-Bellamy also foregrounds the fact that "performance is central to contemporary views of culture as enacted, rhetorical, contested, and embodied. [Performance] functions as organizing trope for examining a wide range of social practices."[10] And while the audience is entertained by the theatrical performance, they are also haunted by the facile way in which Davis-Bellamy makes real how Larsen deconstructs the performance of race and the consequences therein, as to open up new spaces for public discussion on the continuing utility of race as a delimiting construct fueled only by the social investment of skin color—but always and already made known in and through performance.

Hence, the performance of Larsen's narrative text makes real the intense relationship of desire and disdain that race and racial politics engenders in all the characters of the novella (blacks and whites); their investments and divestments—and the ways in which social mobility is tied to the materiality of bodies and the presumption of character therein. It is also important to note that in *Passing Solo,* there is a commentary and critique of the relationship between raced and female bodies that the play barters on and evidences as social constructions of beauty and femininity. Davis-Bellamy particularly flaunts this critical commentary not only in her depiction of Clare, the one of the two women who identifies and is identified by most in the novella as white. But also in Irene, the one who can pass *in strange company* but is married to a dark-skinned African American man—thereby clearly establishing a complicity of either her racial identity or the choices that she has made, impacting, if not reducing, the social construction of her own beauty and allure as a black woman (or a white woman suffering from jungle fever). Onstage, Davis-Bellamy engages a flirtatious femininity in and of Clare's whiteness, while she contains the flamboyance of that performative engagement in her portrayal of Irene. These performance choices, mostly signaled by the novella itself, also reference a historical privilege of flirtation that has most often been afforded to white femininity and not black women.

Second, Davis-Bellamy's performance of *Passing Solo,* while based on a literary text, also wonderfully illuminates the power of solo performance as "political theater"—"a cultural practice that self-consciously operates at the level of interrogation, critique, and intervention"[11] of social audiences and how the performance embodies and illuminates the politics of race that the novella calls to both our readerly and audience attention. And consequently, by virtue of the materiality of her own body—which suggestively allows her to play the characters of this novella with a visual validity—Nancy Cheryll Davis-Bellamy knowingly puts her body on the line, embodying (and taking on) some of the racial politics made present and visible through the novella, onstage. And as performance artist Amanda Kemp might suggest, the black body in question in this performance for some audience members may not be exclusively the fictionalized bodies of Irene and Clare, but also Nancy's body.[12]

In other words, I believe that Davis-Bellamy knowingly calls the audience to critique not only the bodies *in play,* but also to engage in a conversation of the body *at play* in performance; as a strategic component of her commitment to the pedagogy of theater and the politics of theater as cultural intervention. In such case, theater and performance are not just entertainments, but also mechanisms of influencing social perception, cultural action, and political engagement.[13] And of course, by placing her literal light-skinned African American body on the line to portray light-skinned African American women trapped in a web of their own conceits, Davis-Bellamy also places her body as pawn in the politics of racial identity on which the play comments and critiques. And this is one of the risky and dangerous parts of performance, and particularly solo performance, that we do not often talk about. That component of performance that is both desired and potentially feared; that potential in the performance of poiesis and mimesis in which the audience associates *the character played* with *the actual character of the performer in play.* Hence, confusing the virtuosity of the performer in performance with the verisimilitude of realness that performance simulates with particular intent.

Yet, as an act of black feminist performance, I believe that Davis-Bellamy strategically is engaging the politics of performative embodiment as a *feminist framework;* as a particular conceptual structure using Larsen's text in a solo performance format to exemplify, explain, justify, and showcase a set of logics that guide the actions of particular black women (fictional or otherwise) in a social context—and the strategies they engage to end their own oppression.[14] Hence, the performance promotes a series of key arguments that are for me at the core of black feminist thought, in relation to the black female bodies *in play* and *at play* in the text—*Passing,* and in the performance *Passing Solo.* This in ways that use the verisimilitude of realness for a strategic argument of the actual lives of black women in the particular nexus of race, gender, physical embodiment, and the politics of passing.

In other words: the performance presents each of the characters, Irene and Clare, as clearly defined, self-reliant black women who confront and manipulate issues of race, gender, and class to their own advantage. The performance displays each character strategically manipulating and resisting racialized and gender oppression as a continuous social and political engagement both in the public and private sphere. The performance displays each character as a critical thinker and knowledge producer as she navigates her circulation in the racial climate of the times. The performance reinforces the consciousness work that both characters engage as they each contemplate their personal role in the social and political transformation of their times—and the choices that they have made.[15] And it is the knowledge that they gain through this process that determines the particular outcomes of the play—no matter how tragic or dumbfounding they might be. And it is Davis-Bellamy's strategic rhetoric of performance that gives the audience access to her own politics of subversion and resistance; performance as *body praxis*—with difference modulating between the actual materiality of bodies in play and political strategizing that seeks to intervene or transcend both historical and situated moments of being.[16]

Davis-Bellamy's performance of *Passing*, the novella, as a solo performance (*Passing Solo*), forces audiences to critically reflect on the very politics of solo performance, or the one person show—a format that John Gentile calls a focused attention on "a supreme test of assurance and ability, of magnetism and charisma" of a single performer; "the format is seductive and frightening; there's no one to play against, to lean on, to share the criticism."[17] And consequently the politics of a *cast of one* performance—whether in the evolutionary context of platform performance, solo theatre, biographical to autobiographical performance, monologuists, recitals, staged readings, writer-performers, or staged literary texts[18]—the singular performer receives the concentrated focus of audience attention, in which the politics of the performance is neither distracted nor dissipated by the interplay with other actors on stage. Complete charge (both positive and negative) is rendered by and to the solo artist, hence the message and medium become one.

Third, in many ways *Passing Solo* also resembles a foray into performing ethnography. And while performance ethnography is variously described,[19] in this case I am referencing the act of restaging the cultural practices of a particular group for public consumption, critique, political action, or transformation. In such case, actors/performers put their bodies in those spaces, taking on the qualities and characteristics that they most want the audience to be exposed to for the politics and pleasures of performance; as well as the benefits that actors/performers gain in their own self-knowledge through embodiment, further illuminating the pedagogy of performance. Like the work of many solo artists, and particularly Davis-Bellamy, "this means we must embrace the body not only as the feeling/sensing home of our being . . . but the vulnerability of how our body must move through the space and time of another—transporting our very being and breath—for the purpose of knowledge, for the purpose of realization and discovery."[20] And while *Passing Solo* is based on the novella, *Passing* is a presumed fiction; the narrative stands as a cultural text that through performance reanimates what were the foundational social logics that ignited Larsen to write the novel; which I strongly believe was a writing of the culture of her time (or personal experience), which is always the core impetus and methodology of doing ethnography.

TALKING B(L)ACK

At the end of her performance of *Passing Solo* Davis-Bellamy offers a talkback session with the audience that provides them the opportunity to ask questions; questions that range from the (would-be) actors and students of performance—that pivot on issues from her approach, attack, and acclimation to the text; issues of character development, and issues of staging and performance choices; to questions from the academic or lay audience that circulate around the racial politics of identity and passing as foundational to the novella and her personal orientation to the issues of passing in everyday life.[21] Knowing of course that such questions traverse the boundaries of these facile categories of distinction to also bleed the borders of racial identification and commitments of audience members on either side of the reductive black/white binary.

In addition, by special request Nancy Cheryll Davis-Bellamy also offers two postperformance events: one entitled "Knowing Nella—An In-Depth Discussion on the Life of Nella Larsen" and the other, "The Joy of Acting—An Invigorating & Inspiring Acting Workshop." In each case, whether in the talkback after the performance or in any of the special features, Davis-Bellamy engages the audience in what is a sincere discussion about the nature of the text and her experiences in performance, as well as a strategic rhetoric that unpacks the politics of the performance and the novel. It is in these moments that she decouples the characters that she has played from the actuality of her own lived experiences, while also informing the audience of the larger historical, social, and political issues that informed the writing of the original novella, as well as some of the logics that motivated her current reengagement with the text as a solo performance. It must be noted that Davis-Bellamy shares with the audience that she played the singular character of Clare in a full staged production of the novella. Her explication of methodology in establishing the one-person show foregrounds her process as critical, intellectual, and in many ways academic—a thinking actor that researched the origins of the novella, the author, as well as the historical and contemporary racial politics that serve as prisms for viewing her current endeavor.

The talkback session is almost as compelling and engaging as the performance of *Passing Solo*. In this moment, short of the professional biographical description that the audience has been privy to preceding the performance (either from the performance program or a live introduction), the audience gets the curious opportunity to engage the actor that brought forth such compelling characters. After the performance and concluding audience applause, Davis-Bellamy does not exit the stage to break the illusion of the theatrical moment for some other staid off-script performance, or the practice of exiting the stage or closing a curtain to signal a break of character. She stays onstage in costume to engage the audience. And in that moment, the audience views a seamless transition of the artist from text to context, demystifying the sometime facade of theatrical production, and promoting the politics of performance as a pedagogy of continual engagement.

In that moment, as she turns from the theatricalized performance of the script to the performative presentation of herself (another text), the audience gets to see the raw materials of her own personality that Davis-Bellamy drew upon to create the characters of Irene and Clare. The audience gets to hear the modulation of tones in her voice that volleyed between the staid construction of Irene and the dangerous frivolity of Clare. The audience gets to see Davis-Bellamy's physical comportment as dramatically different from Irene and Clare but claiming the same range of expression of both characters. The audience gets to see the psychology of Davis-Bellamy as she critically and strategically responds to a range of questions about acting and performance that makes real and reifies her interpretation of the novella and the particular dynamic of the characters in play.

It is in the moment of the talkback that the audience meets Nancy Cheryll Davis-Bellamy the actor and the artistic producing director of

Towne Street Theatre, Los Angeles's premier African American theater company. It is in this moment that the audience comes to meet the actor as teacher, and begins to fully realize that the performance of *Passing Solo* is really a part of a lesson plan with strategic learning outcomes; the outcomes of which Davis-Bellamy outlines during the talkback session introducing a whole new audience (and generation) to the work of Nella Larsen. When asked in one of the performances at Northwestern University which character (Irene or Clare) is she most attracted to—Davis-Bellamy paused. In her pause there is a flurry of expressions; first Irene's contemplative intensity followed by a relaxed and mischievous expression reminiscent of Clare.

It is a ticklish moment for the audience, because whether Davis-Bellamy was summoning those expressions to remind us of the characters and her facility to go in and out of the characters; or whether she was flushing with a remembrance of each—the audience comes to understand that our immediate experience of these characters is a part of Davis-Bellamy's performance toolbox.[22] Her inevitable response, which was a decline to claim one over the other, was really anticipated by the audience—for to claim one over the other, Irene over Clare, is in fact to rewrite a component of the novella in which even Nella Larsen teases the audience with a similar question of determination, as the play ends in a literal cliff-hanger of speculation.

Passing Solo is a tour de force, a testament to the power of solo performance as political theater and cultural practice. Nancy Cheryll Davis-Bellamy's portrayal of Nella Larsen's powerful characters is a tribute to the novella while the performance reinforces passing as a psychology of performance. The show and the generosity of the postshow discussion offer audiences insights into technique, acting/performance choices, and the politics of racial performance in everyday life. By virtue of her fierce virtuosity as a solo performer, Nancy Cheryll Davis-Bellamy can claim the complete audience applause not only for her solo effort in performance, but also for her success.

NOTES

1. In writing this I am partially drawing on my essay "Passing, Cultural Performance, and Individual Agency: Performative Reflections on Black Masculine

Identity," in *Performing Black Masculinity: Race, Culture, and Queer Identity* (Lanham, Md.: AltaMira, 2006), 69–97.

2. See Gay McAuley, *Space in Performance: Making Meaning in the Theatre* (Ann Arbor: University of Michigan Press, 2000).

3. See Shomit Mitter, *Systems of Rehearsal: Stanislavsky, Brecht, Grotowski and Brook* (New York: Routledge, 1991).

4. Drawn from J. T. Marshman, "The Paradox of Oral Interpretation," in *The Study of Oral Interpretation: Theory and Comment,* ed. Richard Haas and David A. Williams (Indianapolis, Ind.: Bobbs-Merrill, 1975), 83.

5. I am drawing this construction from Richard Bauman's introduction to *Story, Performance, and Event: Contextual Studies or Oral Narrative* (New York: Cambridge University Press, 1986), 2. In this construction Bauman makes allusion to Roman Jakobson, "Shifters, Verbal Categories, and the Russion Verb," in *Roman Jakobson: Selected Writings,* vol. 2: 130–47 (The Hague: Mouton, 1971).

6. See Robert S. Breen, *Chamber Theatre* (New York: Prentice-Hall, 1978); Marion L. Kleinau and Janet Larsen McHughes, *Theatres for Literature: A Practical Aesthetics for Group Interpretation* (Sherman Oaks, Calif.: Alfred, 1980); Judy Yordon, *Experimental Theatre: Creating and Staging Texts* (Prospect Heights, Ill.: Waveland, 1997).

7. See Victor Turner, *From Ritual to Theater: The Human Seriousness of Play* (New York: Performing Arts Journal Publication, 1982), 93.

8. bell hooks, "Performance Practices as a Site of Opposition," in *Let's Get It On: The Politics of Black Performance,* ed. Catherine Ugwu (Seattle: Bay, 1995), 212.

9. D. Soyini Madison and Judith Hamera, "Performance Studies at the Intersections," in *The SAGE Handbook of Performance Studies* (Thousand Oaks, Calif.: SAGE, 2006), xii.

10. Judith Hamera, *Opening Acts: Performance in/as Communication and Cultural Studies* (Thousand Oaks, Calif.: SAGE, 2006), 2.

11. Jeanne Colleran and Jenny S. Spencer, *Staging Resistance: Essays on Political Theater* (Ann Arbor: University of Michigan Press, 1998), 1.

12. Amanda D. Kemp, "This Black Body in Question," in *The Ends of Performance,* ed. Peggy Phelan and Jill Lane (New York: New York University Press, 1998), 116–29.

13. See Baz Kershaw, *The Politics of Performance: Radical Theatre as Cultural Intervention* (New York: Routledge, 1992).

14. See Alison M. Jagger and Paula S. Rothenberg, *Feminist Frameworks: Alternative Theoretical Accounts of the Relations Between Women and Men* (New York: McGraw-Hill, 1984), xii.

15. See Patricia Hill Collins, *Black Feminist Thought: Knowledge, Consciousness and the Politics of Empowerment* (New York: Routledge, 1991).

16. See M. Jacqui Alexander, *Pedagogies of Crossing: Meditations on Feminism, Sexual Politics, Memory, and the Sacred* (Durham, N.C.: Duke University Press, 2005), 329.

17. John S. Gentile, *Cast of One: One-Person Shows from the Chautauqua Platform to the Broadway Stage* (Urbana: University of Illinois Press, 1989), 201.

18. John Gentile roughly organizes his important volume around a focus on these shifting contexts and modes in *One-Person Shows from the Chautauqua Platform to the Broadway Stage*, ibid.

19. See Olorisa Omi Osun Olomo-Joni Jones (section ed.), "Part IV Introduction: Performance and Ethnography, Performing Ethnography, Performance Ethnography," in *The SAGE Handbook of Performance Studies*, ed. D. Soyini Madison and Judith Hamera (Thousand Oaks, Calif.: SAGE, 2006), 339–418; Norman K. Denzin, *Performance Ethnography: Critical Pedagogy and the Politics of Culture* (Thousand Oaks, Calif.: SAGE, 2003); Bryant Keith Alexander, "Performance Ethnography: The Reenacting and Inciting of Culture," in *Strategies of Qualitative Inquiry*, ed. Norman K. Denzin and Yvonne S. Lincoln, first published in the *Handbook of Qualitative Research*, 3rd ed. (Thousand Oaks, Calif.: SAGE, 2009), 75–118.

20. D. Soyini Madison, "Dangerous Ethnography," in *Qualitative Inquiry and Social Justice*, ed. Norman K. Denzin and Michael D. Giardina (Walnut Creek, Calif.: Left Coast, 2009), 190.

21. Here I am riffing on bell hooks, *Talking Back: Thinking Feminist/Thinking Black* (Cambridge, Mass.: South End).

22. Here I am making specific reference to Nathan Stucky's construction of "the performance studies toolbox," that foregrounds *characteristics of theoretical inquiry in performance studies*, as well as *practices in performance studies* that among others include embodiment, social engagement, theatrical resources, ritual practices, imagination and invention, as well as interdisciplinary practices. I believe that Davis-Bellamy draws upon the fullness of these tools, though she might ascribe them more to formal theater pedagogy and methods. Nathan Stucky, "Fieldwork in the Performance Studies Classroom: Learning Objectives and the Activist Curriculum," in *The SAGE Handbook of Performance Studies*, ed. D. Soyini Madison and Judith Hamera (Thousand Oaks, Calif.: SAGE, 2006), 273.

ADVENTURES OF A BLACK GIRL IN SEARCH OF ACADEMIC CLARITY AND INCLUSION

Edris Cooper-Anifowoshe

PRODUCTION HISTORY

Adventures of a Black Girl in Search of Academic Clarity and Inclusion premiered in March 2004 at Intersection for the Arts. A short version was part of the Afro Solo festival in Summer 1997. The short script was developed by Black Artists Contemporary Cultural Experience and Intersection for the Arts as part of a residency in 2004. The technical advisor was lighting designer, Jennifer Bachofner (JennyB). Funding was provided by Zellerbach Family Foundation and Intersection for the Arts.

CHARACTERS

[*all played by the same woman*]
Black Girl, the protagonist of the play; appears at various ages
Voice-Over, the man who hands out the sheep's skins
Mother, middle-aged mother of Black Girl
Hallie, Black Girl's young white female classmate at the integrated school
Hallie's mother, a middle-aged white woman with a drinking problem
Hallie's dad, a middle-aged white man who provides stability in his family
Sharlene, the only other black girl in Black Girl's integrated school
Another black girl, a classmate at Black Girl's segregated school
Mark, a white classmate who sits next to Black Girl
Joan, Black Girl's white friend in high school

All events are true from my memory and happened to me.
Some of the names have been changed to protect the guilty!

[*Dark stage—Square of light reveals* BLACK GIRL *within it. She is disoriented, her back is cramped. Confused, she tries to stand and cannot. She is boxed in. She reads the top of the box.*]

BLACK GIRL: Postmodern discourse.

[*Something is digging into her butt. She pulls it out and reads it.*]

BLACK GIRL: What is this in my butt—Shake's spear? Oh shit, the Patricia Roberts Harris fellowship . . . the University of Iowa . . .

[*She rises hurriedly and walks to a podium, which is now lit. She gathers her papers on the floor, apologizing to the audience. As she is getting her things together . . .* VOICE-OVER *interrupts*]

VOICE-OVER: Uh, Miss Cooper.

BLACK GIRL: Yeah.

VOICE-OVER: Yes, uh well. We've been wondering. There's something we have been meaning to ask you. What is the purpose of your education here at the University of Iowa?

BLACK GIRL: [*matter of fact? sarcastic? unsure?*] I guess to become a better director.

VOICE-OVER: OK . . .

BLACK GIRL: And I am still waiting.

VOICE-OVER: Before you receive your graduate degree we must be sure that you can regurgitate the blah, blah, blah, blah, blah. Now can you name please three playwrights from the Renaissance who wrote in the Romantic tradition?

BLACK GIRL: OK. Uh, let me consult my notes. Uh, three playwrights from the Renaissance who wrote in the Romantic tradition . . . from the Renaissance . . . from the Renaissance. OK, Langston Hughes—

VOICE-OVER: Who?!?

BLACK GIRL: And Zora Neale Hurston.

VOICE-OVER: Who? Who is Zora . . .

BLACK GIRL: Zora Neale Hurston. Oh my, you weren't talking about the Harlem Renaissance?

VOICE-OVER: Miss Cooper?

BLACK GIRL: Yes.

VOICE-OVER: [*pause*] Is Ibsen's *A Doll's House* Romantic Expressionism or Expressive Romanticism?

BLACK GIRL: Oh no, not *A Doll's House* again. What is it the damn question again?

VOICE-OVER [*pause*]: Is Ibsen's *A Doll's House* Romantic Expressionism or Expressive Romanticism?

BLACK GIRL: Honestly, who gives a rat's ass?

VOICE-OVER: Miss Cooper, Miss Cooper.

BLACK GIRL: What is this boring shit!?

VOICE-OVER: Uh, Miss Cooper, we have had the same syllabi for the past forty years. Obviously, it works very well . . .

BLACK GIRL: You've had the same syllabi for the last forty years, man doesn't that strike you as a problem?

VOICE-OVER: Miss Cooper, it is to my knowledge that YOU are the problem.

BLACK GIRL: I'm the problem? Moi?

VOICE-OVER: Isn't it true that you are loud?

BLACK GIRL: I am not louder than Megan Haggerty.

VOICE-OVER: That you disrupt classes, continually challenge your professors and you, uh, made a white girl, uh, cry in class?

BLACK GIRL: I didn't make that girl cry. That girl cried of her own volition.

VOICE-OVER: Miss Cooper.

BLACK GIRL: And I am not louder than Megan Haggerty!

VOICE-OVER: Isn't it true that you direct as if race and gender matter?

BLACK GIRL: Yes. And.

VOICE-OVER: Mizz Cooper, WHAT are Nora's strengths in Ibsen's *A Doll's House?*

BLACK GIRL: Ibsen again, huh?—you know, you could use a little diversity in that fifty-year-old curriculum. I mean I didn't come here to just study some dead white people.

VOICE-OVER: Uh . . . Miss Cooper . . . if you don't like white people, uh . . . why did you come to the uni . . . University of Iowa?

[*She's caught.*]

BLACK GIRL: I didn't say I didn't like white people, man.

VOICE-OVER: What, Miss Cooper is the purpose of your education . . . [*echo*]

[BLACK GIRL *is puzzled. Lights switch. Music plays, James Brown's "Say It Loud." She moves to a chair. Turns it around.*]

MOTHER: You're not looking at it right. You almost died to go to the March on Washington, D.C. Well, this is almost like you are there. You are having your own little march on, well, Fort Sanders.

BLACK GIRL: This is nothing like the March on Washington, Momma. There were a lot of people at the March on Washington. It's just gone be me by myself.

MOTHER: NO it isn't. Your sister is coming next year and John Austin Harris.

BLACK GIRL: I can't stand John Austin Harris.

MOTHER: That is nothing to say about someone. And don't say "gone be." It's "going to be." Don't go down there showing ignorance. Those white folks are just waiting for you to say something like "gone be."

BLACK GIRL: White folks say "gone be." That's who WE got it from.

MOTHER: I am not interested in what white folks say. That doesn't concern me. I am concerned about what YOU say. You know you have to be at least twice as articulate as any of those white people. Twice as smart.

BLACK GIRL: Yes ma'am. They ain't gone be smarter than me, anyway.

MOTHER: Well, they don't have to be smart. They were born white! You, on the other hand, have to be AT LEAST twice as intelligent to even be considered human.

BLACK GIRL: Dang Momma.

MOTHER: Don't say dang and call me Mother Dear.

BLACK GIRL: Mother Dear?! Ugh. That is so prosaic.

MOTHER: Well, you ought to call folks what they want to be called. Not what you like. And be careful of your vocabulary. You don't have to go down there showing off.

BLACK GIRL: Well, if I have to be twice as smart, seems like I would need to use my more expanded vocabulary, MOTHER!

MOTHER: Well, since you know everything, I won't tell you nothing!

[BLACK GIRL *raises her eyebrows at the grammatical error.*]

MOTHER: You figure it out yourself.

BLACK GIRL: Sorry. [*pause*] Momma?

MOTHER: What?

BLACK GIRL: Thanks for pressing my blue dress.

MOTHER: I thought you didn't want to wear the blue dress. You said it was mammy made. I thought you wanted to wear one of your store-bought dresses.

BLACK GIRL [*mumbling*]: They don't have the swing.

MOTHER: What?

BLACK GIRL [*coming clean*]: The store-bought dresses don't swing like the blue dress.

MOTHER: Oh, the store-bought dresses aren't as good as the MAMMY MADE dress?

BLACK GIRL: No, sorry. But really, the store-bought dresses don't swing. And Momma you know—

[*Together*]: It don't mean a thing if it ain't got that swing!

[*They laugh.*]

MOTHER: Well, you need to write your grandmother a letter and thank her for all she went through to get that material for the bouffant.

BLACK GIRL: Yes ma'am. Imo be sw—I mean—I'm—going—to—be swinging all up in them white girls' faces.

MOTHER: Ooh lord, just don't open your mouth and let that mess fall out of it. Now hurry and eat your oatmeal so Mrs. Alexander can braid your hair on time.

[BLACK GIRL *grabs her hair as lights change. The James Brown song comes back in underneath.* BLACK GIRL'*s hair is braided during the following.*]

BLACK GIRL [*as a grown woman*]: They had sent letters to all of the faculty at the local black college and asked them to volunteer their children for the desegregation of Knoxville schools. Well, they didn't want just any Negro children running up in the schools. They wanted to make sure they were clean and smart and not too poor. Ooh lord, if they only knew—that's what we were afraid of too. That we would be surrounded by dirty, dumb as a doorknob, poor white trash!

It was almost fifteen years since Brown versus the Board of Education. Knoxville had first attempted integration in 1968 when they combined black Austin High with lily-white East High. A man named Robert Booker had tried to integrate Austin High before but he had graduated from Austin and moved on to lunch-counter drama with his Knoxville College classmate, a young Marion Berry, when they finally decided to integrate East High. In the fall of 1969 black students from Austin High School had to now attend East High, a few blocks away. Within two years almost all of the white students had transferred to private schools or moved to redistrict themselves. By the time I reached high school, the new integrated and renamed Austin-East was all black and had been for the past six or seven years.

My mother said she thought integration was a good idea. But I was going to miss my old school, Cansler Elementary—named for Charles Warner Cansler—a mathematical wizard (like my father), a lawyer who was admitted to the bar in 1892 and an early black educator in Knoxville.

[*Lights change.* BLACK GIRL *returns to chair which now becomes a car.*]

BLACK GIRL: Momma, I hope there are some teachers that give out candy like Ms. Gray.

MOTHER: Lord, I hope not. That woman had no business giving children candy for doing their work. That is ridiculous. And I know you weren't taking that candy after I told you not to.

BLACK GIRL: No, ma'am.

MOTHER [*doesn't believe her*]: Uhnhuh. I don' know why that white lady taught there all by herself. I always wondered why she couldn't get a job at a white school. Maybe make her feel good I guess. White folks sure do feel good when they think they're teaching you something. She was just giving you all that candy to make sure you all wouldn't hurt her.

BLACK GIRL: Well, all my teachers at Fort Sanders will be white.

MOTHER: Well don't look for any candy there. I doubt if they are that kind.

BLACK GIRL [*after a contemplative pause*]: Momma, what do I do if one of them calls me a nigger?

MOTHER [*thinking fast*]: Like you called Kathy "black" last year?

BLACK GIRL: But Kathy is black, Momma!

MOTHER: But you all just said that because you knew it would hurt her feelings.

BLACK GIRL: That's crazy.

MOTHER: Even still it wasn't right to hurt her feelings by calling her something she didn't want to be called. You ought to call people what they want to be called.

BLACK GIRL: That not the same thing as white people calling you a nigger.

MOTHER: I know.

[*Silence.*]

BLACK GIRL: So what do I do?

MOTHER [*final word*]: Do what you have to baby. Then call me or your daddy, OK.

BLACK GIRL: OK. [*long pause*] It's gonna be OK, Momma?

MOTHER: You just cannot say "mother dear," can you?

BLACK GIRL: Nope [*she grins*].

MOTHER: See you at 3 o'clock baby, I love you.

BLACK GIRL: Love you too—[*exaggeratedly*] Mother Dear.

[MOTHER *watches* BLACK GIRL *go to school and then pulls away from the curb. Someone cuts her off.*]

MOTHER: Watch where you're going cracker!

We fought to be treated as equals, to sit next to whites at lunch counters, in restaurants, bowling alleys, at the movies, in the theaters. But every adult that I knew that had fought that fight had a clear and discernible distaste and distrust for the whites they so vigorously fought to sit next to. The black segregationists almost had a better view of whites than those who fought for integration.

My own mother dear had a narrow, barely tolerant view of whites. She told me once that the French only bathed the parts of their body that rubbed together when they walked and that whites she knew growing up only took baths on Saturdays. She had wild stories of the weird sexual, marrying, and procreation habits of white people. Stories that involved animals, plants, and the proverbial cousins. Some of her stories involved white people close to or IN our own family. Her father, my grandfather could yazza bass better than Stepin Fetchit, but as soon as the door was closed he and my grandmother would yuk it up with story after story that illustrated the ignorance of the white men he worked for. Looking back, at times, it was a bit vicious, but it never had the air of being vicious. It just had air. You know, like a kind of sigh, a sigh of relief. That's what the stories felt like. But if I told you some of them you would think—Damn, vicious! This was the chit-chat of the integrationists. All over Knoxville, parents whose children had been thrust into the chairs of white classrooms struggled to keep their children's heads above the muck. Like dogs treading water, we treaded white people.

[*She begins to tread and continues to through the following.*]

Clothes pressed and sharp, hair always tame, grammar always perfect, diction crisp, but not too—politics—democrat. No ashy knees, elbows ankles, or drunk uncles allowed, shoes. Always. Always expensive and always ugly!—and ABSOLUTELY NO. FAKE. HAIR!

[*Lights change.* BLACK GIRL *leaves the podium, stomping.*]

BLACK GIRL: But Hallie Westhaven has a fall and so does Kitty Carson. Even Missy St. Claire's mother said that she could have one and she's getting one next week!

MOTHER: You done lost your mind! You are not Kitty St. Claire!

BLACK GIRL: Missy St. Claire!

MOTHER: Whatever! You are not one of those white girls. You are not going around with some fake hair on your head like some bald strumpet. Now, get in there and study those words for the spelling bee. You do want to go to Washington, D.C. don't you? You don't want your baby sister to beat you again do you?

BLACK GIRL: I don't care about the dumb old spelling bee.

MOTHER [*shocked*]: What are you talking about? YOU? Not care about winning the spelling bee. Well, I'm just going to have to call your old teachers at Cansler and tell them that you are no longer interested in education and being smart. They just wasted their time with you.

BLACK GIRL: Don't say that, Momma. I wish I was still at Cansler. My teachers there would help me with the spelling words.

MOTHER: Help? You don't need any help. Now, stop crying poor me and get in there and study.

BLACK GIRL [*begging*]: Momma. Not even a pin-on bun?

MOTHER: Girl, if you don't stop worrying me, you better. [*as* BLACK GIRL *stomps off to her room*] I don't care nothing about you being mad. You just better scratch you behind and get glad. Don't make me come in there!

[*Lights change.*]

BLACK GIRL: Hallie not only had a bun and a ponytail but she and Kitty both had full falls that gave them Marlo Thomas hair. I couldn't even get my hair relaxed. I had to be contented with an old raggedy towel.

[*Returning to the podium, she pulls out a yellow towel and demonstrates her "long luxurious blonde hair" à la Whoopi Goldberg.*]

Don't look at me like that! Everybody did it. Oh yeah, we all did it honey!

I was very relieved when my mother let me get my hair pressed 'cause I was tired of answering questions about the part sticking up or the spring in my braids and all. Those girls were always touching my hair, just grabbing it like it was some kind of unexplored territory and they were going where no white girl has gone before. Granted, I did have my share of fights too. I got called nigger quite a few times, both directly and indirectly like, "If I talk to you, then that makes me a nigger lover so I'm not talking to you." Or overheard in the lunchroom, "My dad says that he won't vote for Hubert Humphrey 'cause Hubert Humphrey is a nigger lover." Most of the crap came from the boys. The girls didn't dare. But the nut that cracked it was when somebody said about the Reverend Doctor Martin Luther King Jr., "I'm glad the nigger's dead." Ooh, I just waited after school and started beating everybody's ass. I put them all on notice at recess. "I'm kicking all white people's ass in my grade." I wasn't by myself either. My friend Todd was with me and we had a fight riot after school. We even kicked John Austin Harris's ass for not fighting with us.

[*She leaves the podium to demonstrate.*]

Todd Fisher had just shown up fighting one day. I was kicking some-body's ass for some derogatory remark and Todd just jumped right in. Afterwards, he said that his father had told him that he had better be fighting too 'cause they would come after him next. Todd was a Jew.

BLACK GIRL: What's a Jew?

TODD: I don't know but they hate me too.

[BLACK GIRL *returns to podium.*]

By the time I reached sixth grade, I had surpassed all expectations (not academically, mind you—I studied much less at Fort Sanders and they were a couple of lessons behind my old school, anyway). But socially, I was coming into my own. Shit, baby, I was running the sixth grade. In fact, I had navigated the playing field in such a way I received an invitation to a slumber party—A slumber party!

[BLACK GIRL *dances away from podium in celebration. Lights change.*]

MOTHER [*nose turned up*]: You want to spend the night at those white people's house?!

BLACK GIRL: Mother it is Hallie Westhaven. Her parents have money. Their house is really nice. It's in West Hills. The old part.

MOTHER: Well, you need some new pajamas. No need in them thinking we don't have nothing.

BLACK GIRL: Have anything.

MOTHER: Do you want the durn pajamas or not?!

BLACK GIRL: Hallie Westhaven lived out kind of in the country, near the airport and the Alcoa plant. My mother complained the whole way.

[BLACK GIRL *returns to the chair. Turns it around. It is a car once again.*]

MOTHER: I don't know why anybody would want to live way out here. And with all them planes going by? That proves they ain't nothing but crackers. I don't know why if they are supposed to have money, they live out here down the street from the trailer park. They bet-ter not be living in some old raggedy trailer or you are turning right back around . . . well, the houses are getting better. Ooh, now that's a house. I love those bay windows. Well this neighborhood is not too bad. Still gotta hear those airplanes, though. Edris, you have got to learn to tell a poor country cracker. I told you that girl wasn't nothing special, not with her mother letting her wear all that fake hair like a whore. At her age! These crackers ain't got no money and don't you take no guff offa them either. These are country crackers just like those Carsons and you know what happened when I let you go over there. We had to come out there to get you all. Don't you be up in here showing your behind either. Just 'cause them white girls do it doesn't mean you do it. Now, remember your last name. Oh here's the house. I guess it's not too bad. That is some tacky landscaping, though. Well, here we go. I'm going to the door to meet these people so they can see that you have a mother who loves you.

BLACK GIRL: My grandmother used to say that white people have beautiful landscaping but inside their houses are nasty. Negroes house will be tore up outside but spotless clean inside. I laughed at grandmother's comment when I saw the Westhavens' house.

Her mother greeted me very warmly, a little too warmly—hugging me very tightly and touching me everywhere. We had dinner in the elegant formal dining room.

[*Lights change. Chair is used again.*]

HALLIE'S MOM: The far left fork is for the salad, Edris.

BLACK GIRL: I rolled my eyes.

HALLIE: She knows that Mom!!!!

BLACK GIRL: After dinner, Hallie's father went to bed, her mother to sip cocktails and watch TV, and we went to Hallie's room to play with our dolls. They had Barbie and I had Tressy, the black doll with stretchable hair. I lived out my hair fantasies through her. We were having a good time when Mrs. Westhaven started calling upstairs.

HALLIE'S MOM [*drunkenly*]: Endris! Endris could you come here dear?

HALLIE: What do you want, Mom? We are playing.

HALLIE'S MOM: Send Endris down here for a minute dear. I have something I want her to do.

HALLIE [*whining*]: Mom!

HALLIE'S MOM: Hallie do what I said and sent that little colored girl down here!

BLACK GIRL [*to audience*]: Everybody got deadly quiet. Hallie came back in the room.

HALLIE [*to* BLACK GIRL]: My mom want—

BLACK GIRL: I heard her. We all did.
I stomped down to the front room, where the television was. Television in the front room, something I knew my mother would comment on as being particularly déclassé; Hallie's mother was laying face down on the couch with no shirt on and her bra undone. She had some lotion in her hand.

HALLIE'S MOM: Could you just rub my back dear?

BLACK GIRL: Why would I rub your back? Why do you want me to rub your back?

HALLIE'S MOM: You folks have such good strong hands. Would you mind dear?

BLACK GIRL [*beginning to anger and maybe even cry a bit*]: No, I don't want to rub you back, I want to go home. Can I please call my mother?

HALLIE'S MOM: What? What's the matter with you?

BLACK GIRL [*getting loud*]: I want to go home. Please can I call my mother!

HALLIE: Mother! What are you doing? Put your fucking shirt back on!

HALLIE'S DAD: Helen, what in the hell is the matter with you? I'm sorry darling. Don't cry, we'll call your mother.

BLACK GIRL: Thank you.

HALLIE'S DAD: I'm so sorry.

BLACK GIRL: Hallie went back upstairs and continued playing. My mother came and we rode home in silence after I told her what happened. But I'm sure I hear her laughing under her breath. Hallie and I never spoke about what happened. Other people tried to talk about it but I had enough on Hallie. I really didn't need to milk this. Besides, they weren't my real friends. My real friends were back home in my neighborhood.

[BLACK GIRL *has slowly made her way back to the podium.*]

So you're right to assume that there was not too much learning going on for me in my new school integration experiment. I don't remember what I learned. I remember cool stuff. In that school we had television in class. We saw frightening pictures of the Vietnam War. Cool in retrospect. At the time, we saw pictures so bloody I couldn't eat meat for a week. Cool at the time, was the trip we took to see Washington, D.C. On the way to the wax museum, we saw the Vietnam War protest on Capitol Mall. We got out of the bus and our teachers even let us drag flags around.

Education distracted by the fielding of insults from my classmates and the world, the deaths of black heroes, the rapid insurgence of drugs in my community, and a raging, divisive war. But even that was short-lived as we moved past the comfort and relative innocence—even despite having gotten on the desegregation bus—of elementary school.

My mother, spurred on by the perceived necessity of a privileged, white education was insistent that we get into Webb School of Knoxville, an exclusive (for Knoxville) private school. College prep. I dreamed of traveling to California or New York. I wanted to enter the high school from *Fame*, I was angry about the Vietnam War, Fred Hampton, Malcolm and Martin, and Webb School of Knoxville seemed like prison to me. They had uniforms for god sakes and I was becoming a fashion maven and I didn't need to be prepped for college—my parents were academics and we had not too long ago just moved out of the football dorm!

I successfully fought Webb and my mother and went to Tyson Jr.—and sure enough got introduced to pot, hip-hugger, tie-dye, long-haired hippies. At Webb they were still mooning, at Tyson people were streaking. But still, me and my neighborhood friends, some of whom now joined me, were an unwelcome presence. A fact made known to us in subtle and often not so subtle ways. Social studies always seemed to pose a problem. Those teachers felt they had free license to tell tales of black people. They weren't still saying that we have tails but damn near. We saw pictures of dirty, snotty-nosed black children in leaning lean-tos and were informed that this is actually how most black people live in the South. This is the type of miseducation that led people to question the validity of Steven Spielberg's chosen house for Celie and Mister in the film of *The Color Purple*. Spielberg's team, who I know did their research, were aware of the large and fabulous houses that many black people inhabited in the South, even shortly after the emancipation. In our social studies lessons, we saw more dirty, snotty-nosed black children from the Biafran war in Nigeria and were told that this is actually how most black people in Africa live. When we questioned this, we were told, by my white teacher, that we were a completely "different" kind of black people from the African. We were told that African people hated us and were jealous of how well we were doing in America. That we could never go home again. Now, I was raised on the campus of a black university. We knew about the conflict in Nigeria. We got the news firsthand from travelers who extended warm invitations for us to visit them in Africa. Some even offered to pay for the trip. We had traveled the South extensively and seen firsthand how people lived and many, many that we saw lived well. WE knew better. WE knew our history and then some. Hell, we even spoke some Swahili. We learned it in the settlement house that also housed the Girl Scouts, the Black Panther Party meetings, and Carpetbag Theatre Company.

But what cracked the nut on this one was having to endure Mrs. Jones's Mammy stories. Whenever we challenged the images or information she stuffed down our throats and the throats of our less knowledgeable, more gullible classmates, she would launch into a lovely story about the Mammy whose "teet she suckled as a snow-white babee." One day Sharlene went off on her.

SHARLENE: Lady, if we never hear another word about you and your Black Mammy it will be too soon. I am sick to death of hearing this mess.

BLACK GIRL: And then she left to go call her father. Reverend Ralph Ross was new to our community and quite scandalous for little ole Knoxville. He was the new minister of the Presbyterian church on campus and it was rumored that he had been—a (gasp) Baptist! He grew hair on his face and let the youth choir sing songs by Earth, Wind and Fire. He opened the church doors to everyone—the homeless and the so-called crazy, thugs and homos—come as you are, everyone was welcome to hear the word and boy could he deliver! Fiery rhetoric and a heart of gold. And he really turned it out when he let us have a party and DANCE in the church. My first acting classes were in that church.

But the thing I admired most about Reverend Ralph Ross, I never heard anyone complain about. That was how he preached black power and pride from the pulpit. Now I know he wouldn't call it that but he was a righteous role model. He once threatened to discipline the next child who uttered the term "good hair." And when we're treading white folks in stormy weather he was there with a life jacket. And that day, like many others, he was at that school in a flash! We had all been sent to the principal's office to wait for him by Miss Jones, who pretended to not know what in the world was going on with the colored girls in class. But when the right Reverend Ralph Ross came down and started speaking to the principal, she was summoned and was put on notice. By the time he finished, we were out of her class for good! Homeroom free and I had my first independent study! NO more Miss Jones, no more of the rest of the class's snickers, stares, and embarrassing questions.

But as much as we valued our independent status and privileged education, I began to see problems with being a "special negro." I began to worry about my daily trips to West Knoxville for school and the distance, both physical and emotional, that I had to travel to get back home to my black segregated neighborhood seemed greater and greater. Since my desegregated education began, I noticed right away the role of economics in race and opportunity. It was what we were being educated for. To make good money. To buy a nice home, nice car—to rise above the masses. My parents' generation was upwardly mobile together. It was important to them that the whole neighborhood came up. We were taken from our neighborhood, separated from our peers, singled out as "special." How many times had I heard that I was different from other black people, even from most black people. I wasn't different.—I was separated, a separation that haunted me. My circle of friends had gotten smaller. Now most of my friends were the ones who had decided to go to the white school, too. My sister had it even worse. She was causing scandals skipping down the street hand in hand with her ONE friend—Carolyn Newton, a white girl. Scaring the shit out of people in both her neighborhood and ours.

I had even found white girls that I was glad to call friends. Mabry Benson—who had the one cool-ass hippie mother. Sally and Martha Snyder, whose father, Bill Snyder, was chancellor at the University of Tennessee and who let you cuss in the house and Vicky, a Cher fanatic, who had me drinking Knox gelatin in order to grow long blood-red nails. We bought every bottle in town of Revlon's Raisin when Cher came out wearing it. And my parents were collecting white friends as well. Vicki's dad and my dad played music gigs together and we had Communists and Mafia and Jews at the house. My dad was very popular at bar mitzvahs and Italian weddings—playing with mixed-race bands as well as the local neighborhood gay band Freddie and the Flamingos. Our social roll was truly expanding and it seemed to me that education made the difference. Between who had and had not—who could travel and move through the city and who could or who didn't.

OK, so what was the purpose of the desegregation of the black girl? To diversify her social calendar? I didn't have access to necessarily a better education. The black neighborhood school I came from was several lessons ahead of the white school I transferred to and you have heard just a bit of some of the many distractions. Math, I learned at home. My house was filled with the books I read. School only gave me access through the numerous book clubs you could join and there certainly were no opportunities in the black school to order books on credit.

OK, exposure to other cultures can sometimes be a valuable thing (and particularly the dominating culture) but my white friends, from what I could see, didn't come close to paying the price that I had to pay for this diversity.

So here's some of the things I did learn. I learned to be viciously angry. I learned to talk sassy to my mother, lie to her, drink, and smoke pot. None of which my friends who stayed in the black schools did—except the pot smoking. I guess everybody did that.

I became intimate with paranoia. Dealing with teachers like Miss Jones and other more subtle attempts at racism made me look at every word that came to me from a white person's mouth as suspect. I became confused about what was happening with other black people. I became afraid of black people I didn't know and there were a lot of them. As you grow older, you cover more territory in the city and I would see groups of black kids greet each other on buses and down-town and I didn't know any of them. I was terrified but I asked my mother to send me to Austin-East, the black high school. Yeah right! She knew I couldn't hang. But I fought Webb one more time. That would have just finished me. I think my sister graduated from Webb knowing three black people in the whole city outside of our church. Instead, I was relegated to the neighborhood school, except now we were in a whole new neighborhood. WE finally got that house with the bay windows on the side of town opposite the airport. So I was enrolled in the suburban school which, after several riots, was now well integrated. It was all going down the tubes very fast when the nut cracked again!

At an Austin High School football game where I THOUGHT I was the date of a guy named Charles who was very hot and very popular.

[*Lights change.*]

ANOTHER BLACK GIRL: Hey there she is! Hey little rich black white girl. How come you over here in the ghetto, huh? Don' you live up on the hill with all them other uppity Negroes? Uha, look a them damn ugly-ass brogans, where you get them shoes? Buster Brown's—white people shoes. I bet your momma serve UP some mashed potatoes and peas. You a loser. Charles told us your little scared ass was probably not gone show up but you did. What? You trying to give him some pussy? Go on home and eat some mashed potatoes and peas before my girl Sarita get here and beat your ass for tryna fuck her man. Bitch! Take your ass on back to Holston and don't come around here again. Ha-ha—look at that skinny ass stringy-haired bitch. Black as her ass is she scared of niggas.

[*Lights change.*]

BLACK GIRL: The sad part was—My feelings was really hurt about the mashed potatoes and peas. My mother's meatloaf, mashed potatoes, and peas was my favorite meal. Especially when she didn't use the instant mashed potatoes. What had I become?! Our social life was still very largely black but we were a special breed. WE were supposed to be getting in touch with our community and our roots through organizations like Jack and Jill and the Links, but we went to ice skating parties! Ice skating! My mother could not braid hair and played bridge not bid whist. We went to teas and ate sandwiches with the crust cut off. My mother made tuna fish and potato chip casserole. Instead of Swahili classes we now took ballet lessons. I attended charm school and prepared to be a debutante. A debutante!!!! The most painful times were when we would visit my cousins in the country who were growing farther and farther apart from me and my sister. Too many hand-me-downs and proper speech. When I was there, I would work hard on being a good country nigger, sometimes even selling out my sister for cool points. And through it all I was trying to negotiate through a friendly but still very racist white world. Confusion joined paranoia and began to wreak havoc on the black girls' mind.

You know Hope like in Arkansas—it's where Bill Clinton is from and in the middle of my high school career. We moved there—plunged farther South into the Arkansas interior and there I basked in the clear, lucid, and comforting glow of hateback!

You know Hateback! You gone hate me? Well, I will just hate you back! You know the atmosphere where the whites live, work, play, and shop on one side of town and blacks on the other. Desegregation had not confused this town. They still maintained a clear distance from one another even in their integrated schools. White flight was just one way they dealt with it. Our school was fifty percent black and fifty percent white, not two lone Negroes integrating the world.

They had their student body and we had ours. They had their cools peeps and we had ours. They had their homecoming queen and we had—

White folks had very ugly ways in Arkansas and black people by and large ignored them. They printed racial slurs in the yearbook, raised a statue of a Confederate soldier outside the high school, and in the whole decade or more the school had been integrated not one black girl had been allowed to be homecoming queen. My sister and I were integration veterans and we knew how it was supposed to go down and this wasn't happening. Both my sister and I spent lots of time in the principal's office. She did it while maintaining a four-point-oh average, I rebelled against the whole idea of these devils being the ones to educate me.

[BLACK GIRL *comes from behind the podium. Lights change into something dark and ominous. Rage.*]

Fuck your fucking lies the history teacher is telling! Fuck the skew-ered-ass social and psychology analysis—where black people are rel-egated to all manners of dysfunctional pathologies! Fuck your chapter on South Africa with no mention of Nelson Mandela! The ANC and apartheid reduced to the naked behinds of young African men in a South African jail . . . I was so distracted by all that ass I don't even remember hearing the three-second lesson on apartheid politics.

MARK: God, Doesn't that make you mad?

[BLACK GIRL *looks up confused from staring at the pictures.*]

BLACK GIRL: Huh, oh. What did she say? I was, uh . . .
So, I turned on, tuned out, and joined the only interracial clique in my school. The stoners!

[BLACK GIRL *begins to roll a joint.*]

Oh yes, drugs, substance abuse, contraband—the great equalizer. I was no longer choosing my white friends by circumstance; I was actually choosing my white friends based on something we had in common. And we didn't have to worry about trust 'cause in Arkansas smoking a joint is deep complicity.

[*Having finished rolling the joint,* BLACK GIRL *hesitates before lighting it and eventually tucks it behind her ear during the following:*]

But there was one class, my favorite class. I waited until after that class to drink or smoke pot or doze. That was my Acting class. First class of the morning. Two senior plays. I couldn't wait!

[*Lights change. Music plays, the Chicago sound track "Overture."* BLACK GIRL *sits during the music and pulls the joint from behind her ear. She smokes it with* JOAN *during the following.*]

JOAN: I don't know why you didn't audition for Dorothy?

BLACK GIRL: Joan, I told you. She wouldn't let me.

JOAN: I really didn't want to be Dorothy—

[BLACK GIRL *shoots her a look.*]

JOAN: OK, I really did but . . . I didn't want you not to be. And I didn't want you to be mad at me. And I didn't know why you didn't audition. Couldn't you have talked to her?

BLACK GIRL: I did. You know what she said? "Baby, didn't you see the movie? Dorothy's white." She would only let me try out for the boy's parts.

JOAN: That's discrimination. You should sue?

BLACK GIRL: Sue to be Dorothy, from Kansas with her little dog, Toto?

JOAN: It's not fair!

BLACK GIRL: Well, at least I get to be head of munchkin land.
    I funked that lollipop song up. "We represent . . . the lollipop guild"

[*She continues the song and demonstrates with a funky dance to the "Lollipop"
song from* The Wizard of Oz. *During the following the* BLACK GIRL *dons
an African gelee.*]

The drama teacher loved it. By the time *My Fair Lady,* the second
senior play, came around—I had an epiphany. My father told me one
of his funny Jim Crow stories. He had lots of these kinds of stories.
Some were funny, some were sad, some were scary—most were all
three. This is a funny one.

It seems that my father and a Nigerian friend had figured out a way
around ole Jim Crow and into segregated restaurants and bars. They
would show up wearing dashikis and when they were questioned they
would declare themselves British subjects. This confused the white
folks and they let them in. They had made the laws for Nigras and
they weren't sure if genuine African with British accents counted. So
the next day I showed up to school and we introduced a new character to the George Bernard Shaw acorn. Yes, chile, wherever good
Londoners were, there was Madame Ayo. She was introduced at the
ball. "Introducing Princess Adeyinka Ayokunle." Madame had a seat
at the Ascot races. On the street where THEY lived, she did too. She
was a friend, neighbor, and confidante of Miss Eliza Doolittle. We
even added a scene where Madame Ayo went to Eliza's house to (in
West African accent) "borrow cup of sugar." Now, was I so wrong?
Please, Africans have been in Europe and the rest of the West for a
long time. Check the history. Shit, Shakespeare wrote *Othello.* When?
He didn't just dream up a Nigga!

[*Lights change.*]

True story: The other night I had a dream that I had been locked up in
a mental institution for playing white characters onstage. They were
trying to drug me and do strange things to me and kept telling me I
was crazy for having played these characters onstage. It was frightening. I had finally escaped from the mental hospital, when suddenly
my father appeared. I wondered who had called him. But then I woke
up. Before he could say what he came to say. Like he woke me up.
What was that about?

[BLACK GIRL *puts down the gelee and returns to the podium. Drinks some water. Shuffles papers.*]

Well, when I graduated from high school, I knew that I was going to a black college. Well, honestly, my first choice was UCLA. But my mother would not let me go to UCLA, California was too far way. She said I could go to Puerto Rico or the Virgin Islands but California was out. I had received a scholarship because despite graduating something like 475th in my class of less than 600, with a 2.75 grade point average, I rocked the SATs and the ACTS and had the highest score on one of them in the state and was automatically awarded a scholarship to any school I wanted to go to in the states, Puerto Rico, and the Virgin Islands. So it was just a matter of picking a city that was close enough for my mother's approval—New Orleans—and finding a black school in it.

New Orleans had Xavier and Dillard. Three of my friends were going to Dillard so I picked Xavier. I welcomed the insulated environment of an HBCU [Historically Black College or University]. I felt ready this time to be in an all-black environment. After all, I had gotten a little taste of it in the integrated Arkansas high school. What I wasn't prepared for was what they did with the photograph they asked us to include in the application. They must have grabbed a swatch of that paper bag and placed that shit right up next to my picture 'cause there was an eerie correlation between the complexion of the students in my dorm and the twice as large Katherine Drexel Hall. All hopes of coincidence fell by the wayside when my roommate's mother showed up a week into our freshmen orientation. A creole from Houston, she was dismayed that her daughter had been assigned to St Joe's instead of KD as they had requested. She took one look at my black, dark-skinned ass and high-tailed it down to the Office of Housing to see what had happened. It seems there was an overrun of those Creole girls being admitted and KD was full. I love New Orleans, but it is a place where color matters in degrees but that's another twenty dollars. Though, I kicked myself many times that year for not going to a blacker school. We didn't have a football team and therefore no marching band. But I gained a black self-confidence at Xavier and the city of New Orleans. I got to know all kinds of black people while in New Orleans, on campus and off and I found a level of identification that I have yet to experience since. Unfortunately, I still had not found a desire to study hard, it was New Orleans for god's sake. So my father pulled me from that school and I began to languish in halfway HBCUs—those on their last legs, Knoxville College, University of Arkansas, Pine Bluff (UAPB) Golden Lions. Not much on academics, dorms falling down but they had marching bands! Well, I finally had enough of formal education and decided to get my degree from the streets. And made my way to that heretofore forbidden territory, California! And it was that degree from the streets of California that I used to gain entrance to the University of Iowa. That and the Patricia Roberts Harris Fellowship named for the first African American woman to enter the line of succession to the president. She served under JFK, Lyndon Johnson, and Jimmy Carter and was the U.S. ambassador to Luxembourg. Eighteen of us in each discipline of the arts—creative writing, dance, theater, music, and visual arts—landed in the middle of that cornfield by way of Patricia Roberts Harris. A few of us were from the Bay Area—writer, Cathy Arellano; playwright, Robert Alexander. The loveable and powerful Kabby Mitchell from Richmond, a former dancer with the SF Ballet who summed it up upon landing with a slab of ribs in his bag. "Ooh uh, uh—I can't believe I am in the middle of a cornfield with a bunch of white folks! Imo be out of here very weekend, shit my booty itching now!"

Well the first thing we did as a group was to put some mustard in their potato salad. No we really did. We got to the buffet table at the graduate orientation banquet, everything was that Iowa bland. One of the fellows, Alphonso, just looked around and couldn't take it anymore. He went over to the cold cuts, grabbed the mustard, and started squirting it in the bowl of potato salad and stirring for dear life. Then he grabbed a couple of boiled eggs and threw them in. Complaining the whole time. You know I was cracking up. Well, you know no good negro shall go unpunished. Soon there was some titled woman over there with a pasted-on smile asking brother if everything was OK. He looked up from stirring, smiled, "Oh we fine, just trying to help yaw out. That's why we're here isn't it. Now, that's better." Potato salad done, he politely introduced himself and told her he looked forward to contributing further to life here in Iowa.

We struggled to imagine three years in this isolation. All the white people look scared all the time. They had turned beet red when Kabby said his booty was itching. They kept smiling at me. I noticed it even when they were safe in their locked car sitting across the intersection from—they gave me that smile. I knew that smile. I knew what it meant. I only see it under certain circumstances. One being dark alleys with only me and another woman, whiter than me. I see it if I am in a very, white upper-crusty neighborhood—like Lower Pacific Heights.* You know the tight, forced please don't beat me, touch me, talk to me, breathe in my direction smile. Iowa's motto? You make me smile. And they be smiling!

In the theater department there was no smiling but there was open hostility.

The other directors resented me coming in and working with the black playwrights. They called a meeting to let me know. Put me on notice that they were not taking this reverse racism. They fully intended to direct some of the black playwrights' plays too. Now you know the black playwrights were choosing to work with me. And not to disparage my colleagues but I would imagine they had their reasons. And they told them so in a follow-up meeting. At the end of the meeting they tried to corner me, blaming me for the perceived discrimination in black playwrights seeking black directors.

[*She comes out from behind the podium and charges across the room.*]

When I went off—as you know I did—I had to listen to things like, "Hey don't get you little afro in a wad" and "you know not all of us were lucky enough to be born a black woman to get a free ride and special treatment."

I heard more overt racist comments and saw more hostile action in my three years in Iowa than I had since I left Miss Jones's mammy lesson.

* "Lower Pacific Heights" is what they renamed part of the Fillmore district once whites moved in.

Class discussion on race and culture disintegrated into shouting and throwing matches—when it was a part of the class curriculum. If the class curriculum did not include race and culture and race and culture was brought up it was most times squashed.

[*She returns to the podium.*]

In directing seminar, all of the concepts, references, icons that we studied were old, white, mostly European, male, and dead. At first, I was completely intimidated—this was not like Fort Sanders where the class was five lessons behind me. I hadn't been to school in fifteen years. And we never studied these old dudes in my undergrad theater classes—we studied Bullins, Barak, Shine, Elder, Milner, Davis, Hansberry, Shange, Hughes, Angelou, Childress, Kennedy. When I tried one time to demonstrate my understanding of a particular principle we were discussing with a reference to Mr. Ed Bullins, my teacher looked at me very confused and said, "Well, no." I could tell he knew little about the play I was referencing. I tried to discuss it with him later and he just said, "Well, I am sorry I just don't know those plays."

But the nut got cracked once again when playwright and former student Peter Ullian was commissioned to write a play for Iowa's sesquicentennial.

[BLACK GIRL *comes from behind the podium and matches movements to text.*]

The entire play was narrated by an Indian complete with feather, loincloth, and red makeup. There was a scene a black actress was made to perform where she was a slave escaping through Iowa with flour on her face posing as the queen of England. Jews were depicted as owning all the stores and only owning stores. And the second act opened with an unfortunate minstrel show complete with blackface. It caused a furor among the black students across the campus. I couldn't show my face around town and it divided the theater department horribly. It was very ugly. I prayed a lot but paranoia returned.

I again began to question everything that came out of the mouth of a white person. Whisperings in corners always seemed to be about me—on or off campus. I sometimes slept for days. I drove to Chicago at all hours of the night not knowing where I was going and why.

A professor at Iowa trying to be hip told me well you know you are just here because you are exotic; flavor of the month, I said oh I thought it was my directing potential and my fifteen years of professional theater experience. He say well c'mon—"No you come on man, most of my colleagues have been doing community theater for the last five years and before that they stuck somewhere in this cornfield or they just graduated from some posh ivy league mutual admiration society. I have been in the trenches, working, paying my dues and my rent. Do you really believe that I am not qualified to be here?" He said, "No no that's not what I was trying to say of course not." (me) "Then watch you mouth."

[*Lights change. Music plays, Fela's "Shuffering and Shmiling."*]

It seems my mother's words were just as true today as in 1968. You have to be twice as good to even be on the radar. The irony is those students were there because they could pay the tuition. I had to earn my affirmative action, flavor of the month, set aside, welfare, free ride fellowship on the sweat of my back only. If I could pay for the tuition. would it be worth it? For me? And just how much could this free ride cost? My life?

But, how do you think black students at Iowa fare today? Is the curriculum more inclusive? Has the canon opened up in such a way that Ntozake Shange can be included in the lesson about American playwrights or women playwrights and not be relegated to the lump sum multicultural section that pairs her with Fugard, Linton Kwesi Johnson, Derek Walcott?

Remember that professor who couldn't further a discussion anchored in Ed Bullins's work. Well he has led Iowa Summer Rep in several successful seasons focused on black playwrights and worked with many great African American artists. And most recently, Iowa's theater program received an award for having a diverse faculty. They have three black female professors currently in the department. Can you believe it? The curriculum began to include the work of artists like Rhodessa Jones. We introduced them to Pomo Afro Homos and busted class discussion wide open. Our shows sold out. Our contribution to the university was measurable and enormous. But we were always reminded how big a favor we had received from THEM—the paying customer, the white professor, the white-ass government. Funny, we were never reminded of our debt to Patricia Roberts Harris who I am sure had to work five times as hard as any of her colleagues to come off with a fellowship named after her.

Tha mothafuckin-ass MFA brought me back to San Francisco to teach a class at SF State and those nuts just keep on crackin'! I taught a class called cross-cultural communication through the arts and again made the naive mistake of thinking that race and culture might matter in a course such as this. Six white female students went to the head of the department with a list of complaints. They didn't want to do a project in Nigeria, not the only project assigned, mind you, but they did NOT want to do a project in Africa. They called it racist. They said I couldn't remember their names. The most telling complaint? I taught from an African American perspective. Afterwards, I asked how many of them had ever had a black teacher before. Fewer than half raised their hands.

"And you are not having it for a minute. Your entire academic life you have been taught by a European, white perspective and you're not having the black perspective for a minute. You didn't even give it a month."

I just don't know how much progress was made? I got on the desegregation bus a few times and the ride was rough my friends, let me tell you. I feel much like a sacrificial lamb but for what? But you know what? I have been thinking of going for the big one the Ph.D.—

[*Blackout.*]

What? I'm serious! How bad could it be, I haven't sent out any letters yet—I was just thinking . . .

INTERVIEW WITH EDRIS COOPER-ANIFOWOSHE

Omi Osun Joni L. Jones

Let me start with a question that I think a lot of people have—what does art do? And how does *Adventures of a Black Girl* . . . in particular sit next to that idea? What does your work do? What do you want your work to do?

I'm going to cry! Art saved my life. Period. It saved my life! I'm telling you, I'd be in trouble, if I didn't have the theater to really work out all that stuff I talked about in *Adventures* . . . , the anger was so real for me. And it started really young. I remember my mother had the foresight to put me in the theater—she's a theater person. So my mother took me over to Carpetbag Theatre,[1] and I think that part of what she was trying to do was to get my mind off of racism because in school I was facing it every day. And it hurt so bad. My mother was like, "What do I do with her? She can't get depressed like this!" So she took me to the theater and Girl Scouts, ballet, whatever else she could. The theater was so cathartic for me because these were stories that were giving me a different narrative of myself and my life. My sister and I were doing plays on the weekends, and I wasn't conscious that this was changing me. Only when I look back, I think, "This is why I didn't become a serial killer!" I was there with kids who are doing big things now. We were little theater people. One is an actor in New York, one is an agent in Los Angeles, another one is an actress and a singer in Los Angeles. So we weren't just playing around. This was a serious thing for us. At Knoxville College[2] they formed a little company with the kids, and we did a show called "Knoxville Swinging" that was based on Kool and the Gang's "Hollywood Swinging."[3] We were celebrating the community that we lived in. The line in *Adventures* . . . where I said, "Besides, they weren't my real friends"? My *real* friends were back home. Those were the things that really helped me survive, that I was able to have that Carpetbag experience to go into. And Linda Parris-Bailey[4] I think really recognized that these kids are catching hell. We would be walking home from school and sometimes the Black Panthers would show up, and walk us home, and talk to us because college students were offering us drugs all the time. You know, here I am, I'm ten, and someone's trying to get me to do acid, or cocaine. I got offered cocaine so many times walking home from junior high school! You know, by white people. Now there were black junkies but they never tried to get us high.

So that was an entire education right there.

The black junkies always tried to hide from us—"Oh, here come the kids!"—and would try to straighten up. The white junkies tried to bring us into their den of ill repute. It was amazing.

So you were learning about the dangers of whiteness in the classroom and on the street! What time frame was that?

This was the late '60s and early '70s.

Well, that might be a piece to think about putting in the show—that theater education and street education that you got—

—and how Carpetbag intervened! Yeah! There was something powerful both in the material and the actor training. I remember the click for me was that I get to use my real emotions and that way they don't have to live inside of me and eat me alive. I found that out at nine. I said, "Oh, SNAP! *This* is what acting is!" And so I would go in there and rant and rave, and they would allow it and encourage it. The director would find the part for it! We would do all these improvs. That's what saved me. Rhodessa Jones[5] says that all the time, "Theater saved my life." Rhodessa and I worked together for twenty years, and both of us understand those moments when we've been saved—those moments, they still happen.

Imagine that! Theater as a survival tool for black people! Crossroads, Freedom Theatre, The Ensemble, St. Louis Black Rep, the NEC, Penumbra—there have been so many active black theaters, but many more of them are gone now or doing very reduced seasons. If people imagined the theater as a survival strategy, it would change everything.

If people could understand what really goes on and the type of community that's created, the type of understanding you receive about yourself in the theater. No one likes to look at themselves. I think black people have a really keen eye for looking at ourselves. But what we don't have maybe is the softness of compassion for ourselves. And I think theater gives you that. Not only can you look and say, "Sometimes I'm a black bitch," but you can have compassion for that. I've worked with the Medea Project,[6] theater for incarcerated women. The last Medea Project showed that bitches aren't born, they're made. I have seen people's lives turn completely around after theater. Even in Medea, I was saved again, many many times in Medea. I'm looking at an inmate and there but for the grace of God go I, because I'm making some of the same choices she's making. I might not be crossing the line illegally, but at the time I was thinking her boyfriend is a lot like mine in really bad ways. Why am I choosing *that* in my life? Oh, I have *that* kind of denial going on, too. You can see yourself reflected in the women. That compassion that the art opens in you is very healing.

In *Adventures* . . . you have a scene where a black girl calls you uppity because your family now lives in the suburbs and you are wearing Buster Brown shoes that she calls white people's shoes. Your parents worked so hard to get that house on the other side of town, and now you can't fit in with the black kids from your former neighborhood. In this brief scene, you really get at the class issues that divide black people now. The scene raises painful and complex issues around black authenticity. Why can't a black suburban life be authentic? You make clear that education can create alienation for black people, not having a sense of homeplace. The title of your piece—*Adventures of a Black Girl in Search of Academic Clarity and Inclusion*—we can pay quite a price for that elusive inclusion as our academic credentials create wedges between us.

It's often reflected in how we treat each other, but I think that's more about how we feel about ourselves.

Early in *Adventures* . . . , your mother reveals something of her own scared spaces as she tells you what to do and not do, how to talk, what language to use. Your mother may have wanted you to speak Standard English to protect you in white schools, but that very Standard English becomes a liability in your old neighborhood.

I try to avoid that kind of language training with my son.

We're always under the eye of whiteness. That story with your mother was about survival. The lessons she learned about how to survive with white people, she passed on to you. We have constructed who we are based on protecting ourselves from the physical and psychic violence of racism on the one hand, and trying to prove our humanity, trying to do whatever it takes to prove ourselves to white people on the other hand. We want to get in "the club" even as we are rightfully beating up the owners! Throughout your piece, that's what the academy is about—teaching black people how to be acceptable to white people and demonstrating that black people will never truly be accepted. The institutions say, "How much can you be like us?" "What plays do you teach and how do you teach them?" "For goodness sakes, can you reshape those emotions?" I thought it was so telling that even as a child—before you got to theater, before you got an education in school—you already had the presence of white folk in your house controlling things! That is a deep basic education for black people! The invisible specter of whiteness!

My mother was terrified. I felt like every time my mother let me out of the car at school, she thought she would never see me again! She'd say, "Baby, it's going to be OK!" And I'd say, "When you say it like that, I know it's not! You're scaring me lady!" She was so nervous all the time the first few years that I went there. Because these memories were repressed, I wasn't sure they were real. So I called my sister to ask, "Do you remember this? Do you remember that?" I called to ask if she remembered the fight after Martin Luther King died. She was like, "Oh girl we were beating everybody up!" And I was like, "Wow, she remembers it exactly how I remember it!" I said, "We didn't get in trouble for it." She said, "Daddy came to school with that smile on his face!" And that's what would happen—he would come pick us up with this proud smile on his face! My sister got kicked out of class one time for telling the teacher the word was Negro not nigger, and the teacher said to her, "Well, there's some words in our language that you always mispronounce." And the whole class went off on her! So my sister's like, "Daddy came to the school with a smile on his face." Those were the kind of things my parents would do.

And you had to confer with your sister to make sure it really happened! It's great that she was there to validate it all. But *Adventures* . . . is solo! You're up there all by yourself telling your truth.

You know, I think about that and I always have a talk back, especially with a white audience. They always say, "Now, the story about the slumber party is invented." Could I really invent that thing?

Yeah, the solo thing is scary because one of the ways that society punishes and silences black women is by making us believe we're crazy. They even call us crazy. When we are alone, we can come to believe that we are in fact insane, that the multiple gashes of racism and sexism might just live in our imaginations. But because black folks' lives share similar contours due to racism, your solo piece is really a communal piece. When I saw the show at Northwestern, so many people around me in the audience were like, "Umm humm!" and "Ump humph umph!" and there were those groans of recognition at the pains that you experienced. It seems important that you do this performance at academic institutions since you offer such a critique of academic life—from elementary school through graduate school through teaching in higher education. It seems like when the piece is performed at academic institutions it is more obvious that this solo show is telling the story of many folk.

I find that those people who are used to being around black people can understand what's going on with me. If you're not used to being around a black person, and I don't just mean a person with black skin. I mean someone who's in touch with it all. Some are wearing this horrible mask that so many people in academia wear, and it's not always a whitey mask, sometimes it's a very Afrocentric mask.

But it's a mask nonetheless!

Yes! They aren't getting real with you and they don't have your back! So I've been checking in with Marlon,[7] and he says "Girl! Slow down!" He's got my back! There's always a guest lecture every time we do the play, and when Marlon gave the lecture, he read them so suddenly in his lecture! He's so smart like that. He can negotiate the racial playing field like nobody I've seen. I think it has to do with the gender training, too. He's very clear.

That's fabulous! Because you do have to have your allies. And the allies don't have to be black or female if they are willing to respect your experience and support your truth. You know Pearl Cleage's work? She says this in "Hollering Place." You must have allies and you've got to use them!

And you have to have the language. The right language means that people will get it. Audre Lorde says we have to use our righteous anger, and

I just reread that. I needed to so bad! I've had some really good allies wherever I have had to fight. My revenge comes in the form of public humiliation.

So that's another way that the theater is doing something, right? Because you will get that revenge—with witnesses!

I will go after them onstage! I will go after them on the web! So my second year at Iowa,[8] this play came out, and the headline said, the review said, "Grad Students Skewer University in Hilarious Satire." OK. Later, I realized, at the end of my work there, they were starting to talk to me and pick my brain for how they could be different. Before I left, things changed drastically. Well, [the graduate students] told [the faculty] that we felt we had a federal lawsuit, that if they didn't recruit black actors, that we were not getting the same education that our colleagues were, because we had to use actors who were outside of the theater department. We ran into problems—this guy wouldn't show up because he's really pre-med. You know, we were frustrated because we weren't working with actors who wanted to respect the theater. The third year I was there, more than half of the MFA class was black. It was from zero to like seven.

Wow!

Now, Iowa's, I think, one of the best schools a black actor can go to.

Last night during the talkback a young man was asking you about sexuality in the piece and then Renee[9] was asking you about gender in the piece. There's a way to think about black feminist work in which desire, not just sexual desire, but desire of all kinds becomes really important. It's a way of naming yourself—"This is who I am. I like this person. I am attracted to that person. This is the kind of work I want to do in the world." Name whatever that desire is. As you continue to think about other pieces that you might put in *Adventures* . . . , is there a space where you might include a conversation like that? About growing up and desire becoming a way for you to define yourself? You were talking about the men that you have chosen, and when you met some of the incarcerated women, you realized, "Oh, I'm making some bad choices." So, are you redefining desire?

Absolutely, yeah. And you know, immediately, you think of romance and eroticism. I think I really became clear about defining my desire in that vision with the incarcerated women. And I think the minute it became clear, it became available.

That's a beautiful magic, isn't it?

Yeah, it was like, I was sitting in Iowa and I had decided, I'm not even going to try to date. I'm going to be celibate. And I used that word, but it wasn't this kind of religious celibacy. It was really just avoiding any mistakes, and I felt like there's nothing out here but mistakes. "This is Iowa! You are not going to find anything here, so you might as well start to look at *you*. So when you leave here, you're real clear." I started to really think about it, and I started writing a little affirmation on a piece of paper. I wanted a husband and I narrowed it down to three requirements—spirituality, kindness, and honesty. And I would say, probably three months into this, I met my husband.

In Iowa?

In Nigeria. The other thing, I think, is to define who you desire to be. That's been a little more elusive for me. I can't even decide if I want to do TV next or film! Do I want to do New York or LA? Do I want to do Dallas, or . . .? Do I want to teach? I can't even figure that out right now, and I'm really good at doing nothing and letting something roll by, you know?

Instead of being active about pursuing the thing? Letting things roll by is a strategy, too.

I thought, I'm not going to Nigeria to find no husband, that just would be too cliché! And of course, that's what everybody was saying, "You're going to find your husband over there!" All my African friends. So I was like, "Please!" So when I met my husband, I was like, "I do not want to be bothered with this guy!" As I talked to him, I realized, this is *me*. It was very bizarre. So, two, three months later, my husband turns to me and says, "We need to be married. We need to just go. I think I should be your husband. I think you should marry me." And before I knew it, I was saying, "OK!" We came back to the United States and we went to meet my parents. My mother opens the door, my husband prostrates to my mother, like full flat on the floor, and he starts chanting to her, "Oh my mother! The mother of my wife!" And he walks in and he greets my father and he bows his head to my father and he does the same thing, "Father, I give you respect. Thank you for having my wife!" My parents were done! And then, get this! We're sitting at the table, my husband's there, my sister's there, and my father says, "Well, this is quite interesting that you would go to Nigeria and get married because you were supposed to be born in Nigeria, so was your sister. My sister and I were like, "WHAT?" And he said, "I wanted to go to Nigeria because that's where my great-grandmother is from!"

So it was your firsthand experience with Nigerians that inspired Princess Adeyinka Ayokunle, that transformation you made in *My Fair Lady*! It's great to think of the many transgressions being made when Black Girl dons a *gelee*[10] and gets to pass for high society! What year did you get married?

This was '97. Right after I got married, I came back and went to the National Black Theatre Festival.

I was there, too! Rhodessa Jones did *Big-Butt Girls, Hard-Headed Women*, Shange[11] did *The Love Space Demands*, Sekou Sundiata[12] did *The Circle Unbroken Is a Hard Bop*. After that, like a few weeks later, I went to Nigeria. I had a Fulbright, and I went to Nigeria. Do you know how many people were in the audience that day?

I was there—

Daniel Alexander Jones,[13] who's directing Patrick, was in the audience that day. Robbie McCauley was there, 'cause she and Laurie Carlos[14] did something in that festival. That's the only show I didn't see of that series from—what was it? Cultural Odyssey![15]

It was like the first year of that performance series at the festival. That was a deep, deep period of time. When you talk about that National Black Theater Festival, so much went on.

It really did. At that festival, there was a very distinctive way to think about black performance. Nonlinear, participatory, music-driven, a fluidity of time and place. Cultural Odyssey was putting out work that

you didn't see often. Now, Laurie and Robbie and Aishah Rahman[16] and some others had been doing theater in a jazz aesthetic since the early 1980s, but the National Black Theatre Festival gave them a kind of visibility they didn't often get. They were doing what some folk would call avant-garde work and black theaters were generally more aesthetically conservative than this. They were more likely to have their work done at places like P.S. 122 than say at the NEC [Negro Ensemble Company]. Yeah, that year of the festival really exploded what black theater might be.

And on a personal level so much went on at that festival. I had a woman at the festival walk up to me, she said, "Did you just get married?" I said, "Yeah." She said, "I'm a psychic, and I'm gonna tell you one other thing—you married into your ancestral family!" I was like, "Girl!" Then some of us were all sitting around talking about where we're originally from, Mississippi, Arkansas. One woman said, "I have a sister that lives in Pine Bluff. It's a tiny town." Well, it turns out that I knew that woman's sister—she's my next door neighbor! She had just found out that she even had a sister! All that was happening in that whole period, that was '97.

You have had some powerful adventures—all over the world! In your piece, the Black Girl doesn't have a traditional adventure because she doesn't achieve her goal on her quest. This adventure might be a kind of misadventure given that the heroine never gets what she's seeking! And the lesson she ends with is really where she began—desegregation is rough, its goals are unclear, and the toll is great. So will the adventures continue? Will you add more personal experiences to *Adventures of a Black Girl . . .*?

Yeah! I can't just let these stories sit in my head! I have to find somewhere to put them, you know?

NOTES

1. Founded in 1969 in Knoxville, Tennessee, Carpetbag Theatre is one of the oldest black theaters in the United States. It is committed to the development of new works with an emphasis on storytelling and music.

2. Knoxville College is an HBCU founded in 1875 in Knoxville, Tennessee, through the missionary efforts of the United Presbyterian Church of North America. Originally established as a normal school for the training of teachers, Knoxville College is currently a liberal arts institution that offers students a debt-free work program for meeting their tuition.

3. "Hollywood Swinging" was the first number one R&B single for the 1970s band Kool and the Gang which was known for soul, jazz, R&B, and funk traditions. It has been sampled by a host of artists including DJ Kool in "Let Me Clear My Throat" (1996).

4. Playwright and artistic/executive director of Carpetbag Theatre, Linda Parris-Bailey has led Carpetbag for more than thirty years. Her play for young audiences, *Dark Cowgirls and Prairie Queens,* has been produced at many theaters, including the New Victory Theater on Broadway, Kuntu Repertory Theatre in Pittsburgh, and City Theatre in Detroit.

5. Rhodessa Jones is a performance artist, director, writer, and activist who is the co-artistic director of San Francisco's Cultural Odyssey and the founder of The Medea Project: Theater for Incarcerated Women.

6. The Medea Project: Theater for Incarcerated Women was founded in 1987 by Rhodessa Jones to reduce the recidivism rates among women of color inmates. The Medea Project served as the foundation for the stories Jones gathered into her performance piece *Big-Butt Girls, Hard-Headed Women,* and created a model for the theater production Jones developed with women in the Johannesburg Correctional Service in South Africa.

7. Marlon M. Bailey, a performance studies scholar, is an assistant professor in the Department of Gender Studies at the University of Indiana at Bloomington where he and Cooper-Anifowoshe are colleagues.

8. Cooper-Anifowoshe was a graduate student in theater at the University of Iowa. Much of her graduate school experience is described in *Adventures of a Black Girl in Search of Academic Clarity and Inclusion.*

9. Renee Alexander-Craft is an assistant professor at the University of North Carolina at Chapel Hill with a joint appointment in the Department of Communication Studies and the Department of Global Studies. She provided postperformance comments and facilitated a talkback after the performance of *Adventures of a Black Girl in Search of Academic Clarity and Inclusion* at Northwestern University.

10. *Gelee* is a Yoruba word for a woman's head covering, usually made of a large swatch of cloth that can be elaborately or simply tied on the head depending on the formality of the occasion. The size and fabric of the *gelee* can also denote social status.

11. Ntozake Shange is the author of the groundbreaking choreopoem *for colored girls who have considered suicide/when the rainbow is enuf.* In addition to writing for theater, Shange is also a poet, novelist, and essayist.

12. Sekou Sundiata was a poet, performer, and teacher whose *The Blue Oneness of Dreams* was nominated for a Grammy Award. He frequently collaborated with Craig Harris, and music deeply informed the development of his work. His last work before his death in 2007 was *51st (dream) state,* which was created in response to 9/11.

13. Daniel Alexander Jones is a writer, performer, and director who is currently an assistant professor at Fordham University in New York City. At the time of this interview, Jones was directing E. Patrick Johnson in the premiere of *Sweet Tea* at About Face Theatre in Chicago.

14. Laurie Carlos is a writer, performer, and director who was the original "lady in blue" in Shange's *for colored girls who have considered suicide/when the rainbow is enuf.* She created and curated the Late Night Series at Penumbra Theatre, now presented at Pillsbury House in Minneapolis.

15. Cultural Odyssey was founded by musician and composer Idris Ackamoor in 1979. Rhodessa Jones joined as co-artistic director in 1983. Together, they present socially conscious work that demonstrates that art is activism.

16. Aishah Rahman is a playwright, novelist, director, and professor emeritus from Brown University. Her plays include *The Mojo and the Sayso, Lady Day: A Musical Tragedy,* and *A Tale of Madame Zora.* Rahman is also the editor and cofounder of *NuMuse: An Annual Journal of New Plays from Brown University, 1994–1998.*

"HOW DOES IT FEEL TO BE A PROBLEM?":
EDRIS COOPER-ANIFOWOSHE'S *ADVENTURES OF A BLACK GIRL IN SEARCH OF ACADEMIC CLARITY AND INCLUSION*

Renée Alexander-Craft

> Canon building is Empire building. Canon defense is national defense. Canon debate . . . is the clash of cultures. And all of the interests are vested.
> —Toni Morrison, "Unspeakable Things Unspoken"

> Art is propaganda and ever must be . . . I do not care a damn for any art that is not used for propaganda. But I do care when propaganda is confined to one side while the other is stripped and silent.
> —W. E. B. DuBois, "Criteria of Negro Art"

Adventures of a Black Girl in Search of Academic Clarity and Inclusion begins with the Black Girl trapped in a small square of light on an otherwise dark stage.[1] She is disoriented, frustrated, and angry. The spotlight renders her lone black female frame hyper-visible while obscuring her context. Her link along a historical chain, her connection to other bodies that look like hers, and other consciousnesses that think like her own have been made invisible. As Ralph Ellison illuminates through his famous protagonist, this invisibility is neither an absence nor a phantasmal presence. It is a refusal to broaden the frame of light—a constructed blind spot. In the first words Black Girl speaks to us, she names the means by which she seeks to reveal this trick of light: "postmodern discourse."

Adventures is Edris Cooper-Anifowoshe's black feminist response to feeling crushed within the margins of a Western theater canon that has traditionally excluded or ignored black cultural and critical contributions. More broadly, it represents her ruminations on the project of desegregation. Cooper-Anifowoshe was a member of a generation of black students whose parents placed them at the vanguard of the struggle toward integration—toward the promise that greater resources would evince a better education and thus a more equitable experience of citizenship and belonging. Ultimately, Cooper-Anifowoshe asks us to reckon with whether or not that was true and whether or not it was worth it.

The play uses autobiography as a mode of postmodern discourse aligned with critical race pedagogy to make visible the matrices of power within which the Black Girl circulates and by which institutional power, portrayed in part through the disembodied character of Voice-Over, wields its influence. Writing about critical race pedagogy, Michael Jennings and Marvin Lynn assert:

> Critical Race Pedagogy emphasizes the importance of self-reflection, or reflexivity. Reflexivity is autobiographical by nature . . . exploration of one's "place" within a stratified society has power to illuminate oppressive structures in society. For this reason, narratives constructed by people of color can act as forms of resistance to "othering" that move readily from the private to the public sphere in an effort to examine race, class, identity and other expressive structures. ("The House That Race Built," 27)

Guided by the foundational critical race theories of W. E. B. DuBois and Frantz Fanon, I argue that traveling between her segregated black community and white majority institutions shifts the Black Girl's epistemological orientation from double-consciousness as strategy to double-consciousness as psychosis. In his classic work, *The Souls of Black Folks,* DuBois defines double-consciousness as a "sense of always looking at one's self through the eyes of others, of measuring one's soul by the tape of a world that looks on in amused contempt and pity" (2). Fanon refers to this sensibility as "third person consciousness" (*Black Skin, White Masks,* 110). Both name a way of being in the world marked by suspicion, alienation, and duality. Toni Morrison (*The House That Race Built,* 12) reminds us that double-consciousness is more than a psychosocial state. It may also function as an intentional "strategy" for subversion and survival. While in close proximity to a home community, which supports and sustains her, we witness Black Girl rehearse double-consciousness as strategy. Abstracted into variegated white and hostile communities, Cooper-Anifowoshe experiences what she refers to as "race fatigue" that turns the weapon of double-consciousness back on the self.

Drawing on theories of positionality and voice posited by feminists of color (hooks, "Homeplace"; Moraga and Anzaldúa, *This Bridge Called My Back;* and Collins, *Black Feminist Thought*),[2] as well as Toni Morrison's work on discourses of race and canon-building, this essay examines the ways in which *Adventures* critiques Western theater studies by seeking to take "what is articulated as an elusive race-free paradise and domesticat[ing] it" (x). As Morrison states: "If I had to live in a racial house, it was important, at the least, to rebuild it so that it was not a windowless prison into which I was forced, a thick-walled impenetrable container from which no cry could be heard, but rather an open house, grounded, yet generous in its supply of windows and doors" (*House That Race Built,* 4). I assert that revisiting her early "homeplace" memories gives Black Girl tools to better engage the site of her contemporary isolation and oppression (hooks, "Homeplace"). This *sankofa* gesture (reaching back to move forward) repositions the Black Girl from a state of racial paranoia to a state of critical racial awareness and reflexivity. Through *Adventures,* Cooper-Anifowoshe performatively "talks back" to the canon in an attempt to create a space for broader discussions of race, class, and gender.

Shortly after we first encounter Black Girl, Voice-Over challenges her to respond to a series of questions in order to test her mastery of the Western theater canon. "Name please, three playwrights from the Renaissance who wrote in the Romantic tradition," Black Girl offers the names of Langston Hughes and Zora Neale Hurston, to which Voice-Over challenges "Who????" Voice-Over's question references the European Renaissance while Black Girl's response privileges the Harlem Renaissance. Voice-Over presses on, "Is Ibsen's *A Doll's House* Romantic Expressionism or Expressive Romanticism?" to which Black Girl responds, "Who gives a rat's ass?" (130). More than simply a rebellion against the question, Black Girl's reaction indicates the tension inherent in the project of desegregation. Although *Brown vs. Board of Education* legally ended the practice of "separate but [not] equal" education in the United States and entitled black students to take advantage of resources previously only afforded to white segregated schools, it did nothing to disrupt the hegemony of whiteness, which still dominates U.S. curriculums. Black Girl yearns for integration as a sincere gesture toward cultural pluralism that would necessitate institutional as well as individual change, whereas Voice-Over seeks merely to assimilate her into preexisting conditions. As Black Girl notes, "exposure to other cultures can sometimes be a valuable thing (and particularly the dominating culture) but my white friends, from what I could see, didn't come close to paying the price that I had to pay for this diversity" (145).

In the midst of interrogating her knowledge of the Western theater canon, Voice-Over questions the Black Girl's legitimacy and motivation. "Miss Cooper," it asks, "what is the purpose of your education here at the University of Iowa?" This question is later shortened to, "What is the purpose of your education?" Rather than simply engage the question as a singular enterprise, Black Girl uses her autobiography, which is situated in desegregation's struggle against racism, to pull the audience into the indexical present of her work. As Adrian Piper argues in volume 1 of her two-volume text, *Out of Order, Out of Sight:* "Artwork that draws one into a relationship with the other in the indexical present trades easy classification—and hence xenophobia—for a direct and immediate experience of the complexity of the other, and of one's own responses to her. Experiencing the other in the indexical present teaches one how to see" (248). Addressing the constructed invisibility of racism in this way implicates us all as stewards and dwellers of the Western racial house capable of shining a light on the "racial contract," thereby questioning, critiquing, and revising canons no less than other socio-racial norms (Mill, *The Racial Contract*).

Seen in this fashion, Cooper-Anifowoshe's choice to have Voice-Over raise questions about *A Doll's House* is intriguing given the comparisons that can be made between the predicament of the black integrationist and Ibsen's lead character, Nora. In speaking with her husband, Torvald, about the dismissive and oppressive ways in which he and her father have treated her, Nora says: "You arranged everything according to your taste; and I got the same tastes as you; or I pretended to . . . When I look back on it now, I seem to have been living here like a beggar, from hand to mouth. I lived by performing tricks for you, Torvald. But you would have it so. You and father have done me a great wrong" (Ibsen, *A Doll's House*, act 3). Like Nora, Black Girl yearns to inhabit the space she occupies as a partner and co-creator whose voice and traditions may be valued rather than a radical to be disciplined into subservience and silence. Nora's "doll's house" is fashioned out of patriarchy and norms of nineteenth-century European respectability, which are raced just as much as they are gendered. Ibsen affords Nora the power to walk away from her doll's house by literally and figuratively slamming the door on further discourse or debate. Rather than exist within its structures, she chooses to discard its privileges and strike out on her own. Such a move is contrary to the black integrationist's aspirations and therefore not a viable option for Black Girl. Unlike Nora, she has no interest in walking away from a "home" (i.e., U.S. theater studies) in which she has made intellectual and emotional investments. What, then, is the Black Girl to do with her anger? What is the most productive use of her rage? Audre Lorde argues that "anger expressed and translated into action in the service of our vision and our future is a liberating and strengthening act of clarification . . . Anger is loaded with information and energy" (Lorde, "The Uses of Anger," 127). This is a view of anger with agency beyond simply providing emotional relief or pointing blame. It is a view of anger as reflextive, generative, and reparative.

Like the Invisible Man we meet in Ellison's "Prologue," the Black Girl we encounter at the start of Cooper-Anifowoshe's play is so "bumped and jostled" by decades of fighting against a racial undertow that her initial response to Voice-Over is more of a cathartic middle finger than a constructive intervention. In one of the final scenes of the play, Black Girl places her anger in fuller context. Revisiting the space of the podium, and speaking directly to the audience she says:

> In my directing seminar, all of the icons and the references we studied were old, white, male, mostly European, and dead. . . . And we never studied these old dudes in my undergrad theater classes—we studied Bullins, Baraka, Shine, Elder, Milner, Davis, Hansberry, Shange, Hughes, Angelou, Childress, and Kennedy. When I tried one time to demonstrate my understanding of a particular principle we were discussing with reference to Mr. Ed Bullins, my teacher looked at me very confused and said, "Well. No." I could tell he knew little about the play I was referencing. I tried to discuss it with him later and he just said, "Well, I am sorry I just don't know those plays. (153)

Going off-script, Cooper-Anifowoshe leans toward the audience and adds, "You know, if they don't know it, it don't exist." Black Girl resents having the black playwrights on whose shoulders she stands, her intellectual labor, and her cultural context rendered invisible and irrelevant.

In retaliation, she refuses to symbolically lock arms with Ibsen's Nora in order to create a productive dialogue between their differential standpoints on the axis of whiteness and patriarchy. Because *A Doll's House* and canonical work like it perpetually take the prized seat at the center of theatrical discourses, relegating Black Girl's cultural context not only to the margins, but off the page/stage, she rejects the opportunity to connect Nora's nineteenth-century plight and her own twenty-first-century struggles in order to reveal "deeper meanings" and "other significances" of the workings of whiteness, class, and patriarchy within each woman's context (Morrison, "Unspeakable Things Unspoken," 139).

To regain her voice and better channel her anger in the service of her vision, Black Girl must *sankofa* to an earlier, less bruised and battered self. Traveling back through time with Black Girl, we meet a character self-conscious of her racialized identity, yet confident in her own ability to know "through" race and racism rather than in spite of it. Still in close proximity to her home community, Black Girl uses double-consciousness as a means to navigate the land mines of desegregation. Cooper-Anifowoshe names this sense of duality "treading white people." As Black Girl notes, "All over Knoxville, parents whose children had been thrust into the chairs of white classrooms struggled to keep their children's heads above the muck. Like dogs treading water, we treaded white people" (136). At its most urgent, Cooper-Anifowoshe explicates "treading white people" as a strategy to assert one's humanity and as a means of survival. As Mother chides Black Girl:

> I am not interested in what white folks say. That doesn't concern me. I am concerned about what YOU say. You know you have to be at least twice as articulate as any of those white people. Twice as smart. . . . they don't have to be smart. They were born white! You, on the other hand, have to be AT LEAST twice as intelligent to even be considered human. (131–32)

At its most mundane, Cooper-Anifowoshe articulates "treading white people" as a politics of respectability, mutual suspicion, and "hateback." As Black Girl explains:

> You know Hateback! You gone hate me? Well, I will just hate you back! . . . We fought to be treated as equals, to sit next to

whites at lunch counters, in restaurants, bowling alleys, at the movies, in the theaters. But every adult that I knew that had fought that fight had a clear and discernible distaste and distrust for the whites they so vigorously fought to sit next to.

One of the most poignant examples of this is Black Girl's experience preparing for and participating in a slumber party at the house of a well-to-do white classmate. Although Mother is skeptical about whether or not any good will come of it, she nonetheless buys new pajamas for her daughter and drives her there. "No need in them thinking we don't have nothing" (138). Throughout the ride from their side of town to that of Black Girl's classmate, her mother disparages the houses, neighborhood, and people. When measured against the world she inhabits, Mother finds these things lacking. As Black Girl explains, "Looking back, at times, it was a bit vicious, but it never had the air of being vicious. It just had air. You know, like a kind of sigh, a sigh of relief. That's what the stories felt like" (136). Mother's comments throughout their journey were part of the black "hidden transcript" of racism—the behind-closed-door chatter that helped blacks keep their heads above water (Scott, *Domination*).

Mother's suspicion regarding her daughter's participation in the slumber party is verified when the white classmate's drunken mother asks Black Girl to rub her back because "you folks have such good strong hands" (140). As is the case with the majority of Black Girl's racist encounters, parents more than peers are culprits of racist behaviors. More often than not, Black Girl presents her peers as impotent observers rather than invested agitators, which illuminates them as less powerful but complicit.

Black Girl's in-class social studies lessons in majority white schools were just as fraught as her out-of-the-classroom, embodied experiences. Black Girl cites:

> Social studies always seemed to pose a problem. Those teachers felt they had free license to tell tales of black people. They weren't still saying that we have tails but damn near. We saw pictures of dirty, snotty-nosed black children in leaning lean-tos and were informed that this is actually how most black people live in the South. . . . We saw more dirty, snotty-nosed black children from the Biafran war in Nigeria and were told

that this is actually how most black people in Africa live. . . . We were told that African people hated us and were jealous of how well we were doing in America. That we could never go home again. Now, I was raised on the campus of a black university. We knew about the conflict in Nigeria. We got the news firsthand from travelers who extended warm invitations for us to visit them in Africa. Some even offered to pay for the trip. We had traveled the South extensively and seen firsthand how people lived and many, many that we saw lived well. WE knew better. WE knew our history and then some. (142)

As Audre Lorde states, "We know what it is to be lied to, and we know how important it is not to lie to ourselves" ("Learning from the 60s," 139). The "WE" Cooper-Anifowoshe evokes includes not only her immediate family and circle of intimate friends, but institutions like the black church whose ministry, educational initiatives, and activism help bolster her sense of personhood and actively advocate on her behalf. Speaking of one of her pastors, Reverend Ralph Ross, she tells us, "He preached black power and pride from the pulpit. Now, I know he wouldn't call it that, but he was a righteous role model" (143). His advocacy was not just located in the pulpit. When he learned of the damaging misinformation their social studies teacher attempted to feed Black Girl and his daughter, he "came down [to the school] and started speaking to the principal" on their behalf. "When we're treading white folks in stormy weather," Cooper-Anifowoshe reminisces looking straight out at her audience, "he was there with a life jacket." In close proximity to her homeplace, the Black Girl is surrounded by mirrors that affirm her and lifelines that rescue her.

Even with the support of a loving community, Cooper-Anifowoshe lays bare the bruises the friction of integration has caused the Black Girl. In one of several unscripted moments, she steps away from the podium to speak urgently to the audience:

You are right if you assume that in this environment, not too much learning went on. . . . The distractions and difficulties far outweigh the benefits. I mean, the "race" race overshadowed what was supposed to simply be equity in education.

But what it exposed was an inequity of spirit that plagues us still today. That everyone wants diversity, but people have a real big problem with living and breathing difference.

Although her early memories of self-confidence and cultural-consciousness help keep Black Girl afloat in the muck of racism, prolonged exposure begins to wear on her and weigh her down. Black Girl states, "I began to see problems with being a 'special negro.' I began to worry about my daily trips to West Knoxville for school and the distance, both physical and emotional, that I had to travel to get back home to my black segregated neighborhood" (143). This heightened experience of separation and extended intimacy with seeing oneself through the gaze of another shifts Black Girl's sense of duality away from double-consciousness as strategy and toward double-consciousness as psychosis. She continues:

> I became intimate with paranoia. Dealing with [overt] and other more subtle attempts at racism made me look at every word that came to me from a white person's mouth as suspect. I became confused about what was happening with other black people. I became afraid of black people I didn't know and there were a lot of them. As you grow older, you cover more territory in the city and I would see groups of black kids greet each other on buses and downtown and I didn't know any of them. (145)

Plucked out of black cultural norms yet isolated from those of the white mainstream, the often-violent process of assimilation renders the Black Girl "homeless" (Morrison, "Home," 5). Attending majority white schools prevents her from experiencing everyday performances of black subjectivity in her local community—quotidian cultural practices such as gossiping among local friends, wandering through local spaces, and witnessing local phenomena that underpin one's sense of being and belonging. Cooper-Anifowoshe gives us an eloquent statement about the shift between segregation and integration. Black Girl laments, "My parents' generation was upwardly mobile together. It was important to them that the whole neighborhood came up. We were taken from our neighborhood, separated from our peers, and singled out as 'special'" (144). Whereas blacks in the segregated South often worked primarily within a collective for shared upliftment, young people at the forefront of the struggle for desegregation often moved forward and out like scattered billiard balls—isolated and alone. Reflecting on what these opportunities taught her, Black Girl asserts:

> I learned how to get righteously angry. I learned to steal, cuss, drink, smoke cigarettes, smoke pot, and sass my momma, none of which my friends who stayed at the black school did, except for smoke pot, I think everybody did that. So what was the purpose of this desegregated education? (145)

The fulcrum of Cooper-Anifowoshe's performance rests on this question.

Although focused on the delegitimizing effects of racism primarily in white institutions, Cooper-Anifowoshe acknowledges racism's residue in majority black spaces. As a product of internalized racism, the black community's in-group hierarchies and prejudices often mirror those it suffers in the mainstream. This becomes clear to Black Girl through her experiences attending Xavier, a historically black university located in New Orleans. Whereas learning to "tread white people" meant understanding how to navigate whiteness as privilege, understanding colorism meant learning to maneuver one's way through lightness as privilege as well. Still, it is the oasis moment of rejoining a predominately black community that helps Black Girl regain her voice and sense of self. She states, "I gained a black self-confidence at Xavier and the city of New Orleans. I got to know all kinds of black people while in New Orleans, on campus and off and I found a level of identification that I have yet to experience since" (150–51).

The Black Girl rehearses these memories as reparative and restorative. The cycle of her revaluation of her own cultural context and the power of her own unique voice is exemplified in an exchange between her and her mother about the difference between homemade and store-bought dresses. This scene marks Black girl's transition from the space of the academy, which Cooper-Anifowoshe has marked through a rectangular pool of light, a podium, and an antagonistic disembodied voice-over, to Black Girl's "homeplace" memories with her mother. As James Brown sings "Say It Loud, I'm Black and I'm Proud," Cooper-Anifowoshe dance-walks her way to center stage carrying a wooden chair with a bright swatch of yellow fabric draped over it. She sits in it embodying the voice and performative gestures of both Black Girl and Mother as though the two are seated side-by-side:

> BLACK GIRL: Thanks for pressing my blue dress.
> MOTHER: I thought you didn't want to wear the blue dress. You said it was mammy made. I thought you wanted to wear one of your store-bought dresses.
> BLACK GIRL [*mumbling*]: They don't have the swing. (132)

When embodying Mother, Cooper-Anifowoshe focuses stage left with her gaze fixed lower than her eye level. Embodying Black Girl, she looks stage right as though peering up at Mother.

> MOTHER: What?
> BLACK GIRL [*coming clean*]: The store-bought dresses don't swing like the blue dress. (132)

With her back straight and head high, Mother cuts her eyes to the side, props one arm against the back of the chair, and leans her body away from Black Girl as she repeats Black Girl's statement for emphasis: "Oh, the store-bought dresses aren't as good as the MAMMY MADE dress?" Black Girl angles her head low, fidgets with her clothes, and looks up at her mother with humility when she responds:

> BLACK GIRL: No, Sorry. But really, the store-bought dresses don't swing. And Momma you know—
> [*Together*]: It don't mean a thing if it ain't got that swing! (133)

Ending the dialogue in spirited performative unison, Cooper-Anifowoshe creates a moment where Black Girl and Mother come to a place of shared knowledge, finishing each other's sentence like comrades, pointing to each other like co-conspirators, and laughing heartily like friends.

Mother uses the term "mammy made" to recount Black Girl's dismissal of the homemade dress. The term doubly delegitimizes the dress on the basis of race and class. Like the promise of desegregation to the black integrationist, the store-bought dress appeared better. It was seemingly the product of more sophisticated resources and carried with it the allure of the mainstream. Its quality seemed assured. It was, after all, part of a homogenous lot, which the store saw fit to purchase and showcase. Yet, having been exposed to both, the Black Girl finds store-bought dresses insufficient for her purposes. They are made of different materials, which the Black Girl realizes are not necessarily of higher quality. They also were not necessarily designed to do what the Black Girl intends them to—"swing."

Repeatedly, the strongest moments of the play, which evinced the most head nods, hand-claps, and laughter, were those reparative junctures wherein Black Girl used "homeplace" cultural and critical resources to "trick back" on racist preconceptions. Like Michel de Certeau's theory of subversive consumption,[3] some of these instances point to Black Girl's manipulation of existing resources in ways that exceed their original design. When, for example, the Black Girl is denied the opportunity to audition for the role of Dorothy in *The Wizard of Oz* because, as her teacher stresses, "Did ya' see the movie? Dorothy's white" (151) she uses her cultural repertoire to re-image the role she is given into more than what is scripted. Transitioning onstage between a conversation with a white peer who laments, it's not fair that Black Girl has been restricted to "audition for the boys' parts" rather than any of the female leads, Cooper-Anifowoshe speaks first to her and then to the audience. "Well," she tells her peer, "At least I get to be head of munchkin land." "And Baby," she tell us opening her arms wide, "We funked. That. Lollipop!" Cooper-Anifowoshe begins dancing and singing within a funk and hip-hop vocabulary, inflecting the munchkin song with a revised cadence and aesthetic, "We represent. Hey! The lollipop KIDS. The lollipop KIDS. The lollipop KIDS."[4] Using the resources she had at hand, Black Girl found a way to make room for her voice and perspective within a script and interpretation that excluded black female representation.

As the play moves toward its falling action, Cooper-Anifowoshe offers us another productive example of the ways Black Girl and her peers perform subversive consumption. We rejoin Cooper-Anifowoshe at the University of Iowa as part of a small group of eighteen black scholars funded by the Patricia Robert Harris Fellowship, which was "named for the first African American woman to enter the line of succession to the president" (151). Although they are isolated from mainstream black America, the story Black Girl tells of their experiences in Iowa is one of shared struggle and a politics of making do, which can be illustrated best through an anecdote Black Girl shares about graduate orientation:

> Well the first thing we did as a group was to put some mus-
> tard in their potato salad. . . . One of the fellows, Alphonso,
> just looked around and couldn't take it anymore. He went
> over to the cold cuts, grabbed the mustard and started squirt-
> ing it in the bowl of potato salad and stirring for dear life.
> Then he grabbed a couple of boiled eggs and threw them in.
> Complaining the whole time. You know I was cracking up.
> Well, you know no good negro shall go unpunished. Soon
> there was some titled woman over there with a pasted-on
> smile asking brother if everything was OK. He looked up
> from stirring, smiled, "oh we fine, just trying to help yaw out.
> That's why we're here isn't it. Now, that's better." (151)

Reflecting the process of desegregation—canons no less than institutions—"putting mustard in their potato salad" serves as a fitting allegory.
This aligns with bell hooks's sense of "talking back," and Zora Neale
Hurston's "how to hit a straight lick with a crooked stick." With Black
Girl as his ally, Alphonso used ingredients already prominent on the
host's table to help make the meal better reflect the diversity of those
being fed by it. He inflected it with his own tastes and cultural traditions
in a way that could not be undone. Then, in an act of black significa-
tion, he framed his gesture as one done in the service of his host and not
merely to satisfy his own cultural longings. The master's tools may never
dismantle the master's house, but they may serve to help remodel it (if
only provisionally).[5]

Adventures of a Black Girl not only engages the strategies by which
subjugated people creatively recycle existing resources to better suit their
purposes, but also the ways in which they continue to expand and exploit
the gaps in the U.S. racial contract to better reflect their history, humanity, and voice. Cooper-Anifowoshe shares one such example through
her father's strategy of subverting Jim Crow segregation. Standing center
stage manipulating a rectangular piece of yellow fabric in front of her,
Black Girl speaks directly at the audience:

> It seems that my father and a Nigerian friend had figured out
> a way around ole Jim and into segregated restaurants. They
> would show up wearing dashikis and when they were ques-
> tioned they would declare themselves British subjects. That

confused the white folks and they let them in. It seems old
Jim Crow was written for Nigras [*sic*] and they weren't sure if
genuine Africans with British accents counted. (149)

Among the instructive elements of this retelling, we see that Cooper-
Anifowoshe's father and friend knew better than to simply assert the
friend's Nigerian national identity and have the father pretend to also
be a Nigerian national. In order to confound the restaurant owners and
short-circuit the system, they needed to route their blackness through
European "otherness." Inspired by the potential of using black British
identity in order to create more opportunities for herself within her high
school drama program, Black Girl re-performs her father's appropriation.
Transforming the yellow fabric from a symbolic dashiki into a *gelee* by
twisting it around her head to form a decorative wrap, she tells us:

> So the next day, I showed up to school and we introduced
> a new character to the George Bernard Shaw's classic [*My
> Fair Lady*]. Yes, chile, wherever good Londoners were, there
> was Madame Ayo. She was introduced at the ball. "Introduc-
> ing Princess Adeyinka Ayokunle!" Madame Ayo had a seat
> at the Ascot races. On the street where THEY lived, she did
> to. She was a friend, neighbor, and confidante of Miss Eliza
> Doolittle. We even added a scene where Madame Ayo went
> to Eliza's house [affecting a British accent] to "borrow cup of
> sugar." (149)

The audience erupted in laughter. Cooper-Anifowoshe continued, "Now,
was I so wrong? Please, Africans have been in Europe and the rest of the
West for a long time. Check the history. Shit, Shakespeare wrote *Othello*,
When?" Black Girl's intervention succeeds through the power of her own
imagination and will as well as because the drama teacher/director allowed enough wiggle room in his staging for Madame Ayo to be represented. These are celebratory moments when double-consciousnesses
as strategy give Black Girl the information she needs to undermine a
system that was built to exclude her. They are also kinetic moments of
racial fierceness before the repeated calls to action and activism evince
a sense of racial fatigue. She argues, "The psychological effects of race
fatigue have taken its toll on black females in the academy, resulting in

higher rates of cancer, heart disease and other stress-related illnesses." The greatest individual gain Black Girl admits to having received from her education within majority white schools is access to more resources and the opportunity to socialize with a broader populace. The cost of this access and proximity to Black Girl was exposure to curriculums that were often less rigorous and advanced than those of her segregated schools, a bracketed sense of belonging that, at times, rendered her suspicious of both her black homeplace and a white elsewhere.

Through her use of reflexive autobiography, Cooper-Anifowoshe problematizes desegregation's taken-for-granted premise—that "equal" access would necessarily evince a "better" education. *Adventures* resists easy conclusions. Instead, it offers one woman's personal experience of the unfinished project of desegregation situated within an invisible web of similar stories. These narratives function as an indictment of the trade-offs first-generation integrationists made in the pursuit of desegregation and point to the failure of educational institutions to open their curriculums as well as their doors. Enmeshed in the ongoing process of integrating the Western theater canon, Cooper-Anifowoshe's live performance often exceeded her scripted text. As she states, "All of this was written in the throes of Iowa and a lot has transpired since then that I have wanted to put in this show that I'm just struggling with." Like the racial contract itself, she offers us a performance that is, at times, ad hoc and improvisational. Speaking from the institutional location she inhabited when the performance was produced at Northwestern, she states:

> I am now at Indiana University where . . . I'm on a tenure track and I've been fired from that university not one time but twice. The accusations against me are that I'm lowering the standards by not teaching modern European dramaturgy . . . that I have decided that race and gender matter ALL THE TIME, and that I . . . promote a black agenda. Honestly, what do you think they expected?

In spite of the high personal, political, and intellectual costs of desegregation to Black Girl, Cooper-Anifowoshe's final unscripted renderings make clear the payoff and ultimate beneficiaries—those students who are privileged to engage more diverse curriculums and classrooms because of the sacrifice and perseverance of Cooper-Anifowoshe and those like her. She represents a generation of scholars who have sought to create for their students experiences denied them—courses in which race, gender, and sexuality are engaged through both critical scholarship and personal reflection. "If we're not ready for it," she warns, "if the university isn't ready for it . . . who is? If the university wasn't ready for it, why put me on that damn bus . . . in the first place . . . at nine years old?"

The play concludes with Black Girl returning to the podium, the metaphorical space of the academy and her rectangle of light. She wonders aloud, "How did I get myself into this box? I don't know." Yet, in a final illustration of the vexed relationship the black integrationist has to the academy, she ends by looking out at the audience and stating, "You know what? I've been thinking about going for my Ph.D." The lights onstage dim as Cooper-Anifowoshe screams into the darkness, "What you trying to say? That I need to get out of academia? But how will I write the sequel? There's always gotta be a SEQUEL!" In the end, it is the hope of a sequel—a horizon in which full inclusion and greater representation offer new stories to tell and better endings to claim—that propels Black Girl forward. In this way, the solo/black/woman onstage ends as she began—with a yearning for allies, for recognition, and for horizontal pluralistic discussions of difference that don't leave her yelling alone in the dark.

NOTES

1. The phrase in the title of this essay, "How does it feel to be a problem?," is from W. E. B. Dubois's *The Souls of Black Folk* (New York: Dover, 1994).

2. See bell hooks, "Homeplace: A Site Of Resistance," in *Yearning: Race, Gender, and Cultural Politics* (Boston: South End, 1990) for a discussion of "homeplace theories"; Cherrie Moraga and Gloria Anzaldúa, *This Bridge Called My Back: Writings by Radical Women of Color* (New York: Kitchen Table, Women of Color, 1983) for more information on "theories of the flesh"; and Patricia Hill Collins, *Black Feminist Thought: Knowledge, Consciousness, and the Politics of Empowerment*, 2nd ed. (New York: Routledge, 2000) for an explanation of "standpoint theory."

3. See Michel de Certeau, *The Practice of Everyday Life* (Berkeley: University of California Press, 1984) for a discussion of the ways consumers/users undermine the power of producers/makers by using the materials available to them in surprising ways that subvert or otherwise exceed their initial intention.

4. These words are from the 2010 Northwestern performance and differ slightly from the script printed in this volume.

5. This is a reference to Audre Lorde, "The Master's Tools Will Never Dismantle the Master's House," in *Sister Outsider*, 110–13 (Berkeley: Crossing, 1984).

WORKS CITED

Collins, Patricia Hill. *Black Feminist Thought: Knowledge, Consciousness, and The Politics of Empowerment*. 2nd ed. New York: Routledge, 2000.

Cooper-Anifowoshe, Edris. *Adventures of a Black Girl in Search of Academic Clarity and Inclusion* (unpublished).

Crenshaw, Kimberle, et al., eds. *Critical Race Theory: The Key Writings That Formed the Movement*. New York: New, 1995.

De Certeau, Michel. *The Practice of Everyday Life*. Berkeley: University of California Press, 1984.

Du Bois, W. E. B. "Criteria of Negro Art." *The Crisis* 32 (October 1926): 290–97.

———. *The Souls of Black Folks*. New York: Dover, 1994.

Fanon, Frantz. *Black Skin, White Masks*. St. Albans, Eng.: Paladin, 1970.

Hanchard, Michael. "Racial Consciousness and Afro-Diasporic Experiences: Antonio Gramsci Reconsidered." *Socialism and Democracy* 14 (1991): 86.

hooks, bell. "Homeplace: A Site of Resistance." In *Yearning: Race, Gender, and Cultural Politics*. Boston: South End, 1990.

———. "Postmodern Blackness." In *Yearning: Race, Gender, and Cultural Politics*. Boston: South End, 1990.

———. *Talking Back: Thinking Feminist, Thinking Black*. Boston: South End, 1989.

Hurston, Zora Neale. *Mules and Men*. New York: Harper Perennial, 2008.

Ibsen, Henrik. *A Doll's House*. Trans. Michael Meyer. London: Methuen Drama, 2008.

Jennings, Michael E., and Marvin Lynn. "The House That Race Built: Critical Pedagogy, African-American Education, and the Re-Conceptualization of a Critical Race Pedagogy." In *Educational Foundations*, 15–32. San Francisco: Caddo Gap, 2005.

Lancaster, Roger. *Life Is Hard: Machismo, Danger, and the Intimacy of Power in Nicaragua*. Berkeley: University of California Press, 1993.

Lorde, Audre. "Learning from the 60s." In *Sister Outsider*, 134–44. Berkeley, Calif.: Crossing, 1984.

———. "The Master's Tools Will Never Dismantle the Master's House." In *Sister Outsider*, 110–13. Berkeley, Calif.: Crossing, 1984.

———. "The Uses of Anger." In *Sister Outsider*, 124–33. Berkeley, Calif.: Crossing, 1984.

Mill, Charles W. *The Racial Contract*. Ithaca, N.Y.: Cornell University Press, 1999.

Moraga, Cherrie, and Gloria Anzaldúa, eds. *This Bridge Called My Back: Writings by Radical Women of Color*. New York: Kitchen Table, Women of Color, 1983.

Morrison, Toni. "Home." In *The House That Race Built: Black Americans, U.S. Terrain.*, ed. Wahneema Lubiano, 3–10. New York: Pantheon Books, 1997.

———. "Unspeakable Things Unspoken." In *The Black Feminist Reader,* ed. Joy James and T. Denean Sharpley-Whiting, 24–56. Malden, Mass.: Blackwell, 2000.

Piper, Adrian. *Out of Order, Out of Sight: Selected Writings in Meta-Art 1968–1992.* Vol 1. Cambridge, Mass.: MIT Press, 1996.

Scott, James C. *Domination and the Arts of Resistance: Hidden Transcripts.* New Haven, Conn.: Yale University Press, 1992.

DELTA DANDI
RITUAL/JAZZ THEATER

Sharon Bridgforth

PRODUCTION HISTORY

First presented in Austin, Texas, by Women & Their Work in partnership with the National Performance Network at The Long Center Rollins Studio Theatre in January 2009, *delta dandi* was conducted by Sharon Bridgforth with composer/conductor Helga Davis and choreographer/conductor Baraka de Soleil. The performance featured Florinda Bryant, Helga Davis, Sonja Perryman, and Baraka de Soleil. Monique Cortez, Andrea Edgerson, Karla Legaspy, Leigh Gaymon-Jones, and Azure D. Osborne-Lee also appeared. Set design was by Leilah Stewart, with costumes by Miramar Dichoso. The technical director was Tramaine Berryhill and dramaturge Jen Margulies. Previous versions of *delta dandi* were performed in Brooklyn, New York at Freedom Train Productions Fire New Play Festival in August 2008 and at the Johen Warfield Center for African and African American Studies, University of Texas, Austin, in November 2007.

delta dandi is a 2008 National Performance Network Creation Fund Project co-commissioned by Women & Their Work in partnership with the National Performance Network. Major contributors of the National Performance Network are Doris Duke Charitable Foundation, Ford Foundation, Nathan Cummings Foundation, and the National Endowment for the Arts (a federal agency).

THE SET

Flexible.

SETTING

The past, the present, the future/the living, the dead, the not yet born, coexist.

STAGING

A cast of four or five: two women, one man, and one Identifiably Gender Queer Person.

Movement/layering text/choral telling are integral to the telling.

The Gurl, played by an adult, is working through many lifetimes of abuse.

Elder Spirit/Returning sings text and is the Gurl's spirit guide and future self.

Seer is the trickster at the crossroads, works closely with Baba.

Baba means "father" in Yoruba. Should be played by an identifiably gender queer person. Baba's language is in gray boxed text. These are prayers. They contain properties of different *orisha* (Yoruba deities) that offer medicine to help The Gurl move forward. Baba should be a dancer/ and able to sing.

Conductor (optional), should be woman or identifiably gender queer.

PRODUCTION NOTE

If a Conductor is cast: each audience member receives a randomly distributed sheet of paper with one piece of text from the appendix at the end of this play. The Conductor decides when to bring the audience in and out with their text.

BABA:

> *3. 21. playing.*
>
> *open the road.*

GURL:

i remember i born i remember i born i remember i born

i remember i born i remember jooking with the moon

i remember jumping in the water i remember hiding in the trees i remem-

ber hanging in the sun i remember gold and chattel i remember glitter

and smoke i remember i i i

i remember. when i see me standing across the room

peeking around corners sitting at dusk

in the breeze and mirrors with broken skin

in my dreams

when i wake

all i do is remember

i remember i born i remember i born i remember i born i remember i born

i remember calling me calling me calling me back. i remember

i come screaming into this world bringing what was

with silent cries and whispers

a fallen star they say

i come here baring everything

all at once.

again

again

again

again

me

ELDER SPIRIT/RETURNING:

born in the mouth of the river and sea.

cloaked in kisses that cycle the Sun.

with answered Prayers

naming Heaven where you stand

a chorus of Light/circling your head

closer than that

I am.

hear?

BABA:

playing.

21. 3. the gate.

black candy. red rum. cigars

crossroads messenger.

open the doors open the doors open the doors

GURL:

with beaded crown and bird and staff

from golden throne on backs of men

with iron and stone

armies and slaves

with many wives and many children

i am king. she who rules beyond sight and sound.

i traffic bodies

slavery is divined.

or so i say.

my wealth exceeds assessment

everyone is my servant my slave my concubine

all bow in answer to me.

go.

get me more bodies.

from here and there and there and there

bring them to me.

now!

i've riches to make.

my children glow with laughter and fat bellies

my wives dance my name in the moonlight

i grow stronger in the night

from this bounty of flesh

and prayers/i pay for.

you are the sacrifice for my glory and gain.

this is my birthright.

i don't care what your name is

in the morning

you will fetch me a pretty price

or die.

ELDER SPIRIT/RETURNING:

we/stare.

say go. sorry

i.

your turn.

next time

me.

not born yet.

> *soon soon.*
>
> *so much to do.*

GURL:

i don't know how to die so i just go along. carry all these things. all these

things. till once in the black/blue of day i jump. i jump where the waters

meet. i jump. cold cold cut me. i jump. pray/carry me to the ocean. please.

maybe i find my mama there. i jump. go under. come up. go under. come

up. jump. jump. jump. can't float down. the water won't take me. again

again again i jumping till look see. there right there a woman tall tall

naked and shining in the water stand laughing laughing down at me in

the water. i run out. run stand under giant tree with weeping arms. look

through bending branches. still still. no breathing. can't move. can't turn

head. can't close eyes. no look away. the woman tall tall naked and shining in the water stand. stop laughing. stare. stare. stare. stare telling me

something

i don't know what.

BABA:

> *silver pearls and turquoise. yams and seaweed. blue skirts 7 layers. peacocks*
> *and fish*
> *watermelons and grapes. monday. shifts.*
> *north star half moon rivers and pound cake.*
> *strength.*

SEER:

dirt in the blood dirt in the blood dirt in the blood where did it go can't

remembercan'tremembercan'tremember turn left no see turn right right

right left how it go how it go how it go i i i can't remember

i know it i know it i know i i i mama said mama said

always Pray.

always Pray. this i know this i know

this is what i know

circle circle circle

dirt in the blood/i. clay

salt in the night/i. moan

deep from belly/i. rain

waves crash sun/i. sand

earth turn run i/i i i

am

GURL:

i lay on dirt bed next to mama. scared not sure why. i pray every night. i praying please don't let nothing happen to my mama please don't let nothing happen to my mama please don't let nothing happen to my mama. say it ten times turned to left ten times turned to the right ten times on back and stomach. curl knees to chest be very still say it again.

i don't know this god i'm praying to but maybe this god hear better than mines. please don't let nothing happen to my mama. one night he bust in. one night late late with friends he bust in. just before they storm just before they force the night on my mama she push me push me so hard i knock against dark in small corner away. stay hide she say. i so scared can't move. i hear hit and hit and wail and cry.

mama fight. they too many. i close eyes. i praying please don't let nothing happen to my mama please don't let nothing happen to my mama. i keep praying through crash and knock and scream and hit and hit and wail.

till later later later outside i hear

that nigger woman bled like a gutted pig.

then laughter walk away.

i always wonder. did i know what coming.

or did i thinking make it happen.

i stop praying. god can't hear i think.

was i three

BABA:

> *honey wine. yellow amber gold. crocodiles and vultures. sweet things.*
>
> *oranges pumpkins and perfume. Love beauty flowing.*
>
> *fans and mirrors. release.*
>
> *Joy.*

SEER:

railroad tracks biscuits and bacon grandma and and and ma'dear aunt sweety and dem dat ole moonshine baddshittbaddshitt sour pickles daddy done picked hisself right out the garden right out the garden ain't nuthn but cucumber a a a cumber treated special you know neckbones greens chit'lins and cobbler and and and mama's sweet potato pie head don't work no mo don't work no mo just don't work sometimes but i remember everything just too much at one time see there was big pretty tom fruity and mr gladys say big pretty tom fruity and mr. gladys yessuh they was always kind useta give me a nickel for stirring the gombo just stand there and stir the gombo cause you know you got to stir the gombo and they wasn't gonn never stand still that long too busy getting ready for friday to come but i always have liked stirring gombo just stand there listen i i i try to not remember but can't help it listen it it it

keep
coming
back
all
those

things

keep

coming

back

my

mind

sees

too

much

i i i dem peckawoods they took my baby brother they took him and they beat him beat him beat him so bad till oooooooh they took him they they they just took that baby boy cause he wouldn't turn around when they said hey nigga and and and well we just wasn't raised like that we just knew who we was mama raised us men we walked like men my my my baby brother wasn't no nigga he always walked like he was going some-where cause he was and why in the hell would he turn around cause some teenage peeckawoods calling him out his name like that

he

had

on

his

uniform.

just back.

i told him he should have just stayed gone.

BABA:

> iron. cowbell and machete. coral crown. bronze horse.
>
> beach sand river dirt. goats. an owl.
>
> thimble. thread. scissors. ivory.
>
> fight.

GURL:

i free when i run so i running all the time. the dresses they make me wear

choke my skin and heart so i run till the touch of no fit leave my mind.

always i wonder why they yell these dresses on me.

why boys look like i feel but not how i look.

i know things i think.

like i remember i was king once. a woman looking like she felt. i see her.

just before i running sometimes she come whisper to me.

she scares me.

i feel she reach for me with the mean of her soul

ELDER SPIRIT/RETURNING:

God mask face

veil the calling.

ruffle hairs

brush past

surround spirit

unborn and dead pull.

blood moon circle waters

trees wave birds rush

thunder call she name.

tiny fingers first. she come reaching

rip the life out she mama /she own mama the sacrifice

she mama spirit turn right back round/quick

reborn unto sheself

catch last breath/gasp

she mama go back/come out through dead mama sheself.

no cry.

quiet.

water hush birds sit wind tight

blood moon turn white

this is how they born

this is how they born

this is how they born/tiny hands slow move touch face

feel eyes

press cheeks

pull chin

lift slow

lift veil

up up

pull pull

look round see who there.

tiny hands stuff veil in mouth

she eat she veil.

wind lift stars burst moon cycle.

we still

in Light

we see

eyes look

no smile

no cry

we watch

we stomp

fast fast

we shout

clap right

she look

we spin

turn left

we praise

dance sing

we call

spin right

we know

now now

we say

hear hear

we pray

this time

she hear

this time

she know

this time

her time.

NOW.

GURL:

the room was dark always dark. standing in the dark i watch her in the mirror as she brush her long black hair. flowing down her body her long black hair the brush brushing she look herself in the eye and smile. come here gal she whisper. every night every night the same

she hit me she hit me she always hit me with brush and broom with stick and fist she hit me in the night. cursing she drag me to the shed in the woods and slam and chain the door. **nobody hear you crying gal cept the devil out here in the dark.** scared to scream to tremble to moan i stop breathing don't breathe till morning. shed not big enough to stretch. i stand in pools of piss with maggots swarming. wake in a ball on the floor

in wet with stink and bugs and heat and haunting. i hear her through the broken slats. always she fling the door open with the sun and pull me out by my hair. must tend field and house before eat.

why nobody come. why they not come get me. why i here i wonder every

day every day every day   i hate her. must hide thoughts. can't breathe.

no talk. no mumble. no scream. my kin live down the dirt road.

they sold me i think to the devil for a few chickens and

a barrel of shine.

with bruised body and heavy eyes i sag in my spirit and spine.

i five. i think.

ELDER SPIRIT/RETURNING:

the first hands that took me was black/dark as the night.

grabbed my mama

used our own traditions to take us/used prayers we prayed

to hold in place what already was.

our king sent them to carry away carry away many.

they got my mama. i was in she.

nobody knew.

i grow in the pen/in mama.

they keep her caged

wait till price high enough to sell she.

they feed and watch till then.

BABA:

thunder. drums. fire. dance.

red white.

bananas green.

friday saturday.

good times.

okra. cormeal. rooster. apples.

double axe. 6.

ache now

ache you

ache king

ache.

ELDER SPIRIT/RETURNING:

full moon. blood red. follow follow mama.

packed sealed.

below deck.

backs open.

flesh stench.

blood vomit. bowels loosed.

mucus and broken spirits.

she born to that

SEER:

she was a boy born a girl till she became a man then a woman now both

i i i he was a girl then a woman till she became a young man with flowing

hips and hair i i i he a man then a boy i i i she a man she a woman i i

i him. she perfect perfectly made perfectly made for us for we himshe

boygirl manwoman girlwoman man young woman spirit man girl child boy grown now now now himshe now now now herhe now now now weus i i i

GURL:

she raise she fist in the air always before swing down look up see long scar thick under chin down neck and tip of chest. always i think just before hitting the ground i wonder who strong enough to open and close she skin.

finally one morning after field and house before eat and sit i hear knock on door swing open. in step man. he make her smile. they smile and talk. she snatch me to shed before eat and night that day.
i feel trouble in my sleep. more than familiar or past.

days nights field house shed days later i see he play piano while she brush hair in the night. he see me and smile. tell her he gone teach me play. she say do what you want. he teach me to play piano. say i got to pay him first. days pass. everyday when she go get wash cross town
he play piano i play him. i learn things.

the day he gone she stop smiling. i run. go past the shed in the woods cross creek run walk walk walk along tracks. can't move no more. see big tree with long braids flowing to the ground all around it. i go in sit between trunk and braids. cry.

i ten. maybe.

moon sun moon sun. hungry. i step into the sun. look around. everything sparkle. see water moving soft. birds bees butterfly frogs fish. peaches on ground. buds open. color everywhere for all my eyes can see. i in heaven i think. breath catch in chest. bee land on arm. no sting. butterfly land on head no fly away. maybe it okay to breathe. i try.

i walk to water.

jump in.

ELDER SPIRIT/RETURNING:
rocking i tell she babyself we gone be alright
rocking i tell she gurlself to hang in there
rocking i tell she young womanself to fly fly fly
rocking i tell she grey   We be back
rocking rocking
rocking/I
smile smile smile
waving walk backwards towards the Sun.
i call loud pull everything
give instructions
push everything everything everything
tell all

kiss mark on forehead
blanket eyes

whisper whisper
soft
i am here

i am here

i am here

whisper whisper whisper

soft.

rocking we come into this world

wearing the Veil

bringing the message.

Love.

GURL:

they said i needed to get the religion

like something wrong with me

they said i needed a saving

have the gods watch over me

like they wasn't already.

they said it would help me not die early/and i don't want to die early

so i said i needed to get the religion/like something wrong with me

i said i needed a saving

have the gods watch over me/like they wasn't already

i said that it would help me not die early.

they took me to the water to the water to the water.

the water moved for us/came to shore fast and hard

the water moved to us came over over over and down

they lost hold of me in the water/may have just let me go

i could not breathe i always could not breathe why i can't never breathe i

wonder as the water coming so fast tall and crashing it came down hard
carried me way out away from they hands. the water took me down down
down tossed me here and there way out i found myself standing on sand
not on the shore. i couldn't make sense of it way out there standing on
sand wasn't no body around i turned towards the sun and there i saw the
water standing high high high the water was standing up painting the
sky and all space with itself. i knew it had come to take me. i knew wasn't
nothing to do but go. i said this must be my time early after all.

they said they took me to the water to save me but the water had its own
plan it seemed. so i did the only thing there was to do in the face of the
water standing up tall and painting all the sky and space. i walked into it.
gave myself willingly. the water then came down from standing up came
down from standing tall and painting all sky and space and knocked me
down down down into itself it threw me up in the air and caught me
then
the water pulled itself back and laid me on the shore. i lay there on my
back at the foot of the people staring down at me
staring down at me quiet.

i knew then that the water had saved me. not from itself not from the
wrenching that life had done to me. the water saved me from the people.
they were careful with me after that. only used me a little.
in a distant kind of way.

ELDER SPIRIT/RETURNING:

full bodied. beauty tall. tall open. too wide. like the sun. hot road.

thirsty. raised bent. for all to see.

bruised heart.

reaching. beyond rain.

one day. shed what was.

one day. you smile. one day. you leave.

go.

just like momma. just like granny.

go.

pulled apart flesh. torn dreams.

go.

paint sky.

go.

now!

go.

GURL:

i think i might be broken.

can't feel anything most days.

hear things. see things. know things.

why

SEER:

and and and what i wants to talk about i i i thats just what happened

himshe and and and boygurl i i i wants to talk about sweet sweet sweet him yessuh she mighty fine and and and could sing too. so fine done broke up many a happy hometown band and church house with him her she he man woman gurlboy sweet sweet sweet self. awh lawd wasn't never enough room in the joint with all that there folks pushing and hollering like like like a pack a hungry children trying to to to just want to see himshe lawd just to be close to the sweet sweet sweetness just want to smell it. they they they just tear up everything. married ones boyfriends girlfriends neithers. sweet ones evil ones gamblers and holy rollers just just just. which is how i i i gots my good eye knocked out see see see awh lawd the sweet sweet sweetness

just

GURL:

shut up shut up shut up shut up

go away go away go away go away

leave me alone leave me alone leave me alone leave me alone
i no see you i no see you i no see you i no see you
no no no no

SEER:

blood is everywhere blood is everywhere blood is everywhere. blood. there is blood. i scream. no one hears me. why no one ever hear me. i i i all i see is blood. i i i there is no sound. help. please somebody help me. why nobody ever come help me. can't lift my feet.
i i i turn my head. see people bleeding open scars running running in the night running from dogs with flesh and bones and fangs and growling

and running i i i father i i i see father he floating above his body hanging from

a tree. somebody snatched grabbed me is dragging me past bodies that hang from trees and the smell of flesh burning. i i i it's the lady from the water tall tall and shining she drag me to the river pull me in. swim. float. run. swim. swim. float.

is this where father going

GURL:

floating

i tear my flesh. i pull my hair. i crush my teeth. i run no breathe. i say no eat. no use.

i just come back again me.

why why why why

SEER:

gimme some a that fried chicken dark meat an an an put somea that warm honey on there warm the honey pour it on there pour it on there umhum and i want somea them greens and cornbread somea them cheesegrits an an an i'ma need some hothothot peppers and salt i said i'ma need some hothothot peppers and salt i'ma have cobbla you got peach i want some peach cobbla and some gimme some more thats right and sweet tea. baybay i sho love you you look so good to me right now with that serving spoon in yo hand. can i marry you. i i i don't care if you married you cook so gotdamn good i be yo second wife. i be your third husband.

i be your your your side dish. ummhumm yes and gimme some of that

some of that i i i

a little butter too

BABA:

himshe

father king

white cloth crown.

sunday thursday peace.

cool head 8.

sky bones snails.

riding elephants

and snow.

coiled snake

ELDER SPIRIT/RETURNING:

i know in dreams in the hard of my own heart

they always sell always sell we people

black hands to black hands.

for animals some brass. because.

always been made go away

before there here

always borned sold

always been slave.

SEER:

i born with the curse of grief clawing my soul to shreds.

stop the noise stop the noise stop the noise i i i can't stop this noise in my

head chatter passing passing passing my mind i can't let go of what i i i

don't want to know all these all these things all these things true.

ELDER SPIRIT/RETURNING:

i see your scarred back

i know your heart is shattered

and you are holding your breath.

your world has been built by ghosts

every promise has been broken

and your body is a prison

but you are here.

the dead whisper in the trees

memories take you captive in the night

and you are afraid

but you are here.

you are not your suffering.

you don't have to jump

right here

right now

in this moment you are safe.

no need to pray yourself to sleep.
you are here
i am with you.

and you are Loved
hear it
it's alright
you are Loved
say it
you are Loved
know it
you are Loved
Love.

SEER:

they say i'm crazy say i i i crazy cause i keep telling it all the time all the
time they know i know they know i know they know but they act like i
don't my my my mama she tell it to me in the night when i sleep whisper
every night every night every night help me sure i ain't crazy i i i never get
no sleep daddy they carry me off to to to all them places in my dreams i
wake up feet wet sometimes blood on the pillow they tell it tell it tell it
they say i i i my mama my dear sweet mama my mama that man he killed
her my dear sweet mama he killed her cause he felt like it like her life
wasn't nothing like her like her life

wasn't nothing they they they and in they silences everybody lie everybody lie everybody lie everybody lie my mama she i i i daddy come they smile in the night daddy all the time every time she come he he he there with neck and body and hands no rope no tree he he he smile and in the daytime i say this is what happened you have to thats how we know we know what we know and i just i just a white man kill my daddy

mama daddy kill she

why they won't talk about that

remember?

BABA:

> eggplants. coins. maroon. magic. wednesday. 9.
> fly whisk whirlwinds and masks. lightening buffalo
> red wine. the dead. the gates. cemeteries. hurricane.
> change.

ELDER SPIRIT/RETURNING:

put his still beating heart deep in the earth
put his still beating heart deep in the earth
put his still beating heart deep in the earth
put his still beating heart deep in the earth
throw in all the clamped-down names not ours

pack tight the pulled-back dirt
for she mama she mama we mama for us
for all before/for them to come/for We and They

call her

call her

     louder

call her

shatter shackles

break iron

spit bit

crush collar

     blow dust

     blow dust

     to the Wind

     to the Wind

     to the Wind

     to the Wind

walk away

walk away

walk away

walk away

NOW!

THIS

STOPS

HERE!

SEER:

my mother laughs in the night. i i i think she that bellowing in the breeze with long arms that that that can not hold me. just beyond her eyes is the light/lingering where i i i stand.

for for for this i cry

ELDER SPIRIT/RETURNING:

for she who never flew

for her.

for us whose dreams were taken in the night

i i i

for her

we we we

i am my mother.

GURL:

i pull your name off me. i give you back your stench. you keep your fists your screaming the beatings. i refuse your ghosts and all the mean they make you. i take away your right to call my name. i will not hate you i will not hate you i will not hate you. i did not die. i do matter. i will love me i will i will i will learn to love me. i i I Am.

ELDER SPIRIT/RETURNING:

born in the mouth of the river and sea.

cloaked in kisses that cycle the Sun.

with answered Prayers

naming Heaven where you stand

a chorus of Light/circling your head

closer than that

I Am

hear!

GURL:

i see her in the thickened grass

standing under moss and hawk

slowly she turns/scars run raised down she back

a rooted tree

i see her tall tall naked and shining in the water she stand there reaching

with wounds closed by silence

i see her on piano bench glittering

head back tilted shot glass banging keys and laughter

scars rushing down forearm to finger tip

i see her with dead eyes and fists raised in fury in the night

i see her swinging down at me stick belt back of hand shredded heart

i see she sold me black hands to black hands

her curse running through the blood in my veins

i see her under the full red moon

i see her with veil

i see her circle and snap

i see her

i i i in the swollen thickness of her skin

the tone of her voice the feel of her gaze

i recognize her.

she me.

when i wake from/dreaming wake

with sand on feet

no no no fear no sweat/this time

I say Yes.

come i will tell you the future. this is what i know

miracles are made of Love miracles are made of Love

miracles are made of Love.

ELDER SPIRIT/RETURNING:

you are never alone.

rest now

little girl go to sleep

dream sweetly and free

right here

right now

in this moment you are safe

i release you to this

the Truth.

this is what you're born to.

and you Love.

little girl running past the shed i love you.

slave woman shattered i love you.

old man stuttering i love you.

Veiled baby i love you.

African King who sold me i love you.

jooking woman i love you.

woman praying at the river i love you.

himshe i love you.

this is the message i'm bringing

i love you

this is the reason i'm here

i love you

scared beaten neglected

i love you

drunk mean abusive afraid

i love you

hear me now or come back to it again

i love you

this is my prayer for you

i love you

this is the road we choose

i love you

this is the magic we make

i love you

this is the Change we bring

i love you

i love you

i love

you

GURL:

me.

SEER:

i i i laugh long into the night and rising morn my daughters my daughters my daughters i are free now. my Souls we gathered in this body/this time

said enough!

i see everything.

my name is Freedom.
and I Love.

GURL:

i quiet. all in head and heart. quiet. this is new. quiet. i sit in it. feel like all around all around i floating. and held. like many many i can't see holding me. softly. this make my heart open open open and burst wide into forever. i crying. for the first time not from scared. not from hit. not from pain. not from alone. i crying from feeling beauty. from feeling beauty wail inside me. i sit in the sweetness of this.

open and bursting. old things fall away. i sit. i float. i feel like a feather.

carried away. i fly. i giggle. i twirl. i swing. i sing. and run.

i play now.

now i free.

BABA:

yes yes yes yes yes yes yes

GURL:

Yes

Yes

Yes

Yes

Yes

Yes

Yes

SEER:

Yes

Yes

Yes

Yes

Yes

Yes

Yes.

GURL:

Yes

Yes

Yes

Yes

Yes

Yes

Yes.

ELDER SPIRIT/RETURNING:

Yes

Yes

Yes

Yes

Yes

Yes

Yes.

GURL:

i wear hat and suspenders

pants with high waist and cuffs

tie and pointed shoes shining.

i carry my staff and veil. flow into all my selves.

i am King. now and always. girl woman. seer. in this body

today i say

i am right to be here

today i call my own name proudly

today i take old skin off and eat it

i am made new.

this is where it all comes together.

this is where we meet. the shift is now.

the Change has come. it is time.

i move from the crossroads

stand where all the rivers meet.

life flows through me.

i wait for you.

come to me.

ask your question child.

APPENDIX

delta dandi is ritual/jazz theater. The work is made of polyrhythm, simultaneity, and circular narratives. Multiple realities coexist. Layering text/choral telling and song are integral to the telling. The script is therefore a musical score. The audience are active witness/participants helping to create a soundscape in support of the story. The Conductor should make decisions accordingly. If a Conductor is cast, each audience member should receive a randomly distributed sheet of paper with one piece of the text below on it:

0

THIS STOPS HERE!

0

put his still beating heart deep in the earth

put his still beating heart deep in the earth

put his still beating heart deep in the earth

put his still beating heart deep in the earth

1

i remember i born i remember i born i remember i born

i remember i born i remember

2

guns beads brandy. SOLD!

3

Freedom

Freedom

Freedom

come

here

NOW.

4

so much/so hard/so many things to face

whisper whisper/i

in breeze right here

right here

always

with you

remember?

5

we/stare. say go. sorry i.

your turn. next time/me.

not born yet.

soon soon.

so much to do.

5

for she

who never flew

for her.

for us whose dreams were taken in the night

i i i

for her.

we we we

i am my mother.

6

water falling all around her. water falling

all around me

6

circle circle circle

dirt in the blood/i. clay

salt in the night/i. moan

deep from belly/i. rain

waves crash sun/i. sand

earth turn run i/i i i

am

7

i love you

this is my prayer for you

i love you

this is the road we choose

i love you

this is the magic we make

i love you

this is the Change we bring

8

we spin

turn left

we praise

dance sing

we call

spin right

we know

now now

9

come here gal

9

nobody hear you crying gal

cept the devil out here in the dark.

10

full moon. blood red. follow follow.

mama. packed sealed.

below deck. backs open.

flesh stench. blood vomit. bowels loosed.

mucus and. broken spirits.

she born to that

11

born in the mouth of the river and sea.

cloaked in kisses that cycle the Sun.

with answered Prayers

naming Heaven where you stand

a chorus of Light/circling your head

closer than that

I am.

hear?

INTERVIEW WITH SHARON BRIDGFORTH

Anita González

My first question is about your work. I would like to know how you think your work as a theater artist intersects with other genres like poetry or music.

I actually identify as a theater artist. People look at my work on the page and they call me a poet, and I don't mind that, because I feel like my heart is a poet's heart and that's how I came to writing. I write performance literature, and sometimes performance novels, because for me, I'm working in a black aesthetic that assumes that the oral tradition is valid, that stories are performative in their nature. I kind of go back to my mother's kitchen as a kid where there's a party, there's singin' and dancin', the food is cookin', there's laughter and cryin', and all kinds of things are happening at the same time, and great stories are being told. For me it's important that my collaborators put their vision inside of the work, and my goal is to make the work . . . the text . . . musical in its nature, so that there is space and room for other ideas without changing the text. I assume that there's going to be dancing and there's going to be singing. It's not musical theater, it's jazz theater, there will be multiple layers of things. It's always prayer, and it's ritual.

I'd like you to talk now a little about how community and geographic locations have influenced your aesthetic.

I identify as Southern. I grew up in Los Angeles. My father is from Louisiana. I didn't grow up with him, but I have blood memories and I am very haunted by the voices, the history, the people of that area. My mother is from Memphis, and her family went from Mississippi, Arkansas, Memphis; then they moved out to Chicago and L.A. I spent quite a bit of time in Memphis, so I went back home a lot when I was growing up. When I was living in L.A. the black people had migrated, they weren't from L.A.; they were from the South—lots of Louisiana people. I grew up in what they now call South Central L.A. Every black person there was from the South. And so it really was like being in a Southern community . . . except these young people, the people my mother's age, they were a little faster. The home people weren't there watching their every move; they created their own new sense of protocol. They were there to create better lives and explore freedom. And so I pull on that voice, and I feel that my heart voice, my real writing voice, is a Southern voice. But I am a jazz artist, so I like shifting contrasting rhythms, I like multiple explorations of time and space, and I like spirit—always—as the point.

How were you were introduced to the jazz aesthetic? Did the words themselves always sound musical to you, or were there special jazz artists that influenced your work?

I came into theater late. I started writing when I was fifteen, but I didn't even go to theater until I was in my 20s, and the show that I went to see was *for colored girls*. That changed my whole life. When I bought the book, it affirmed what I knew was possible and important—words as music, storytelling as black and female and spirit. It just changed everything for me. *For colored girls* freed me up to experiment, and I experimented by myself for a while. And then when I fell into theater, I pretty much immediately started my own company. When I was thirty, I moved to Austin. I fell in with this group of people that were doing work, so I was the artistic director, the writer, and in a collaborative process directed with the performers; the same basic way that I'm working today. Omi, Dr. Jones, in '91, did intensive workshops with us. She brought her expertise in, and it helped me to flesh out my ideas. She also brought in language that helped give me context for what I was doing, because her specialty is African and African American performance aesthetics. And she is the leading scholar on the "theatrical jazz aesthetic," and she was starting that work then. So I fell into my tribe and we toured until '99. Michelle Parkerson came and worked with us. At first I was just working from intuition but with some shaping by Omi, and Michelle, and Marsha Gómez, over time you get better. You keep trying new things. Marsha Gómez has passed now. She was indigenous, called herself Red Cajun . . . Geechi. She was from a little bitty town in Louisiana—wild crazy—but also a very serious human rights activist. She was one of the founders of the Indigenous Women's Network, and a sculptor. The theater company was called the Root Women Theater Company and she was the set designer for our first piece. She helped me come up with this idea, she said "girl you just tryin' to pray. I'm going to build you a living altar, and just don't have the actors ever leave the stage, because they're always praying." I was like—that's it! So my working process got set early on, but I was working from intuition. Later in the '90s I met Daniel [Alexander Jones], I met Laurie Carlos, and then I was able to deepen my own understanding of the living context that I was working with. But basically I've been doing the same thing.

Do you ever work with jazz musicians?

I did that once. Helga [Davis] conducted *love/conjure/blues* in 2004. The first time we did it, we did it a cappella, and the second time we did it with musicians. I liked it, but it was better a cappella. I'm blues in my foundation—in my writing voice—but you can't have jazz without blues. I am a jazz writer theatrically, but my sensibilities are blues. My heart, my voice, my foundation, is around blues stories, and blues idioms. I go back to my mom and the kitchen. For me the text is the music. I prefer the layering of breath and singing. Like that kitchen where everybody's talking at the same time, maybe talking over each other, or somebody's crying in the corner. That's the world that I love to explore.

How do you view the relationship between soundings and breath, especially their connection to spirit and memory?

The thing that I pull from is the old folk, their deep prayers and their deep desire for life to be better for me and for the coming generations. They repeat the same stories over and over and over. They were telling me the family history and talking about how to survive. They were telling me who I was, and it was kind of like a mantra . . . of prayer.

Give me an example.

Well, my great aunt, Auntie Bea, who I lived with for a while, she knew every part of L.A. She knew everybody and everything, because she migrated there when the black people migrated there, and it was still like a Southern village. She'd be sittin' on the couch, lookin' out the window, and she'd be tellin' me people's business. It was like this longing for home. She'd talk about the family, and she'd talk about Memphis, and she'd talk about growing up. She'd talk about some of the hard and horrible things that happened to her . . . just life . . . sittin' on the couch lookin' out the window, looking over her shoulder every now and then.

And to me those were life lessons. This is how I love constructing narrators, as griots, as people holding history in tension and prayer,

What does it sound like?

It sounds like repetition. It sounds like crying. And it sounds always like laughter. In my family this is a blues thing, a Southern black thing. They understand the medicine of laughter. So while they may be telling a story that's really hard and haunting, there is always some element of humor.

So how do you translate that into words and language for plays?

It's why Honey Pot is woven into *delta dandi*. Honey Pot is carrying medicine, grounding information about who we are as black people in this country, with a Southern perspective.

There are several spiritual influences in your work. Could you talk a little bit about those?

I always go back to everyday prayers, which were stories that held the deep desires and intentions, hopes and prayers and dreams of my family for life to be better. It's the prayer that was their life, the sacrifices, that caused them to leave home and then to grieve. Because they left home and you can't go back. It's different when you're gone.

Some people have described your work as being like a church ritual, but I find it more earth-based.

I'm talking about my family but I'm also talking about black people. I know I'm generalizing because we're all so different and especially if you're in the South or you're in the East or the North or whatever, but I think I'm talking about a particular time, space, and context that is part of our history. We were forced to leave home with the middle passage. I believe that Africans have been coming here for a long time, but with the middle passage it's this ripping away from home that is very old for us. There was slavery. There were many free blacks and there were many maroons. It was very complex. Many cultures were inside of that blackness and it's something about grieving for home, the deep prayer that is the life that holds the possibility for the future. That's the whole point of the work for me. The prayer is the life, and that's one basic spiritual component for me. I'm trying to be better and grow and be more myself in my humanity so my daughter will be better than me, so that she will be able to aspire and attain and manifest her dreams and her full potential. That's one level of the spiritual aspect of the work for me. I am very influenced by Marsha. Some of my other indigenous friends took me in and I've done sweats, and I understand. I have been privy to Native American spiritual practice, and I don't often publicly say this but I identify as a black Indian. That's why that fit for me. I've also been part of a Yoruba religious tradition. At the moment I consider myself trans-denominational, so I'm not practicing one thing. Spirituality is part of my blood memory and where I, without knowing why or how, drew from to create the work. But I do really make worlds that are black American. But we are people of the universe. And I think the more specifically we are artists. The personal then becomes something that speaks across all these boundaries.

How does gender move through your work?

[*Laughter*] People who are queer in their gender and queer in their sexuality are just part of the world. It's not separate. They're part of the world, and they're part of the spiritual matrix, part of the community, it's a given. If we were all free in our hearts and spirits, without danger and complications to be who we are, I think gender and sexuality would be much more fluid. I kind of like dreaming in that world.

How does that come across in your writing . . . as queer?

I intentionally, organically, always have him/shes. People who are complicated in their gender, queer characters, lesbians, gay men as holy people, and people who are part of the communal process of invoking change. I love the juke joint. In them juke joints, they was doin' everything, and they didn't have the hang-ups that we have today.

You've already talked about artistic influences in your work. Now could you speak about other plays and past productions, especially favorites or ones that marked changes in your aesthetics?

With Root Women we toured three pieces: *love rituals and rage, no more blues,* and *dyke warrior prayers.* I feel that I was growing as a writer, and so those are painful for me to look at right now 'cause they just weren't that well written. But we had a great time, and this is how you learn, by doing. Those were markers for me because I grew into myself as an artist. I wrote a piece called *blood pudding*, which I'm returning to now. It was the piece that exorcized my Louisiana blood memories so I'm going back to flesh it out. The change was when I did a piece called *con flama*. It was the first time that I was able to write and not have three or four jobs. I received a Theater Communications Group/National Endowment for the Arts playwright's residency at Frontier at Hyde Park theater in Austin, Texas. Vicky Boone was the artistic director. I could just write. My idea was to look at the cultural landscapes of Los Angeles. When I was a kid, I took the bus from fifth grade on, and I knew how to navigate the whole city. By the time I got to high school, I would go from South Central L.A. to Echo Park. That was a two-hour bus ride each way. On that bus ride, the cultural languages, the smells, the protocol, everything changed probably six times 'cause the city was so segregated. On the bus, you're moving out of all these people-of-color neighborhoods. The white people live in the suburbs, so it was mostly people of color, and there were sections that were very Jewish as well. My question was: why did these people come from all over the world to this city, and what was their story? So I wrote this very poetic thing, and Vicky Boone and Frontera invited Lori Carlos to direct it. Lori had directed *blood pudding;* she knew that I trusted her. I look back at the script, and I'm like, Oh my God, how'd she do that? The first day of rehearsal, Lori basically waved that script in front of me and she said, "This is pretty but you ain't telling the story. This story is not about this city and this poetic bull. This story is about this girl, and why this girl was on the bus, and where was her mother. You've got to tell *that* story." So I went home and wrote in the girl's voice and the piece really became a generational piece: the girl, her mother, her mother, and then there's a daughter that comes. It became something else, and it changed my whole life. I feel like that's the first script that I really look at and still love, and I'm proud of it. And after that was *love conjure blues*, which was published as a performance novel and then after that, *delta dandi*. Now I'm working on a piece called *ring shout*.

So it sounds like that girl is also at the center of *delta dandi*?

Yeah. It is. It's an older story, and it's a deeper exploration. But it is that girl. And Omi suggested that I probably have a trilogy. She thinks *blood pudding, con flama*, and *delta dandi* are a trilogy, and I think she's right.

Because there's a certain kind of self-hatred and cruelty with black people in the South, particularly people in Mississippi . . . Memphis, that area, that I don't understand. It hurts my heart. And I experienced it. They love, and they love hard, but there's something that is just painful. It's so old, and I wanna understand it. I think that in my family, I broke—forever shifted—the cycle. I did it through *delta dandi*. I had cancer in 2005, and right before my surgery I said, I really want to live. You know, I was a functional alcoholic; I was somebody who started drinking when I was ten. I drank until 1995, and then it took me a long time to learn how to behave. I feel like this is a common story that has something to do with grief, and fear, and self-hatred and hope, all at the same time. When I got well, I felt like the cancer has been, in part, many things that I had held that did not serve me: sadness, anger, fear, and self-hatred. And so my question was, how do I release this? I was involved in the Yoruba tradition, but it was clear to me that was not going to be my answer. For me, the evidence of spirituality is joy, generosity, and kindness. And I thought: how do I get to that? I had to start with myself, and figure out what to release. So, *delta dandi* is fictional, but *that* is my story; the story ends with the girl's transformation. It ends in a place of love, that's really the beginning of living.

In *delta dandi*, you talked about the "cruel grandmother," and you talked about Auntie Bea and she had a "cruel grandmother." What did you mean by that; how were you thinking?

My mother's mother, my mother, and I were all born here in Chicago under similar circumstances. All of our mothers got pregnant at a young age, and got kicked out. They ended up in Chicago because there were relatives here. My grandmother, she was young—sixteen—loved Chicago. But she lived hard and fast and she sent her child back to Memphis. Auntie Bea raised my mother, and she never felt loved. And Auntie Bea never felt loved because her grandmother, who was cruel, raised her and beat her. So my mother's way to love me is to push me away, but I know that she didn't know anything else. She wanted me to survive and be strong. She would say that to me. "You have to be able to make it. " What I wanted to do [in *delta dandi*] was to name the cruelty because I don't think it's uncommon. I also wanted to imply that the African sold the Africans. I went to Nigeria, and that was a hard experience for me. I saw they didn't give a damn about us as black Americans. They didn't talk about slavery in Nigeria. It wasn't the middle passage; it's like we [black Americans] are just weak and stupid. And white. We're strangers. I still haven't figured out how to talk about this. As African Americans we want to talk about that we was African kings and stuff, and we probably were. But that's not how they see us. We weren't all kings, most of us were slaves. And most of us were born into slavery in Africa. I had such an extreme reaction, and I was so angry that it took me a couple of years to even talk about Nigeria. Maybe in a past life I may have been one of those cruel kings. I do believe in past life—that we come back to work on stuff and we keep coming back. That's why the king was in there; because I consider it a possibility, as one of my past lives, but also as this girl's beginning.

I want you to talk a little about the characters, the structure, and the communal voices in *delta dandi*.

There are four primary voices. There's the girl whose story it really is, and everybody is her in some time in her physical life experience. All are living at the same time, 'cause I'm working with the idea that the future and the past exist right now. So, it is her story, everybody is her, and there is an urgency for her to learn how to love herself. This was my big life lesson. This is why I came this time, so I was trying to work this out for myself. But it is fictional in this piece. There is an urgency for this girl, despite all the hard and horrible things that have happened, to know that she is loved, that she can love and for her to love herself.

And her name is Gurl.

Gurl. Her name is Gurl. There is a voice called Elder Spirit Returning, and this is gonna be the girl's next incarnation. There is an urgency for that voice to be heard by the girl, 'cause it's like her spirit guide, but she's also herself—unborn. Her language is actually primarily sung when we do it with the performers. There is the Stutterer, who is a seer. He's like that crazy person who's really a spirit, but you pass by him all the time. He's talking and saying all kinds of things and has really got post-traumatic stress syndrome from being black. But he's a holy person. He would be a griot, but I'm not calling him that. He's a seer. Then there's the Blues, who represents the base sensibility of the piece. The Blues is a voice, and the Blues tells the Honey Pot stories, but the Blues also represents a deity—Oshun. The Blues is so important for black people, for jazz, the Blues is bigger than one person. I want Honey Pot to be bigger than life—legendary—so her story probably changes a lot every time it's told. The idea is that there's always a lead voice, and in the process of telling a story, there are multiple voices that communally come together. They're all a part of it in their different existing spaces.

How do you structure these communal voices into a nonlinear piece?

I want my collaborators to embody, and that happens in rehearsal. Some things are clearly songs. It is clear who the lead voices are because I use the fonts to say that, but I love, invite, and need the collaborators—who to me include the actors—to discover through process where this happens.

Is this something where the structure of the performance will change each evening?

It would not change each evening. It's set in rehearsal process. But it would change if we bring in different performers. From my performances at the Long Center for the Performing Arts in Austin to the Fire and Ink National Conference the show was very different because some of the performers were different. Now I'm figuring out how to put myself in it, *and* the performers, *and* the audience (laughter).

How does the actual construction of the work help people connect to blood memories; and who do you want to connect to the memories: audience, actor, playwright?

I have what I call blood memories and the girl in the piece speaks about it a little bit. My work comes to me through my right ear. What I've learned is to just release to it. I just know stuff, and I don't know why I know it, but I do. One of the reasons why I love jazz as a structure for my theatrical work is that I wanna go past the place that language can go, past the intellect. This is why it's ritual. It's like the juke joint, the ritual that happens in the grove, what happens in a black church, it's all the same thing. You combine the spoken word. First of all, it all has to be from an honest and deep place of being present and seated in an openness and desire for something bigger than yourself. But you take that and you combine singing with movement, with sound, with some kind of visual component, and magic happens. So that's the conjure. And when that happens, then what I find is that people—it doesn't matter what their race, their background, their life experience—it moves into people. And it is the place where we touch each other in our humanity. That's the place where we all meet. And it's been very interesting over the years because what I've found is that there are a wide range of people who I would expect to get it and be moved, who are not, and who I would never expect and are. And then the ones who of course I think would be and they are.

My last question is, you've done a lot of work with community activism and "Finding Voice" facilitation, however it seems as if *delta dandi* is doing it through an aesthetic experience, more of an artistic experience, than the health care work that you've done before. Is community activism still relevant to the way you want to work, or are you moving in a different direction?

That's a great question. You know, I developed this method of facilitation called Finding Voice, and basically, I've figured out how to articulate and walk people through the process I use to create work. So for years I have been facilitating creative process for people, some of whom don't even identify as artists, and some who are very experienced. For years I facilitated so much that I wasn't focusing on my own work. I lived in Austin for twenty years, and my decision to move from there was to push myself to be in a new environment so that I wouldn't be always the teacher, and I could focus on my work in a different way. I realized that I can't facilitate as much as I used to. The great thing is, I have people all over the world that I've worked with, that I can depend on, that have been in circle with me, that I love, and that support me. So I'm eternally grateful for that. Now I have to focus on my own work as a writer and a theater artist. This new way of doing *delta dandi* allows me to do that. I will not facilitate as much, but I'll do it more intentionally and mindfully connect it with theater work.

What are your future goals and new directions?

My goal is currently to have my work produced professionally for long runs around the world: to be a very active member of New Dramatists, and enjoy the opportunities that provides, to have my work adapted for film. I think my work is very visual, but I don't want to write the script. I want a filmmaker to adapt the work. And to continue to write performance novels which will live as literature. And to spend more time writing and eventually go back home to L.A. so that I can hang out with my family and go to the beach.

Now I'd like to return to the question about spirituality and the African American church. I think critics of African American drama are anxious to connect our work to the black church, when there are so many other spiritual influences. I was thinking that the spiritual influences that you were recognizing in Nigeria are actually present in the way that black people understand themselves as Christians. And so that Christianity in a certain sense, particularly with its relationship to Judaism, is a misnomer for the way African Americans practice Christianity. And I just wanted you to talk through that.

Yeah. I was a child of someone who migrated from the South. A lot of that generation wanted to reclaim their freedom and independence. My mom didn't go to church. Now she is a church lady, but when I was growing up, she wasn't trying to go to church. She was working two jobs. She was partying hard. She was a single parent raising a child. Sundays she did play the church music in the house, but now, I can see in retrospect, that our whole living room was a freakin' altar, you know? You've got the pictures of the dead, you've got the plastic on the couch, there are velvet pictures everywhere. There's certain areas you can't go into and there are certain things that happened in certain parts of the room. In Memphis, too, it's always this veneration of the ancestors—raising or calling on the ancestors by naming them, by telling you about their lives, by passing on the hope from them to you. So of course, when I went to Catholic school, from fifth grade until my first year of college—I loved that, because that was the same thing. The altars, the chanting, the ritual, the incense, all the pomp and circumstance, the languages. What I now know is of course that on this soil, we placed our traditions in the church, particularly in the Catholic church. This is also true in the Baptist church. Eventually, when I was in my twenties, I was baptized Baptist where it was the music and the spirit that moved through the room and the oratory, a contribution of the preacher and the deacons and everybody. Then, when I got with my indigenous people and my African practitioners and I did Buddhist, it's all true and everybody's saying pretty much the same thing. The people get in the way but the spiritual concepts are pretty much to me all the same.

AQUANOVA: COLLAPSING TIME
IN THE LIVES OF SHARON BRIDGFORTH'S *DELTA DANDI*

Stephanie L. Batiste

In performance Sharon Bridgforth's *delta dandi* is a jazz quartet of vo-cal sound volleying the sonic lead between voices, characters, times, and histories. The gorgeous nonromanticized soundscape of black experience is localized in the experience of "Gurl" and loosely tells the story of her pushing her way through a lifetime of generations of violence and abuse. A delta is the place where fresh river water meets the saline ocean. In their more conventional capacity of representing birth and rebirth *delta dandi*'s waters usher Gurl's survival and resurrection forth from horrific pasts. The waters of the rivers, oceans, and deltas in their meeting become a metaphor for time, history, community identity, and selfhood in what Bridgforth calls performance literature. These help the main character to develop, but in a sense they *are* her as well. Harry Elam Jr. describes how notions of the past animate black theater performance as artists drama-tize black American memory, aspiration, and liberation.[1] In her unique way as a writer, performer, composer and conductor, Bridgforth not only imagines a present that incorporates a past in art, but also theorizes their simultaneity and collision in a collapsing of time. Through a nonlinear, chronologically layered journey, *delta dandi* links the development of the subject and subjectivity to this process by layering spirit/voices that have felt the past and witness the future.

Gurl's story becomes both specific and universal in Bridgforth's use of the "i" to stand in for a collective "we." Bridgforth's solo-voiced perfor-mances of *delta dandi* permits the possibility of imagining that each voice and historical era might be reincarnations of the same spirit finding its way through time to redemption and divinity. In the solo show all of the voices collapse into one body highlighting the multiple lives and phases of black history being visited fully upon each succeeding generation and each succeeding voice. The voices accomplish the capturing, collapsing, and extension of time such that the past, present, and future exist in the same moments, words, and gestures. The multi-character soundings make it possible to perceive a story, without the imposition of a clearly linear plot in the piece largely because of the environment created. Episodic happenings linger in the sound of the theater—perhaps like a film's flashback or overlay, but in live memory. Embodying Omi Osun Joni Jones's discussion of the "jazz theater aesthetic," Bridgforth calls upon vocal rhythms of a jazz quartet and a structure that mirrors its collaborative improvisation on the stage.[2] The show emphasizes language and atmosphere promoting an imagistic, rhythmic building of narrative. Text and performance bear out sharonbridgforth.com's description of the show:

> An interdisciplinary theater piece, *delta dandi*, is a re-imagining of sacred concerts and tone poems that jazz icons Duke Ellington and Mary Lou Williams innovated. Through glimpses of the transmigration of one Spirit's many lives, *delta dandi* asks, how does collective grief and trauma inform the Black-American experience? What must a Soul do to heal? What is the traditional role of Queers in ritual? *delta dandi* is ritual/jazz theatre, conjuring Love. The past the present/the future. In this world the living the dead the unborn co-exist.[3]

It is not just this "co-existing" that inspires the notion of collapse that runs through my analysis. Aquanova suggests the powerful rush of disparate currents and flows crashing and commingling, fresh waters meeting salt, swirling and changing substance to forge something altogether new—like the skies' supernova, only river and sea-bound. The aquanova borrows the mystery and vastness of outer space in its suggestion of the multiple layers of cosmic existence—time, location, distance—as a primary element in waters' movement between and across spaces. In this way, the work moves as needed through time and space, reinforcing how these are one and are interdependent. A literal water baptism offers a significant transformation for *delta dandi*'s main character. The "aquanova" suggests an end, a transformation, and a beginning that incorporates and exceeds spiritual sanctification typically associated with such libation. The waters of this play include the oceanic depths and stagnant pools of the Middle Passage, river waters of boundary nourishment and escape, southern gulf waters, and uterine waters that all resist containment. Likewise disparate forms and voices, identities and histories not only co-exist but also crash, commingle, and collapse in the spaces of the page and the theater, forging coextensive "i"s and "we"s.

Four characters interact in a journey that traverses space and time. A typical cast calls for two women, one man, and one identifiably gender queer person.

> *The Gurl* is working through many lifetimes of abuse.
> *Elder Spirit/Returning* is the Gurl's spirit guide and
> future self.
> *Seer* is the trickster at the crossroads.
> *Blues*[4] is a jooking woman voice that offers healing.

In its Northwestern University (2009) performance and in other conducted solo renderings, the script contains boxes of numbered text (0, 1, 2, and so on through 12)[5] delivered by the audience that acts as an additional collective character. The text in these boxes is primarily drawn from the script, sometimes echoing a character's lines and spoken at the same time as another character's primary narrative. The eye travels over the page seeing shifting sounds and experiencing a collapsing of voices as Gurl, Elder Sprit, Seer, and Blues interact in telling the history of Gurl's struggle. An alphabetic score, the letters dance like so many notes on sheet music. In this way Bridgforth accomplishes something new through words' performance on the page in her poetic rendering of black drama. Exuberant phrases grow, undulate, and diminish on their own in shifts between different characters, and repetitions. Characters' "lines" jump from margin to margin, with phrases unevenly spaced and broken in unexpected ways that redound to dramatic direction by the text itself. The voices and times flow like the waters conjured in the title and resolution of *delta dandi*. The overwhelming visual effect encourages the reader to let go and flow affectively with the shifts.

"Gurl" is a child-slave born into bondage and then over again into violence during subsequent generations. In the life we first encounter she witnesses her mother's rape and murder. Her mother delivers her from this fate by shoving her into a corner where she cowers hidden in the darkness. The rest of Gurl's story is suggested episodically and seems to occur in many eras in her roles as slave, servant, and unloved orphan. Gurl's ages appear intermittently in the text, making clear that her initiation into violence begins early: she is three years old when her mother is killed (193), five when her physical and mental abuse in service emerges (199–200), and ten when she is sexually abused by her piano teacher, her mistress's boyfriend (202). Even as this development occurs chronologically, these ages do not represent a single lifetime. Gurl's lives happen simultaneously in time and out of time. Gurl's pain is a form of sacrifice ensuring the survival of future generations. Her endurance of physical abuse is a labor of love. Hers was a spirit that did not fly back over the water to the motherland, "for she who never flew" (214), but instead was born born born again to try for a new future in a new place and birth new generations.

Bridgforth positions a tangible South as a key symbolic space and transitional node in black history and movement. The forced movement of slavery transitions historically to the chosen movement of migrations from plantations and farms to towns, cities, and new states. For Bridgforth, this movement signifies the aggressive push for a new future in different, re-newed spaces. Bridgforth's *delta dandi* becomes the goddess under the waterfall rising out of the waters. The blending of waters signify this motion, difference, transformation, and blending of gender, time, and space. In this way Gurl is linked to attempts at survival that include migrations and geographical shifts of generations over time looking for a new life. Through Gurl *delta dandi* gestures not only toward past and present, but also to the future in its pregnant possibilities of motion.

Of the remaining characters, the Seer is a stutterer whose vocal rhythms stop and trip over time. Seer emphasizes Bridgforth's idiosyncratic use of pronouns. S/he repeats "i i i" (214) in a search for and, at the same time, insistence upon selfhood in his/her stumbling over the word. The Seer's temporal era remains unclear as s/he slides through history seeing into each of Gurl's lifetimes. Multiple "i"s pushing forward in time into being become articulations of communal selfhood(s). The use of lowercase in the articulation of "i" indicates a sublimated ego until finally at the end Gurl utters "I am" (214). Selfhood diminished and asserted at the same time. Elder Spirit is a force of love and protection ushering Gurl through release from pain. Elder Spirit is unable to protect Gurl's body, but guides her heart and soul to peace. Blues is a traveler, commentor, and bearer of history.

Solo renderings of *delta dandi* emphasize the power of this performance novel's language. Language and sound establish both character continuity and distinction since multiple bodies do not distinguish the characters. "her," "me," "she," "he," and "i" swirl and separate only through pause, crescendo, the rhythmic and perspectival shift of the characters' voices. Although the audience participates as a wave buoying the performance, the single voicing of *delta dandi* affects a containment of diverse characters and manifestations of selfhood and community in one (collectivized) body. The single voice articulates the shattered and reconstructed "I" in an ironically unified way as Gurl, and her collective analogues, black community and black creativity, become almost interchangeable. In doing so, the singular performer embraces multivalent affect and identities— traumatized, joyous, abject, centered, genderless and genderful, articulated and silent. When her voice is echoed by the audience, particularly from the first-person's perspective of "i" and "me," we also take on these identities. In the participation of the audience reverberates the shattering of the primary subject and performer like a wave breaking over the theater space. The dispersal and reconstitution of voice and narrative through the interplay of performer and audience echoes the constitution of the individual, of racial subjectivity, and of history theorized in *delta dandi*.

In performance, the black box manifested a choral, dramatic, jazz theater aesthetic that extended from the stage to the seats. The effect was sonic and atmospheric. For "solo" performances a series of lines or vocal contributions are assigned to audience members. Printed creatively on single sheets of numbered paper like poems on pages, our lines waited on our seats. When Bridgforth signaled our number, we chimed in with our words, phrases, and songs. Audience voices coalesced as an impromptu choir. Bridgforth accomplished a beautiful circularity of call and response by transforming audience into participant. Sound emanated singularly and at times from the entire room in modes harmonious and cacophonous, sympathetic and aggressive, in accord and in contradiction. This gesture evidenced a risky trust of the audience as collaborators and perhaps a model of democracy. The show exploited the multiple rhythms of strange voices and guided them into improvisational unity. The theater experience became unfamiliar, presentist, and personal as we watched, listened, and attentively awaited our cues. The words rendered us part of the show's history and at times transformed us into its characters via articulations like #6, "water falling all around her. water falling / all around me." In such moments we became Gurl. Voices too flowed like the waters gathering and swirling, lifting and pulling under. Gurl is tortured and aided by audience voices reading #9 "come here gal" and

#3 "Freedom Come Here Now." The audience became complicit in op-
pression and compassionate in caretaking. We became a part of the show
implicated in history and survival both personally and collectively in our
vocal blending with strangers across the room. The structured participation provided a conduit for speaking back to the performance and responding to the feelings the show aroused in real time. The feeling of #8
"honey wine. yellow amber gold. crocodiles and vultures. / sweet things.
/ oranges pumpkins and perfume. / Love beauty flowing. / fans and mirrors. Release. / Joy" that describes *delta dandi*'s linguistic richness, as well
as its moments of narrative decadence, became ours.

Bridgforth's costume included a black tuxedo, white untucked shirt,
and bowtie undone or perhaps never done. As a conductor orchestrat-
ing jazz Bridgforth gestures forcefully out while gender, character, narrative, time, and plot collapse. Bridgforth's attire casts her as tired, in
control, hard-working, and perhaps a tad spent. An invocation of spirit
also existed in the set. Idioms of birth and baptism, cleansing, and
prayer suffused the language and feeling of the performance. Bridgforth
stood alone on a white prayer mat before a microphone and music stand.
Glasses and pitchers filled with water, honey, black-eyed peas, sea salt
surrounded her. These substances amounted to remnants of moments,
wishes, and experience, of joy, sharing, hunger, and survival in black history. Salt from the distillation of ocean in black lives together with the
honey signifies flavor, riches, and preservation. The water refers back to
ocean and river—to crossings and to washings. It holds the place for the
meeting of river and sea in the waterfall that appears near the end of the
play. Together these render the simple set an altar of offering, prayer,
and preaching. The collective environment of *delta dandi* becomes one of
healing and transformation.

Other performances of *delta dandi* have looked very different from
Northwestern's solo showing. A Long Center for the Performing Arts
(2009) production at the University of Texas at Austin presented a large
cast of dancers and speakers. Distinct actors, singers, and dancers played
the show's four primary characters. In addition, a chorus of dancers provided a narrative of movement that supported the words and interaction
actions. At the Warfield Center's Fire and Ink Cotillion (2009) four professional actors dressed in white delivered a dynamic blend of voicing and
movement from a set of four chairs.[6] The element of dance that makes

its way in to collaborative performances of *delta dandi* embodies the jazz theater aesthetic as movement. Thomas DeFrantz connects black social dances to language in that they "physicalize a continuity of performative oratory for Africans in diaspora."[7] The script of *delta dandi* almost demands a kinetic layer in order to manifest and direct the thick energy generated in its spoken layer. The body in motion captures the complex vernacular rhythms embedded in Bridgforth's syllabic play and releases the drama's multidimensionality through embodied form. Fire and Ink's choreography mirrors *delta dandi*'s meetings of histories and spaces in its combination of West African and jazz movements. It also manifests the text's location of freedom in the active body. "i free when i run so i running all the time. the dresses they make me wear choke my skin and heart so i run till the touch of no fit leave my mind" (196). Freedom in the body occurs in *delta dandi*'s ritual dance's accelerating movements. The audience simultaneously vocalizes #3 "Freedom / Freedom / Freedom / come / here / NOW," and #8 "we spin / turn left / we praise / dance sing / we call / spin right / we know / now now" (223, 225), calling this freedom back to the characters in embodied exchange.

One of *delta dandi*'s earmarks is its atmospheric character and the palpable emotion produced in the images and drama of the story. *Delta dandi* crafts a textured world of scent, color, and feeling. *Delta dandi*'s emotional texture resonates in a three-year-old baby Gurl's ritual prayer (193). Through the emotionally devastating fear of a child, the play establishes the urgency of Gurl's journey. Gurl's futile desperation for her mother's safety and presence drives the narrative.

> just before they storm just before they force the night on my mama she push me push me so hard i knock against dark in small corner away. stay hide she say. i so scared can't move. i hear hit and hit and wail and cry.

> mama fight. they too many. i close eyes. i praying please don't let nothing happen to my mama please don't let nothing happen to my mama. (193)

Gurl wishes and prays even though she's had a premonition of violence and even though her prayers contradict what her senses tell her. The supplication for "mama" articulates a need for a useable past, an ancestor, and the knowledge and nurturing possible through that connection.

Overlaid with #9 "come here gal; nobody hear you crying gal / cept the devil out here in the dark" and #2 "guns beads brandy. SOLD!" this scene collapses time and experience in a manner violent and emotionally traumatic for the characters and theater participants.

The melée of voicings in this scene accomplishes a shifting and collapsing of historical and geographical spaces. "Guns beads brandy. SOLD!" occurs in both Africa under the watch of the Yoruban king and the United States under the slave trader's gavel. Whether the words of a black slave collector, white trader, or abuser, "come here gal" communicates the vulnerability of a slave, servant, or sharecropper in an ante— and postbellum—era. The audience's "come here gal" (#9) mouths the command of the white woman in the mirror ominously beckoning the bonded child whom she permits her music teacher boyfriend to instruct and molest (202). "Come here gal" marks the rape and murder of the three-year-old's mother and the physical abuse of a slightly older Gurl in a dark, putrid shed (193, 202). "Come here Gal." Usage of this terse phrase is unequivocal in its violence and foreboding. "nobody hear you crying gal / cept the devil out here in the dark." Bridgforth's rendering of bonded childhood makes the representation of the horrors of abuse that much more poignant.

> why i here i wonder every / day every day every day i hate her. must hide thoughts. can't breathe. / no talk. no mumble. no scream. my kin live down the dirt road. / they sold me i think to the devil for a few chickens and / a barrel of shine. / with bruised body and heavy eyes i sag in my spirit and spine. / i five. i think. (200)

Gurl's battles are unending, her powerlessness pervasive, her psyche and spirit undermined. Her innocence and pain engenders the audience's deep investment and hope in her survival. Our abuse of her becomes that much more painful and our participation in her renewal that much more jubilant. In her capacity of allegorizing black people, black histories, and futures, her youth opens up a space for growth and possibility, even as it intensifies the horrors of her experience.

Delta dandi's story operates like a puzzle. It refuses order and develops through voices colliding and overlapping in nonchronological, seemingly unrelated descriptions and voices. The narrative quickly travels between spaces, experiences, and eras of slavery including African shores, ship-holds, American auction blocks, sharecropper cabins, and big-house sheds. The characters take shape and gain coherence (and sometimes dissolution) over time. The age of Gurl is noted in memory and at intervals interrupted by adventures into a deeper past and a spirit world that redefine the temporal geography of human life. Life occurs in multiple spirit spheres and places at once in arriving at the present.

Like the story's telling, time itself is not linear in Gurl's own lives. Gurl's mother seems to have survived the middle passage and to have been murdered as a slave or as a sharecropper; Gurl herself seems abused by a mistress as a servant sometime after the Civil War (after 1865) at the age of five, though she should have been born no later than 1808 when the U.S.-African slave trade was officially ended; Gurl sees her "daddy" lynched, though if this is her biological father the middle passage would make her knowing him highly unlikely; her brother is attacked after a world war which would be around 1919 or 1945. To be linear the youth of two generations of this one family would have to extend over 100 to 150 years. The temporal and historical nature of Gurl's familial relationships and of her life are vague and would be impossible were her life singular. This broken temporality emphasizes the recursive, multigenerational nature of Gurl's existence. Time is related to lives and not the other way around. It is violence in the characters' lives and memories that provides experiential and geographical specificity. The violence of these lives disarticulates family from time and underscores the repetitive, transcendent nature of the violence. Violence stretches temporality between generations and collapses it in the lives of Gurl.

Often the same language signifies all of the spaces and times at once as in, "guns beads brandy. SOLD!" to signal the multiple spaces and times of the auction block and the signature phrase, "water falling all around her. water falling / all around me" (224) as a placeholder of the middle passage, literal birth, and mystical renewal. Such moments recur out of sequence and repeat in new ways in the process of Gurl's lives. Blues, both the character and the rhythm embedded in the characters' speech, links black musicality and orality to these redefinitions of time and experience. The capacity of the language to signify multiple spaces and moments in short resonant phrases simultaneously collapses and extends time and the past. Bridgforth's very use of language theorizes the process of history as layered, recursive, and, in fact, invaginated, that is, falling into itself, continually re-embedded, and productive. As Jacques Derrida explains, "with the inevitable dividing of the trait that marks membership, the boundary of the set comes to form, by invagination, an internal pocket larger than the whole; and the outcome of this division and of this abounding remains as singular as it is limitless."[8] In *delta dandi* Bridgforth lifts Derrida's concept of invagination from genres and objects to a consideration of history, Atlantic and Gulf geographies, and subjectivity through sound, character, and print.

In this way Bridgforth genders the operation of language and diaspora as female in a redefinition of history and subjectivity. Similarly the waters pull, absorb, and reproduce, "i walked into it. gave myself willingly. the water then came down from standing up came down from standing tall and painting all sky and space and knocked me down down down into itself it threw me up in the air and caught me then the water pulled itself back and laid me on the shore" (205). The water becomes the symbolic structure through which Bridgforth's reimagination of live(s) comes into being. In this way, Bridgforth crafts the "aquanova," a productive meeting of substantial, intangible forces, like water, time, and palimpsests of historical spaces, that flow and crash together in the birth of new perspectives, epistemologies, and subjectivities out of the re-forming or, even, destruction of something old.

Delta dandi opens with a conundrum, "i remember i born"—an impossible telling, and telling impossibility, that repeats twelve times in the first twelve seconds of the production. No being remembers their birth. With this opening line the central character of the piece performs a speech act whereby she calls herself into being via memory. "i remember i born" might be a dialect rendition of "i remember that i was born," rendering born a past event. "i remember i born" positions the subject as seer of that event positing an existence prior to the self. This element of her identity connects Gurl with Seer. The out-of-body, out-of-time previous version of I witnesses the birth of the new creature. In this simple sentence Bridgforth suggests the presence of the ancestors in the current generation both watching over and coming forth. Furthermore, the phrase connects thought, particularly memory, with existence. Without punctuation or passive structure, "i born" becomes an active verb, a declaration of a present event parallel to the present tense "i remember." The speaker becomes birthed via memory and speech. "i born" declares the coming into being of the subject in the further impossible present and continuous iteration "I am born." Both actions determine, perhaps even cause, each other. "I remember [therefore] I born," something like "I think therefore I am." The grammatical structure of the utterance "i" paired directly with the action alone articulates a subject in development by reproducing the new speech of a young child presently coming into language. The lowercase "i" sublimates the individual and suggests the possibility of its growth, until later when a capital "I" finally replaces the lowercase on the page (226, #11). Thus the first line of the play suggests the past, history, renewal, regeneration, continuity, and radical self-creation. i remember, i born. If "re-member" deploys the word "member" as a reference to a section of the body, then the "i" reconstructs the members of the body as she physically remakes the personal or collective self by "membering" (building) the body together over and over again. The possibility of historical or personal change resides in active re-membering—the always present act "i remember." In this way, thought becomes clearly embodied. The repetition of "i born" enacts the birth of the subject over and over in the present moment—a continuous present. The repeated "i iii" can simply be insistent upon existence and also can be the same subject renewed. She can be a different, newly voiced subject of a forthcoming or subsequent generation. Bridgforth toys with time in the construction of the subject in her tripled and quadrupled "i i i"s. Each possibility is simultaneously articulated through a single voice of universalized "we" all speaking together as "i."

At the same time that the subject gives birth to herself through language in an articulation of the possibility of renewal, the phrase "i remember i born" also indicates that the past is born with us into the present via the ancestors, memory, and learned or absorbed behaviors. In *delta dandi*, these learned behaviors include violence out of which the generations of characters in the play must be delivered and redeemed—"borne" out of and through difficulty. In the script the repetition always begins and ends with "remember" opening on the page to things whimsical, impossible, and previous. The length of the word "remember" contrasted against the brevity of "born" performs a rhythmic extension and contraction when spoken of a life lived and a life begun, perhaps also mimicking the contractions of birth and the gasping and exhaling used to bear its physical labor. "i iii." The rapidity of the repetition forces a smooth regulation of breath that acts as a secondary rhythm underlying this declaration of life. History and the future, mind and body, meet in the phrase. "i remember i born." And in the play Bridgforth's language in *delta dandi* bears out the theme and content of the narrative. The opening phrase foreshadows the story's development as much through language as through plot.

The repeating "i" spoken by Gurl, the Seer, and the audience provide a resounding blues repetition of birth and renewal. We encounter the same "i" and many generations signaled in the repeating "i" of different characters and speakers.

> always Pray this i know this i know / this is what i know / circle circle circle / dirt in the blood / i. clay / salt in the night / i. moan/deep from belly / i. rain / waves crash sun / i. sand / earth turn run / i/i i i.; . . . #6 circle circle circle. / dirt in the blood / i.clay / salt in the night / i. moan / deep from the belly / i. rain / waves crash run. i. sand / earth turn run i/iii / am. (192)

The "i" of many generations arrives, speaking at once in the single and multiplied voices. The shifting voices mix the temporality of generations as well as the plot structure. Understanding this extension and circularity of the subject illuminates the invaginated relationship between Gurl, her mother, and herself. In performance this knowledge is imparted through impression and feeling as the language washes over the space and audience.

> tiny fingers first / she come reaching / rip the life out she mama /she own mama the sacrifice / she mama spirit turn right back round / quick /reborn unto sheself / catch last breath / gasp / she mama go back / come out through dead mama sheself. / no cry. / quiet./water hush birds sit wind tight / blood moon turn white / she born. / tiny hands slow move touch face. (197)

In this *singular* passage mother and daughter collapse into single and continuous lives. The child climbs free, hands first in the creation of herself. Subjectivities flow and crash into the creation of someone new.

In Bridgforth's writing black voices embody the jazz theater aesthetic through improvisational, colloquial, and vernacular speech and rhythms.

They trade soundings like instruments in a jazz quartet. In many instances, the four primary voices merge, telling each other's experiences along with the story of "Gurl" and the woman she becomes. In solo shows the audience participates in the quartet, borrowing and repeating the voices of the primary characters. The collapse and simultaneity of voices occurs as Blues, Blues/Gurl, and Elder Spirit/Returning all tell Gurl's story in the first person. The indeterminacy and overlapping of the character voices and narrative positions forges an aquanova of sound and identity in the theater and on the page. Blues speaks in Gurl's voice to tell her story, "the first hands that took me was black/dark as the night. / grabbed my mama / used our own traditions to take us/used prayers we prayed / to hold in place what already was" (200). Blues's and Gurl's voices merge in the telling and blend in Gurl's first-person voice:

> i i i my mama my dear sweet mama my mama that man he killed her my dear sweet mama he killed her cause he felt like it like her life wasn't nothing . . . my mama she i i i daddy come they smile in the night daddy all the time every time she come he he he there with neck and body and hands no rope no tree he he he smile and in the daytime i say this is what happened (211–12)

Elder Spirit/Returning tells Gurl's story as "i," "*the Prayers of all the me's I Am.*" All of the voices merge, overlap, and collide in a visual, sonic aquanova resolving in Gurl's "miracle" made of "Love."

In the performative blending of time, voices, and spaces resonates the gender blend of male and female and of manifestations of sexuality. Bridgforth's loose tuxedo tie satirized the title's "*dandi*" that signals the blur of the gender and sexual identities. Sexual identity, gender identity, and gendered narratives of power are not *necessarily* binary. Spirit gods that preexist and are outside of bodies manifest both sexes. A queer sensibility undoes the bounds of gender specificity in a moment of mental and physical freedom for Gurl. When alone and running she says, "always i wonder why they yell these dresses on me. / why boys look like i feel but not how i look . . . i remember i was king once" (196). The stuttering seer takes on Gurl's voice to articulate the gender blend of the spirit world and the individual and collective past while the audience provides the sonic layer of her signature phrase #1 "i remember i born,"

> she was a boy born a girl till she became a man then a woman
> now both / i i i he was a girl then a woman till she became
> a young man with flowing / hips and hair i i i . . . .i i / i him
> . . . himshe / now now now herhe now now now / weus i i i.
> (201–2)

Male gender codes complicate the nature of Gurl's she-ness as gender becomes temporal and linguistic as well as embodied.

The collisions of language in constructing gender and time ripple in the plot's collapsing of Gurl with Mama (224, #5). The audience vocalizes the mother and daughter's intersubjectivity with different groups simultaneously chanting different #5s. #5 "we/stare. say go. sorry i. / your turn. next time/me. / not born yet . . . ." and #5 ". . . for us whose dreams were taken in the night / i i i / for her. / we we we / i am my mother" (224). As #5 continues to flow, Elder Spirit joins with them in a further collapsed "we." Ignoring boundaries of time she says *"rocking i tell she babyself we gone be alright / rocking i tell she gurlself to hang in there / rocking i tell she young womanself to fly fly fly / rocking i tell she grey We be back"* (203).

Gurl becomes Seer, Blues, Elder Spirit, mother, goddess, self at the crossroads of the water. In *delta dandi* the middle passage occurs in the life of a pregnant mother's capture, transport, and sale (200). "Mother's" figurative birth into violence via the middle passage occurs in the hold of the ship, #10, "full moon. blood red. follow follow. / mama. packed sealed. / below deck. / backs open. / flesh stench. / blood vomit. bowels loosed. / mucus and. broken spirits. / she born to that" (226). She carries a child at the same time that she is born / e over water. Blues tells the story about the middle passage so it is unclear whether she is this "Gurl's" own mother or some earlier mother. Circular beginnings, as births and transformations, occur through water. During a Christian baptism Gurl experiences a rebirth and deliverance other than the conventionally spiritual one intended. She is redeemed not from her life, but into a new, safer relationship with her oppressors and a revised relationship with her past.

> they said they took me to the water to save me but the water
> had its own plan it seemed. so i did the only thing there was
> to do in the face of the water standing up tall and painting
> all the sky and space. i walked into it. gave myself willingly.

> the water then came down from standing up came down
> from standing . . . knocked me down down down into itself it
> threw me up in the air and caught me then the water pulled
> itself back and laid me on the shore. i lay there on my back at
> the foot of the people staring down at me staring down at me
> quiet. i knew then that the water had saved me. not from itself
> not from the wrenching that life had done to me. the water
> saved me from the people. they were careful with me after
> that. only used me a little. in a distant kind of way. (205)

When Gurl sees her father lynched, he "floats" in air above his body hanging from a tree. It is unclear whether this memory overtakes her just as the "lady from the water" "drag(s)" her into the river to "float. run. swim. swim. float" or whether it occurs the other way around with the lady from her future saving her from this moment (208). In both doubled temporalities, the racist violence of the kind that took a mother (200), a father (208), and brother (195) collide in the dangerous intensity of re-birth in Gurl's transformation by the water. As she is swallowed by the waters, she wonders, "is this where father going / floating," and imagines her own floating as articulated, perhaps necessitated, by his (208).

The tallness of the water symbolizes the woman Gurl meets there. The disorienting apparition of the woman "right there a woman tall tall naked and shining in the water" happens early as Gurl encounters this si-lent specter of deliverance from amidst the dark trauma of her lives (191). With the repetition of #6 "water falling all around her. water falling / all around me," from the first few pages of the text throughout, the woman reemerges in different voices, places, and times (224). This woman, who is described in the blended voices of every character, acts as a guide for Gurl and as a vision of her future. The woman in the water takes shape finally and clearly in the memory of Gurl's spiritual passage in the water (224).

> so tired i i i am so tired. finally i stop running in the night.
> this time when there there there right there a woman tall tall
> naked and shining in the water stand smile smiling down at
> me in the the the water.
> #6 water falling all around her. water falling /
> all around me   . . . i listen/and i i i hear old Souls sing-
> ing the water gently pouring /

the Prayers of all the me's I Am /
sweetly round my head. a little girl me/there there there. (191,
224)

While the audience repeats #6, "water falling all around her. water falling
all around me," the voices of Gurl, Elder Spirit, and Blues intermingle in
describing Gurl's renewal after she has been taken by the water (191). A
similar commingling of character voices accompanied by the audience's
offering of two distinct #7s brings the play's resolution, #7 "i love you / i
love you / i love / you / me," and #7 "I love you / this is my prayer for you
/ i love you / this is the road we choose / i love you / this it he magic we
make / i love you / this is the change we bring" (225). The coalescence
of the theater's voices in the resolution of Gurl's arrival into womanhood
offers the possibility of collective deliverance from the violence of the
past in the radical possibility of love.[9] The past brings legacies of pain
and abuse, but also ancestor comfort in Elder Spirit's tonal libations, *"you
are never alone. / rest now / little girl go to sleep / dream sweetly and free /
. . . in this moment you are safe"* (216). The very name of "Elder Spirit/
Returning" signals the past's offer of emotional succor (216).

Gurl seems to arrive beyond birth, torture, or pain in her ultimate
merging with the woman in the water. This merging signals an incorpo-
ration of the past that accompanies her achievement of mental and spiritual freedom. Being swallowed by the water purges Gurl of her recursive
experience of violence, allowing her to become a conduit to change. The
water encapsulates *delta dandi*'s implosions. The return of rich natural
imagery and transcendent impossibility surround this aquanova until
Gurl returns willingly to the water.

> moon sun. hungry. i step into the sun. look around. every-
> thing sparkle. see water moving soft. birds bees butterfly
> frogs fish. peaches on ground. buds open. color everywhere
> for all my eyes can see. i in heaven i think . . . i try. / i walk to
> water. / jump in. (202–3)

When the group lifts Gurl to her deliverance in voices of love she offers
love back, beckoning the future in the form of a child:

> this is where we meet. the shift is now. / the Change has
> come. it is time. / i move from the crossroads / stand where

all the rivers meet. / life flows through me. / i wait for you. /
come to me. / ask your question child. (221)

Girl arrives in a new place and time into a radical present. Beyond violence
and pain develops opportunity and hope for the future. Gurl as *dandi*
emerges in the *delta* as a personally liberated, gender-liberated subject, a
queer woman closest to the manifestation of the goddess in the waters.

NOTES

1. Harry Elam, Jr., *The Past as Present in the Drama of August Wilson* (Ann Arbor:
University of Michigan Press, 2004), ix–xix.

2. Omi Osun Joni L. Jones, "Cast a Wide Net," *Theatre Journal* 57, no. 4 (December 2005): 598–600.

3. http://sharonbridgforth.com/content/bookscdsdvds/theatre/my-newest-work/.

4. Originally, a series of blues stories focused on a hard drinking, blues singing,
piano playing woman named HoneyPot was in *delta dandi*. HoneyPot "and dem"
offered laughter as medicine, as is the way with the blues. These stories therefore
served to thread Gurl's journey, and to ease the hardness of the telling. During the
development process of the play, however, Bridgforth discovered that the blues voice
did not belong in *delta dandi*—that, in fact, HoneyPot demanded so much attention that she didn't serve Gurl at all and thus the character of Blues was removed.
Instead, the character of Baba emerged. Bridgforth made the decision to remove
the Blues character after the writing of this essay, which is why she continues to be
referenced here.

5. These audience assignments will be noted in the text of the article with the "#"
sign even though they do not appear this way in the text of the script. Citations from
delta dandi will be noted in the body of the article by page number, i.e. (1).

6. *delta dandi*, Fire and Ink Cotillion, University of Texas, Austin, John Warfield
Center for African and African American Studies, OrangeMoon media, 2009.
Future performances promise to morph further as Bridgforth gives the work over to
the talents of new collaborators.

7. Thomas F. DeFrantz, "The Black Beat Made Visible: Hip Hop Dance and
Body Power," in André Lepecki, ed., *Of the Presence of the Body: Essays on Dance and
Performance Theory* (Wesleyan University Press, 2004), 76.

8. Jacques Derrida and Avital Ronell, "The Law of Genre," *Critical Inquiry* 7, no.
1, "On Narrative" (Autumn 1980): 59. Derrida offers a gendered spacialization of the
boundaries between genres and our ability to know (in particular to know a thing
from its signifier).

9. Omi Osun Joni L. Jones, "'Making Holy': Love and the Novel as Ritual
Transformation," in Sharon Bridgforth, *Love Conjure/Blues* (Redbone, 2005).

QUIET FRENZY

Stacey Karen Robinson

dedicated to
my ancestor angels
chester & evelyn

my guardian angels
irene, krystal & karla

PRODUCTION HISTORY

Quiet Frenzy was initially presented at the Wild Project, in New York City, in August 2010. It was directed and performed by Stacey Karen Robinson with lighting design by Melissa Mizell and sound design by Colin Whitely. The production stage manager was Itunu Balogun.

There were subsequent performances of *Quiet Frenzy* at The Pillsbury House Theatre in Minnesota in October 2010, as part of *Non-English Speaking Spoken Here: The Late Nite Series,* curated by Laurie Carlos and E. G. Bailey; The Longwood Art Gallery at Hostos Community College in New York in December 2010, presented by the Bronx Council on the Arts; Northwestern University in Illinois in February 2011, as part of the solo/black/woman Performance Series presented by the Department of Performance Studies; and The University of Texas at Austin in September 2011, as part of the Performing Blackness Series, presented by the John L. Warfield Center for African and African American Studies, Omi Osun Joni L. Jones, Executive Producer. *Quiet Frenzy* received developmental support from the Hourglass Group, Ltd.

CHARACTERS

LaShonda, A celestial city girl on the verge. She extends her burst-open heart. She is the one that remains. Deep within her, a multidimensional tear. Sometimes she sees what others do not. Sometimes she unveils Other World.
The Angel of Death, Dead-dead/cemetery-dead dead-looking woman. Maybe she's an apparition, maybe she's an ancestor. She appears to/through LaShonda.

TIME

Spiral time. Journey the circle to unearth the line where strangers, spirit, memory, and magic collide.

PLACE

The ephemeral ground of remembrance/rebirth.

PRODUCTION NOTE

A vibrant movement story is essential to this work; it is the thread that spins and illuminates the web.

PROLOGUE

BOOM

LASHONDA: [*with Breath. Movement*] BOOM.
My heart
popped.
A crack in time—all the stars snapped inward.
The earth fell off its axis, all of a sudden, was standing up straight.

[*Breath. Movement*]

BOOM.
I was scared. I wanted to hide. I wanted to press out my memories,
deflate myself. I wanted to run backwards into yesterday so I couldn't
be a witness. I wanted a way out.
I scratch my skin

to

enter

sky.
My tears fly off my face—form an arc of invisibility.

I didn't want no part of it.
I didn't know then.
I didn't know that
there are some things you have no choice about.
I didn't know/

everything
everything
disintegrates.

CELESTIAL

LASHONDA: He says,
"*I think you're celestial.*"
I say,
"Yeah . . . Aiight."
Funny thing is—he had already made my day.

I had seen him earlier. You know with all the drama I got going on, you know my drama, I had to get out of the house. I was just in the street. He stopped at a red light, rolled down his window, *"Hey Ma. You look so beautiful."* I don't know, you know? He caught me on a day I could really hear it 'cuz

[*Pause.*]

I wasn't feeling beautiful. I looked him dead in the eye. "Thank you. You made my day." Then I was feeling a little good. Took myself to the basketball game.

OK, five minutes left in the half. Coach called a time out 'cuz the Riff-Raffs were getting sloppy. Vinny missed a wide-open three-pointer that would have tied up the game. Why he's even in the game, I don't know. Vinny's in the game while Airborne's on the bench?? Fine–

I look up, who do I see but HIM.

What is this?

Who is this? Never seen in the neighborhood before—now I see him twice? Is God trying tell me something? 'Cuz I'm single. My horoscope said, "Get Ready. Big Things Are Coming."

I'm like, I could deal with Big Things.

I look up again, he's gone. Which is fine with me 'cuz you know how I am with basketball. I'm serious. Don't mess with me. Don't bother me. Don't talk to me when I'm watching the game. I mean, you could do it, but you might get your feelings hurt. You could do it, but you might get your feelings hurt. OK–

Eleven seconds left in the game. My team's down 1. Airborne misses a layup that even Vinny coulda made. Someone puts their hand on my shoulder. *"Hey shorty."*

Who's touching me? 'Cuz, first of all, you know I don't like anyone putting their hands on me like they know me. Second of all, let me find out I have to school another Brother about bothering me when I'm watching the game. I turn around, ready to fight—

[*She ooh's with great delight.*]

Ooooooooooooooooooohhhhh!

I think I'm in love.

He says,

"*I think you're celestial.*"
I say,
"Yeah . . . Aiight."

ANGEL OF DEATH

LASHONDA: Angel

of

DEATH—

she be
stalking me.
Trying to catch me round
every
turn.

I be trying to do basic simple things. Order an egg roll, some chicken
wings.
Here SHE come,
peeking round the shoulder of the man behind the counter. Talking
'bout,
"*Gotcha!*
You can't hide.
HEH. HEH. HEH."

I be like,
[*Aggressively*] "You better back up lady!"
'cuz
that ain't right.

[*Pause.*]

But she don't seem real intimidated.

Sometimes late-late/early-early
I
shiver/
awake
shuddering/

hear her
enormous
laugh

all
around
me,
sucking me into the deep.

Angel

                       of

DEATH.

[*Pause*]

But I don't—
I won't

I never
open my eyes.

SUBWAY/STOP

[LASHONDA *sits rigidly on a subway bench. She speaks to a stranger standing nearby.*]

LASHONDA: I was wondering. I was hoping.

[*Pause.*]

I can't move.
I've been sitting here for a while . . . I think.
I can't seem to move myself.
I was wondering.
Do you think you could you help me get on the train when it comes?

[LASHONDA *speaks her heart. She is not aware that her words are audible.*]

I can't mooooooove.
You are gone from me.
Come back,
it hurts too much.
Come back.

I need you.
I'm drowning in my own breath.
Where are your fingertips?
Your deep waves of silence?

[LASHONDA *speaks to the stranger.*]

I, I, I, feel like I'm um, uh, underwater.
Am I here?
Is this happening?
It feels like a dream. This whole thing feels like a dream. I can't seem
to wake myself up.
I haven't been able to get myself up.

[LASHONDA *speaks her heart.*]

Where are you?
Where you be?
I'm undone.

All
folded
over
myself.

[LASHONDA *speaks to the stranger.*]

I can't get my legs to move.
I thought I wasn't real.
I thought I had ceased to exist.
I've been sitting here. No one has said anything to me.
Until you said hello.
Then I realized I'm still here.
I'm really here.
Right??
My legs are not working right. I'm not working right.
I can't move.
Please, this makes no sense to me.
Can you help me?
Do you think you could help me get on the train?

RIDICARONI

LASHONDA: So–

Yeah girl,

I gotta stop drinking.

Not because of that/this sickness—Because I woke up in some strange room completely naked. As the day I was born.

It was pretty scary for a second there. I woke up. I didn't know where I was. Not only was I nude but my clothes were nowhere to be found. Bad feeling.

When I found out what really happened—Worse feeling. OK?

You know J.J. right? My friend from college, J.J.?

Yeah, J.J.! J.J. had a dinner party.

Now you know I love J.J. but he can't keep his my mouth shut. About fifteen minutes after I arrived I realized that not only had he told everybody about that/this sickness but also he had shared with everyone that I've been unemployed.

They knew too much without knowing.

Everyone was incredibly, overly nice. One of his friends came up to me.

"I hear you're unemployed. Well, you're in good company."

"Oh, are you unemployed?"

"Nooooo."

What does that mean, you're in good company? What? "Where's the Makers Mark?"

I remember making that choice. I'm going to drink. That's about the last thing I remember.

Anyway-

According to J.J. by nine o'clock I was totally wasted/ aggressively flirting slash antagonizing his friend Bradley.

I don't know, I don't remember any of this.

A bunch of them were having some big political discussion. J.J. said anytime Bradley spoke I said, [*exaggeratedly*]

"BLEH! BLEH! BLEH! Blehblehbleh!"

That's odd.

I don't know why J.J. didn't take me out of the situation. But because everyone knows that I'm "*sick*" they all feel sorry for me. They think I'm drowning my sorrows in alcohol. So they all just ignore me and continue to have this big political discussion while I'm Blehblehbleh barking at his friend.

J.J. said I got incensed that I was being ignored.

I proceeded to scream at Bradley.

"You think you're so smart. I think you're Ridicaroni. You're just RIDICARONI!"

Which isn't even a word, but it's close enough to a word to be quite offensive.

Before he left he asked J.J. to make sure we are never/ever invited to the same event again.

But I guess the highlight of the night came when Priscilla, you remember Priscilla? The interior designer–

was talking about some plastic surgery she's about to get. J.J. said I immediately began to weep and wail. [*Immoderately*]

"Why do we hate our bodies? Why are we taught to hate our bodies? Maybe that's why I got this—Maybe I hate my body."

Then it seems, I decided that we could all heal ourselves of our self-loathing if we samba'd. The dance samba.

I demanded that everyone there take a samba lesson from me. I lined everyone up, took off my shirt, threw up all over myself.

At which point J.J. finally removed me from the situation. He took off my clothes, cleaned me up, put me to bed.

So,

yeah girl,

I gotta stop drinking.

WALK THE EARTH

[*Movement and gesture are necessary throughout.*]

LASHONDA: I want to
    walk the earth
    in search of you
    but they say
    there is nothing left to find/no traces.

I'm searching for story—
Outlines to exist inside.

Just one pure wish.

I usedta be beautiful,
remember?

I was ripe,
full of scent
before I knew what life was all about.

I'm searching for story
to give me form.

I haunt myself.

I feel like I've been
walking the earth
looking for you

but

really

I've been in this
room
of
sleep.

I keep
crawling
into the cave of mourners
by mistake.
Mothers
everywhere/
leaping
at the echoes
of the too soon
dead
dead
dead
dead.

I cut off all my hair—
an isle
set
free
from
itself—
be seeking.

I'm searching
for
your
body
your
hair
your
flesh
your

[*She vocalizes inhalation.*]

AAAaaah.

[LASHONDA *tries to conjure with palms outstretched.*]

All the magic in my palms
all my heat—

[*Pause.*]

still

you do not
emerge.

The body.
No!
Not the memory of skin.

Somewhere
exists
the
house

of
my
heart/here

[*She inhales.*]

there is a faint smell
of
HER/Here

[*She inhales.*]

Round joy.

[*She inhales.*]

Sweetness

of
Sun.

MOURNING SONG

[LASHONDA *is in a doctor's office.*]

LASHONDA: Why am I here, Doc?

[*Pause.*]

Because I lost it. Because I asked a woman to help me on the subway, she called 911 instead. Because of the car accident. Well yeah, God saved me. I'm the one that remains but instead of getting up, moving on, embracing life—I'm always holding my breath. I often catch myself not breathing.
That's funny, right? There's a punch line there, somewhere.
I'm stuck, sick. I reek of . . .
Doc?
Do you think your spirit can leave you? I've been thinking about this. I think my spirit is somewhere resting on an egg, in a nest, in a tree far away from here.
I don't mean across oceans,
I mean across time.

I'm having a problem with boundaries.
I can't seem to locate myself.

I feel my
binding
coming a loose.
Stitches a loose.

It's not how you would think,
falling apart
is
so
very
mundane.
Stitches opening. Me a loose.

What do I want?
I want to
arise
in song
soaking the earth with my lamentations
but
I can't get back
to where the story begins.
The yesterday before yesterday before yesterday before/

Maybe I'm
missing
some
essential
something.

Trying to
flip
without the
sacred
syllable
that animates.

What hurts??

The sun coming up.

Night
seeps into/
darkness
insinuated
under my skin/
instead of
music
there is crushed bone
molded flesh
leaking sound.

No one told me
stories
too long
shelved
implode.

I just want to say good-bye one last time.
Doc, may I start again?

[*Pause.*]

I want to live/
so that I may
Start Again/
Take my past/
take what I know of myself
do what you must–

I'll give you everything.
Here—
Take this
HA!
I have nothing to give.

Take this
bag of
breasts

belly
shame.

Seize this poor offering.
What is it you need?
I am yours.
Peel me clean
of myself.

I scraped off my skin
tried to
pull
every
sin
to the surface.
HA!
I got stuck somewhere
in my sufferings.
haaaaaaaaaaaaaaaaaaaaaaaaaaaaaaaaaaaaaaaaaaaaah.
I give you
every
fractured word
spit
into my womb.

Every
un-birthed
imagining.

Here—
I'm
extending
my
burst
open
heart.

HERE—
The

slivered
fragments
of my dreams.

HERE—
My
brilliant
unfolding
sorrow.

I give you everything.
HERE—
TAKE THIS—

Please

Make off with it.

I
I surrender.

INTIMACY DANCE

[*This scene is a word/movement/gesture eruption.*]

LASHONDA: BOOM
       Pop
Stand
Hide

Press/Run

Scratch/
Fly

                                           Nooooooooooo.

KABOOM

[*The setting is for the same doctor's office.*]

LASHONDA: What?

[*Beat.*]

How'd I get my scar? You know this Doc. Long story short—I was in a car accident with my sister. She died. I survived.

[*Pause.*]

No, there's really not a whole lot more to tell. I don't have any memory of it. The actual crash.

[*Pause. She tries to remember.*]

It was hot.
The first heat of spring.
A record breaker.
A Saturday.
We hadn't seen each other in a long time, my sister and I. We put on tight-short shorts. Went to stroll. We spent hours walking circles. Holding hands. The people, they couldn't take it. We were looking too good. But we weren't wasting no time. We were together. It was our day.
I remember—I felt fully *alive*. Even my skin was breathing.

[*Beat.*]

She kept holding me up. I kept falling over 'cuz everything was funny.
All day her tummy was tickling. When she was happy her tummy would tickle. We was moving as one, so my tummy was tickling. Not just the twin thing. You know as a twin sometimes you hear the other's thoughts. But this was more deliberate. As if she was directing herself into/out of me.

[*She makes a quick movement.*]

It made me giggle.
We were eating sun.
Must've been 'cuz all of a sudden it was late/dark.
It's so stupid. We were seven blocks away.
Later, a cop told me there were a lot of DUI's that day. 'Cuz it was so pretty. People all over the city had been celebrating the surprise holiday.

Anyway–
Who pulls up beside us but the Op-Shop Boyz, these guys we grew
up with. They insisted on taking us home. Juke gave us the front seat
'cuz Bobo was real fat. There wasn't enough room for all of us in the
back. We wouldn't have been comfortable. They always treated us
real gentle, like real ladies.
We were in the front. She was on my lap—
KaBoom.

[*Pause.*]

Not that I remember.
I just remember losing breath—
Seeing Neecy,
my sister,
everywhere.
She was multiplied–
many, many, many, many, many, many, many, many times.
All
around me was
Neecy!
Dancing.
Holding me.
Hugging me cheek to cheek.
Tugging my ears.
Kissing my eyelids.
Every part of her was singing this song we made up as kids—

[LASHONDA *sings a peppy playful song.*]

> angel,
> oh angel.
> my angel,
> Oh-o angel.

I was bliss.
I was erupting. All these little explosions of me.
I was, all of me was, embraced by her.
She kept singing.

I kept saying,
"Neecy!
Oh Neecy!
My Neecy!
Isn't this the BEST day?"

ORI ORI ORI/THE ANGEL OF DEATH

[LASHONDA *is in transition. Something is happening beyond her control. She breathes deeply, tries to regain herself.*]

Ori Ori Ori
DoGo
Ori
GoDo
Ori
DoGo

[*She vocalizes inhalation.*]

AAaaaaaah.

Ori Ori Ori
DoGo
Ori
GoDo
Ori
DoGo

[*She vocalizes exhalation.*]

AAaaaaaah.

LASHONDA/THE ANGEL OF DEATH

[THE ANGEL OF DEATH *partially possesses* LASHONDA. THE ANGEL OF DEATH *begins to slowly, gently incarnate.* LASHONDA'S *voice and gestures begin to change.*]

Ori Ori Ori
DoGo

Ori
GoDo
Ori
DoGo

[*She vocalizes inhalation.*]

AAaaaaaah.

Ori Ori Ori
DoGo
Ori
GoDo
Ori
DoGo
SO

[THE ANGEL OF DEATH *possesses* LASHONDA *completely.* THE ANGEL OF DEATH *speaks.*]

THE ANGEL OF DEATH: You've come to
    Ask—
    I should tell?
    Why?

[LASHONDA *recovers and speaks with her own voice. For the rest of the scene* LASHONDA *will fall into and out of possession, fluidly effortlessly embodying* THE ANGEL OF DEATH *then speaking as herself et cetera.*]

    I keep having this CRAZY DREAM.
    Crazy/Vibrant
    Waking Dream
    Or
    Visitation
    Or
    Something . . .

THE ANGEL OF DEATH: You SEE me.
    Want to
    talk
    with me.

Then what
HAH?
What
will you do
with
my
Stoooooory?

LASHONDA: I keep seeing this
Ancient
Blood/Mud
Dead-Dead/
Cemetery-Dead
Dead-
Looking Woman.

THE ANGEL OF DEATH: You come for visit—
Expect me
toooooooooooooooo
shake every secret from my hips.
The key
under all
these rolls
this weight
this burden.

[*Pause.*]

Enter my tomb.

[*Her arms open wide.*]

It's empty!
HA!

LASHONDA: I usedta think she was the angel of death coming for me.
Like when an old timer tells you,
"*If you have a dream—*
with a man all dressed in Black/
with a Black top hat/no white in his eyes—
He tells you to put on your shoes/

Points to a Big Black Door—
You better tell him, 'GET THEE BACK SATAN!'
Because if you put on your shoes/
walk through that
THRESHOLD—
You'll fall into the BIG BLACK NIGHT/
never wake up."
Usedta think she was death coming for me, like that.
But now I'm calling to her, conjuring her.
I keep begging this dead-dead/cemetery-dead
Dead-looking woman
Please.
Tell me.
Please.
Please, please, tell me, please.
Please tell me your story.
She does.
I think.
Maybe . . .

THE ANGEL OF DEATH: I was born
    into
    a
    curse
    forced upon my mothers/
    heart popped.
    SHE carried the bits around/
    squeezing the juice onto her skin.
    Gaping hole
    under SHE breast—
    But the surface of her?
    BA BUM
    BA BUM
    BEAT-TING

LASHONDA: Crazy/Vibrant
    Waking Dream
    Or

Visitation
Or . . .

THE ANGEL OF DEATH: BA BUM
BA BUM
BA BUM
BA BUM

All
the veins of my pain.
I fold you into my story?
[*Playfully*] *Nooo.*
I want to be folded into yours.

I want
suckle your shade
be wrapped in your innocence.

You there.
Me here.
What
a
difference!

LASHONDA: Dead-dead/cemetery-dead
Ancient
Blood
Mud

THE ANGEL OF DEATH: Someday I will begin again—
Gathering all the little pieces of myself.

I have outlived them all/
You say/
I have something to offer.

I say—
I have given
everything
back to the earth
already.

I know you want your
redemption
through me
but grant me
some mercy first.

[*Pause.*]

It's simple.
You must be willing to disappear.
Ha!
Then you will know
what it's like to
walk with the dead.
HAAAAAAAAAAAAAAAAAA!

LASHONDA: Tell me.
Please.
Tell me how . . .

THE ANGEL OF DEATH: Stop. Enough!

[*Elongated ssh's. Like the sound of wind.*]

Sssssssssssssssssssssssssssssssssssssssssssssssssssssssh.

Beware.
There are triple dead things.
Things that produce no life.
Be still.
Listen.

[*Pause.*]

There is rejoicing.

[THE ANGEL OF DEATH *dances a Spiral Dance.*]

Awake
HA!
Awake
HA! HA!

Awakeninnnnnnnnnnnnnnnnnnnnng
Day of
Reckoninnnnnnnnnnnnnnng
HA! HA!
HA-HA-HA-HA-HA-HA-HA.

Everyday is born
a new sun.
Everyday anew
my only one.

Walk the earth child.
Walk the earth child.
Walk the earth and shout!

Ori Ori Ori
DoGo
Ori
GoDo
Ori
DoGo

[*She vocalizes inhalation.*]

AAaaaaaah.

Ori Ori Ori
DoGo
Ori
GoDo
Ori
DoGo

[*She vocalizes exhalation.*]

Aaaaaaaaaaaaaah.

[*The dance ends.*]

GARGOYLE

LASHONDA: Giiiiirl—

I was walking to the subway late one night when this Brother steps in my path, literally right in front of me. I'm dumbstruck.

Before I could even say anything he's speaking the good speak, *"Evening Sista. I don't mean to take up any of your precious time. You just look so heavenly, I'd be angry at myself if I didn't tell you so. Would you mind greatly if I walked with you just a step or two?"*

I'm digging him. I'm thinking,

[LASHONDA *sings.*]

Isn't this romantic?

Wouldn't it be ideal if my soul-perfect-life-partner just appeared?
I was looking crazy.
I had just come from the gym, let's say. Nooo, I wasn't coming from the gym. I was having one of those—
Now I know I shouldn't be walking outta the house looking like this but I just don't care days. But then, of course, I did care. By that time it was too late. I was way downtown before I caught a glimpse of myself in a glass window. Long story longer—
It was nice he could appreciate me in my natural state. I was thinking, "Maybe he can see my inner light."
We begin to walk.
He asks my name. I say, "LaShonda."

"La—WHO? La—WHAT??"

"LaShonda."

He asks where I'm from. I say, "the Bronx." He says he hates the Bronx. Every woman he ever met from the Bronx was a gold digger who wanted him for his Cheddar.

"Cheddar?"

"Cheddar/Paper/Money."

He asks what I do. "I'm a secretary but if I could do anything, be anyone, I would be Mae West meets Nina Simone on the Grand Concourse."

[LASHONDA *sings, sultry and stylized.*]

I've got
indiscreet notions & indiscreet motions.

I've got
indiscreet physics & indiscreet time.

I've got
indiscreet faces in indiscreet places.

I've got
indiscreet poetry & indiscreet rhyme.

Where can I get
a decent cup of coffee?

Where can I get
a decent Joe?

If you see me
why don't you see me?

If you see me
where did I go-o?

[*Without a beat,* LASHONDA *returns to her story.*]

He says he hates singers. "*Everyone in the entertainment business is so phony.*"
Do you remember when that was the biggest insult? "You're so phony."
Like when you're in the ninth grade, riding on the bus, telling your new best friend, Jennifer, about last summer when this high school basketball player named George tried to kiss you. This mean girl, Lauren, interrupts. "*You're so phony. No basketball player named George ever tried to kiss you. You're so phony.*"
The whole bus went, "Ooh." Remember phony??
Anyway—
I was starting to think this brother was not really feeling me. Though I found his invitation to sit in McDonalds and get to know each other better, intriguing, let's say—
I had to decline.

"We're not compatible. But I truly hope you find what you're looking for."

"Nah. No you don't. You don't hope I find what I'm looking for."

[*Long pause.*]

"OK."

"It's because of my swag, I got way too much swagger for you."

[*Long Pause.*]

"OK."

As I walk away, I begin to hear this chant behind me, *"gargoyle, gargoyle, Gargoyle, GARGOYLE!"*

I'm a little surprised by this. I look over my shoulder-

"You know what you are. You know what you do. GARGOYLE!!"

At this point I did hesitate for a moment to ask myself, What World is This?? I wanted to run to him—

"Baby can't you see what I'm made of? All this . . ."

But I just kept it moving.

MISS GERALDINE'S LUCKY FIG TREE

[LASHONDA *sings a with a Country Western twang.*]

> All my life I been
> a-waiting
> for that
> extra
> special
> something
> to occur.

[LASHONDA *speaks.*]

Got this Country Western tune stuck in my head.

[LASHONDA *sings.*]

> Sitting back
> anticipating

all the sweetness
that the good life would offer.

Got a system with the Lotto
only play
every third
Thursday of the month.
When I hit I'm headed for Morocco.
Marrakesh,
Fes,
Casablanca,
or Bust.

[LASHONDA *speaks.*]

I made it up. This little ditty doesn't exist anywhere outside of me. I
checked, I Googled it. I mean it's stupid enough to be an original.

[LASHONDA *sings. She really goes for it.*]

All my life I been
a-waiting
for that
extra
special
something
to occur.

Sitting back
anticipating
all the sweetness
that the good life would offer.

Got a system with the Lotto
only play
every third
Thursday of the month.
When I hit I'm headed for Morocco.
Marrakesh,
Fes,

Casablanca
or Bust.

[*The song ends.*]

Do you remember your first kiss?
I don't.
I know who I had my first kiss with, Delroy Barnett, but I can't recall anything about it.
I do remember the first time I thought I was gonna get kissed. It was the first summer I spent without my sister. She was in Vermont at art camp. She painted, beautifully—Won a scholarship for "kids with promise."
My father sent me South.
There were no kids my age on my Aunt's block so I got paired with my Aunt's best friend's grandson, George. A star basketball player.
He was rumored to be some star basketball player but I never saw him shoot no hoops.
I was with him all day, almost every day. Monday to Friday, 9 to 5, like a job. Actually—that probably was his summer job! I never saw any money exchange hands but he probably was getting paid for it.
He mostly ignored then teased then tolerated me. He called me Peach Fuzz because of the hair on my upper lip.
I avoided him.
Spending my time reading or daydreaming or writing letters to my sister. I wrote her a letter every day and she me. My letters were looong, bulky! I remember, I always had to press the crease really hard to fit them into the envelope. Hers were more like postcards.
"*The turkey meatloaf here smells like butt. Love, Neecy*" "*Discover Odetta. Please.*"
She was full of silence, not shy, like people always thought. She was about the loudest quiet person you ever could meet.

Bold
bright
inside herself.

Sometimes she would catch me staring at her—

[*Pause.*]

"*Shonda, Leave me be.*"

She was spacious.
Effortless.

She was my sister . . .

[LASHONDA *hears something.*]

Did you hear that?
Thought I heard . . .

[*She makes a quick movement.*]

Got a chill. Anyway—
George. George spent his time listening to Public Enemy, on his headphones, inside the house.
He was a bad babysitter.
I passed my days on the porch. I wasn't allowed to leave the porch without George. I wasn't interested in leaving the porch with George. I followed the rules.
Except, one Friday, I got tired of hanging around. I had one of Neecy's letters ringing in my head. "*Don't be polite. Seek. Seek adventure.*"

[*She makes a soft incantation.*]

Don't be polite. Seek adventure. Don't be polite. Seek adventure.
So—
At 2:57 I ran off the porch down the block. I didn't know where I was running or why I was running or why I was screaming

[*She screams.*]

at the top of my lungs, I just was.
I made it three blocks before I heard George, "*Whatchu doin' Peach Fuzz? Peach Fuzz—Whatchu doin'??*"
I'm steady running, still screaming.
I see Miss Geraldine's Lucky Fig Tree about a block and a half away. I start thinking, Miss Geraldine's Lucky Fig Tree equals victory.

George is coming up behind me quick. His legs were as long as I was, I'm sure it was just a little jog for him. I knew he was close but so was I.

I'm bounding now, exhilarated, still screaming.

Just as I make it to Miss Geraldine's, George lifts me from behind. Holds me high in the air for a few.

Flying in a dream! To be airborne so unexpectedly.

Everything falls hush.

[*Pause.*]

George puts me down. Turns me around. Looks at me.

I look up at him, realize his hair is cherry brown. The dimple in his left cheek looks about a mile deep. We're both breathing heavy. He traces my upper lip with one finger. *"Peach Fuzz. I didn't know. You were. Like THAT."* I lean in. I could smell mustard on his breath. I felt this specialness rising in me, the promise of new-new-new.

[*Pause.*]

Out comes Miss Geraldine. *"Now Master George,"* she called all the young men master. *"Now Master George—Would you please be so kind as to explain to me the reason for all this preternatural hurly-burly?"*

That day I wrote Neecy my only skimpy letter.

"Miss Geraldine's Lucky Fig Tree equals VICTORY!"

FREE-FALL

LASHONDA: I was temping at the Chrysler Building—

Do you know that the elevators at the Chrysler Building free-fall?

They free—FALL when it's windy out.

Something about the age or the construction of the building, I don't know. All I know is—

I stepped in, the wind howled.

You could hear the wind howling while inside the elevator. Note to self, if you step into an elevator and the wind howls, STEP OUT.

The elevator

[*She makes a gesture.*]

dropped.

I was at the edge of myself.

When I got off, I said to the people waiting to get on, "Um, I was just in this and it dropped several . . ."

Everyone was very casual about it. "*It's windy out. It does that sometimes when it's windy.*"

[*She speaks mockingly.*]

Just a windy Wednesday at work.

As they brushed past me I replied, "But I don't even like roller coasters." I found myself confessing that all day. "I don't go to amusement parks. You won't find me at Great Adventure. I don't even like roller coasters."

The second time it happened, I was in the elevator with two other women. As we're falling, I'm thinking—Oh, I will have a freak-out. But one of the other women beat me to it. This little petite thing scrunched up in the corner, trembling like a fluttery bird. "*I just can't take this. I'm not made for this. This is the fourth time today. I just can't take this! I'm not made for this!*"

[LASHONDA *agrees with the petite bird with an emphatic:*]

Thank you!

The other woman with us looked over to me. I gave her no sign that I was in any way equipped to deal with the situation. She was one of those take no mess/scare your spit dry-looking women. Real authority.

She turned to the little bird.

"Listen up.

You are not.

Going to lose it.

In here.

With me.

TODAY.

SO

GET

YOURSELF

TOGETHER."

And she did.
Like that.

[*She makes a gesture.*]

By the way, so did I.
Turns out I just needed some direction. Get yourself together. OK—
OK
Alright . . .

NEECY

[LASHONDA *sees* NEECY*!*]

LASHONDA: Is that you? Have you come to me? Ooooooooooooooooooooh
Neecy!

[LASHONDA *falls into an excited silence and is girlish when she speaks.*]

Have you nothing to say? It is for me to speak?

[*Pause.*]

Forgive me for this. I've been so guilty because you were so deserving
of life.

[*Beat.*]

Do you remember that game we usedta play as little-little girls when
we tried to kiss each other's open armpits?

[*Beat.*]

Neecy, I want to love and be unafraid. I want to be undivided.

[*Beat.*]

Niece-Niece, I had a bad dream. I dreamed I was Old Man Waits
from Norfolk, Virginia.

[*She speaks in a rush of language. In a wave.*]

Do you remember that story that Daddy usedta tell us about that
old man from his neighborhood who waited at the bus station all
day/everyday for the last ten years of his life because his wife woke

up one morning saying she had a dream of a white stallion running backwards, so she had to go see her folks but that she was sure to be back on the last bus, the 7:50. But she never did come back. He never stopped believing that she would come back. He died at that station/ standing up. Fresh Bluebells in one hand, small bag of Mary Jane's in the other just as the 7:50 from Newport News pulled in.
In my dream—
I saw that old man sitting, waiting at some dusty small-town bus stop but then he turned into me. Stuck on the subway bench that day I lost mobility.
I'm like that old man, Old Man Waits.
I've got all this love, this immensity of love. It's all grabbing at the past, all directed into the memory of you. No.
To be honest. Not into the memory of you. Into the absence of you . . .
I miss you.
I love you.

[*Pause.*]

That's all I really wanted to say.

[*She laughs.*]

Thank you.
Thank you.
Thank you for being my

[LASHONDA *grabs her heart and makes deep inhalation.*]

GREAT BIG NOTHING

LASHONDA: I was handing the cashier at the supermarket
3 dollars 33 cents when—
her hand
brushed mine.

For
one
moment
I didn't know who was who.
I didn't know where her skin ended and mine began.

Odd
ecstasy,
not knowing.

Vast
Embracing . . .

[*Slow, long inhalation.*]

I took one step
to grab my groceries off that whirling whatchamacallit—
I had the strangest sensation
I was
lifting
into the secret name of things.

One minute you're
struggling
mourning
waiting
getting peanut butter at supermarket,
then—
It hits you.

Life
is

[*She searches for language.*]

on the move.

Now.
                        Now.
        Now.

That great big nothing
that you been feeling inside you.
That great big nothing
that you've been thinking
is a great big something
that needs to be
filled up

washed out
scraped clean—

Is
really

a great big nothing
that's
EVERYTHING.

[*Pause.*]

What the hell?

[*She laughs.*]

Don't know.

A
luminescent
mystery

on
the
move.

NOW.
        NOW. NOW.

I walked out of the store—
Saw a little girl
playing with the wind.

What a big life!

I dropped my groceries–
Waving to the little girl's mother, she was on her cell phone, "She has
the right idea!

Let's/

[LASHONDA *plays with the wind.*]

Shall we/
Let's.

I want to celebrate with you child! I want to celebrate."

NOW.
NOW.
NOW. HA!

EPILOGUE

FEELS SO GOOD/INTIMACY DANCE #2

LASHONDA: Woke up this morning
feeling good
in spite of myself.

[LASHONDA *struts playfully.*]

So good
for
no good reason.

I'm broke
but I'm still sexy.

Earth is still earth
sun is still sun.

Feels
so good
to be
in skin.
I'm real thick with myself.

[*She makes Movement/Gesture/Dance.*]

Life.
I want life.
I confess.

Give me
grace
to
embrace
all

Life.
I want life.

Break my heart open to love.
I want to rise from mud spitting fire.

Here/
This
fleeting
preciousness.

Exquisite
aching
impermanence.

NOW.

Here.

Right
Here

Right/Here

Right
Here

YES.

[*The dance ends.*]

INTERVIEW WITH STACEY KAREN ROBINSON

Diana R. Paulin

Thank you again for taking the time to speak with me about your work and your performance, which I want to reiterate again how much I enjoyed.[1] I also want to congratulate you on receiving the Brio award—Bronx Recognizes Its Own—for best playwright in 2009.[2] I want to start off with a bit more background about your experience both as a playwright and as an actress. I also want to give you a moment to talk about how you moved from thinking of yourself as a writer to thinking of yourself as a playwright.

I've written since I was a child. In high school I discovered playwriting. In college, at Brown University, I took an introductory acting course in order to become a better playwright and caught the acting bug. I worked on a monologue from Ntozake Shange's *for colored girls* and became excited about performance.

I'm going to interrupt you to ask if that led to other performance work, either at Brown or in the surrounding area, before you left Providence.

I performed at Rites and Reason Theatre quite a bit. Rites and Reason Theatre is part of Brown University's Africana Studies Department. It's also one of the oldest black theaters in the country.[3] My first professional appearance was with the Perishable Theatre in Rhode Island. I was a member of their Shows for Young Audiences Company for one summer.

You didn't play a tomato or something . . . You said it was for children.

A gargoyle. I played a gargoyle. It was a sweltering summer. I remember sweating profusely under this big, orange gargoyle head. It was a funny, delightful first professional paid acting job. Anyway, I didn't truly consider pursuing a career in theater until my final year of college. After Brown I went to the actor-training program at Juilliard.[4] Juilliard is a four-year program. I completed two years there. After Juilliard, I worked as an actor, appearing in regional theater productions and [in] Off-Broadway [shows] in New York. I still wrote occasionally, but I didn't actively pursue a career as a playwright. Then, a few years ago, I felt strongly compelled to return to writing.

Well, I wanted to go back to one of your comments that you made about your original decision to take acting, to become a better playwright, and how it has contributed to your voice as a playwright. And, even though you weren't writing publicly, or preparing anything in particular during that time you were acting, are there ways, when you're thinking back now, that those experiences contributed to your skill as a playwright? And, did you, in fact, accomplish what you originally intended to accomplish [becoming a better playwright by becoming a better actor]?

I'm sure being an actor has influenced my writing. The way that I approach acting, what I do first, is try to get to know the text as a text. I read and reread the play, trying to understand what story the playwright is telling. Then I begin the process of embodying the character. The acting process is one of interrogation. You're constantly asking questions, of the script, of yourself. It's transformative.

You mentioned that a few years ago you were inspired or somehow led back to this work [playwrighting], which I'm assuming is *Quiet Frenzy*. So, I want to talk about your return to this particular piece.

I felt compelled to return to writing. Actually, I was both compelled and afraid to write. I was having a lot of nightmares at the time. The dreams were abstract but incredibly disturbing. It sounds silly to say now. For some reason, I felt that if I sat down to write, the nightmares would worsen. But the call to write would not cease. Finally I surrendered. For several months I wrote feverishly. I wrote all the time: on the subway, before I went to bed, as soon as I woke up in the morning—all the time. I wrote until I felt emptied out. Then . . . a kind of silence. I looked at everything that I had written; I write by hand, so it was pages and pages of material. I couldn't find a play. I couldn't find a consistent character. It was a hodgepodge of seemingly disparate monologues, scenes, and poetry. I went through the work, looking to understand myself and I couldn't. I couldn't understand why I was so afraid to write. I couldn't understand why I was compelled to write. I didn't enjoy the work that I had written. I was disgusted by the whole episode. Honestly, I almost threw all of the work away. Instead, I put everything in a box and put it aside. A few years later, I was invited be part of the Hourglass Solo Lab, a writing collective for female solo performers sponsored by the Hourglass Group [Theatre].[5] When I received the invitation, I thought, I've got to deal with that box. So, I took out the box and began a long process of investigating the material inside. I would make piles. This pile was work that had similar themes or imagery. This pile, monologues, this, poetry, etcetera—just trying to figure out what was there, trying to find my mind.

And did you stop having that nightmare after you started writing?

I did. The feeling of being compelled to write didn't go away. But the nightmares stopped almost immediately.

Which is interesting because you talk about how you physically write and, for you, it sounds like this process during this particular period was very physical, in that as you were writing you were putting your different monologues in piles. Not discounting the creative and imaginative part of it, but the physical piles of themes, and writing out [everything] by hand, putting the pages in the box, then taking them out, and resurrecting them from the box; there's a lot of movement and physicality to it [the process of developing a one-woman performance] that I really hadn't thought about until you were talking about it.

I even put bits of text on pieces of colored construction paper scattered around the room. Eventually I came to [the] point where I had a series of monologues that intrigued me.

Have you always conceived of it as a solo performance piece?

The piece is different than anything else that I've ever written, in that I didn't begin with any conception of where I would end. I took the opportunity, when I was invited to be part of this writing collective for solo performers, to try to get at that box of writing. Rather than a decision, it was a question. If I go back to that box is there a solo piece in there? That was the exploration. The initial process was about surrender and discovery. Once I had the foundational monologues, another phase of writing began. Once I could hear the play, so to speak, I began to craft it.

I [also] want to talk about any pieces that you wrote before or after *Quiet Frenzy.*

My first solo show, *Deja and the January River,* is about a little girl named Deja and her brother and their adventures in a magical play-world. During the course of the play, we learn that the brother is imaginary, that the little girl created him and the play-world to escape and transcend the trauma of her real life. I did a semester abroad in Brazil.[6] I studied at the Pontifical Catholic University in Rio. As part of a project for one of my classes, I interviewed several women. Part of the assignment was to translate the interviews into English. I did a translation for meaning. Then, just for fun, I translated one of the interviews, an interview with a woman named DeJaneira, word for word. When I translated the interview word for word it sounded like a little girl talking. *Deja and the January River* is not directly about the life of DeJaneira or the interview, but I was inspired by the word-for-word translation and the interviews with the women and my time in Brazil. I wrote a one-act play called *Wounded Heart.* It's about a couple dealing with the loss of a child. The play takes place on the birthday of the child who has passed. It's a play about trauma. In *Wounded Heart,* I was responding to a tragic family story that I only have a few details about. It was a way for me to process my [own] known/unknown history.

Right. As you were talking about both of these plays, I was thinking about *Quiet Frenzy,* and this idea of trauma; you made the comment—although I think it's the opposite—you made a comment in reference to writing about subjects or characters that you don't necessarily know that much about; it seems so much like this building [process], this progression toward *Quiet Frenzy,* was also generated by something you couldn't really work out at first. You didn't know what it was about. And it's interesting that these other two, *Deja and the January River,* as well as *Wounded Heart,* are also about a kind of discovery process that each seems informed—and maybe you can tell me more about each instance—by an event or a moment in your life. *Quiet Frenzy* was, in part, compelled by dreams, and *Wounded Heart* by this event from unknown past [events] in your family. Maybe you can tell me more about *Deja and the January River* and these stories. I imagine the setting outside of the United States and coming back, and your knowledge of the Brazilian space, a Catholic space, has its own way of shaping or pushing you toward the unknown. But [at the same time] it [also] seems like you *do* know, each time you tap into something that is part of your unconscious or something that you're wrestling with.

I think writing is a way for me to deal with my restless, unresolved, deep underbelly stuff. That's why I think the nightmares and feeling compelled to write were intermixed. I'm unearthing, uncovering my shadow or unconscious, possibly. One thing I haven't mentioned. For a long time I was consumed by the Egyptian Isis/Osiris myth.[7] It's a story that I used to think about a lot that really got inside of me. In one part of the story, Osiris, Isis's husband, has been killed and dismembered. Pieces of his body are scattered all over Egypt. Isis travels the country trying to gather the body, trying to recollect the discarded pieces of his body. There's something about that in my work, some mythos about recollecting the discarded pieces of oneself in order to come to wholeness, about having to journey to recollect and reclaim oneself.

At so many different levels travel, both literally and physically, but also through the layers of history, is often fragmented for so many of us. But also psychically, like when you have those moments of inspiration or connection or spiritual awaking, and you try to find out what it means. And that [notion] made me want to ask you to talk about the title, *Quiet Frenzy,* and the oppositions [invoked by it]. The title is very compelling.

The title came very late in the process. The play was untitled for a long time. When I started to get to know LaShonda, the protagonist, I realized a juicy thing about her. While she's living an ordinary life, all these extraordinary things are happening in her inner life. *Quiet Frenzy,* to me, describes the epic depth of our everyday experience. We're at work or the supermarket or waiting on the subway and huge—multifaceted, multidimensional things are happening inside of us . . . so, that's part of it. Also, *Quiet Frenzy* is a description of the tension, duality in LaShonda's experience. There are a lot of opposites at play in the play. There is fragmentation and integration, there's breath and breathlessness, there's loss of memory and created/imagined memory. The event that has plagued LaShonda, the event that has been the cause/site of her disintegration is the accidental death of her twin sister. The car crash is the most awful thing that has happened to her; yet, it's her best memory. She has no memory of the instant of impact. Instead, she remembers this astonishing moment of seeing her sister multiplied. It's her worst-best day. So the title tries to get to all of those things. The epic-ness of our emotional lives, the tension of complex experience . . . Yes. So, the title is trying to capture some of that.

And it does. I think it captures the tension, even in the words that you choose. I mentioned to a friend of mine that I was seeing your play, *Quiet Frenzy*. She immediately, without knowing anything about your play, said, "Oh that describes my life. That is my life right there." And I think that it speaks to that multidimensionality, the sense in which everyday moments carry these different levels of meaning. And, going back to this idea of trauma, there are these little moments of trauma but there are also moments—these coping mechanisms and survival tools—that have enabled us to survive over centuries or we wouldn't be here. It's the trauma that you forget or remember in a different way or reconstruct in a way that enables you to move forward. And I think the way in which you describe the memory of her [LaShonda's] twin sister's death as this beautiful memory, the worst-best day really encapsulates the complexity of how we deal [with trauma]—particularly in thinking about African American identity and women who literally embody or repress so much of those everyday traumas and cope with them, whether it's through laughter, whether it's through an imaginative moment, or seeing beauty where others might see horror. And these ways of using other psychic spaces, not just for disintegration but also for healing and rebuilding, really emerge in your performance. I think it was also what the audience, that I was fortunate enough to be a part of, responded to so intensely and was so moved by—that complexity and multidimensionality in your performance, and by the different moments that you literally played out onstage.

Thank you. It's really important to me that even though this woman is in crisis, she's still fully alive in the world. That's why it was important for me to put so much humor into the play. LaShonda is in crisis but it's a healing crisis, a fertile crisis. Like all those descent-to-the-underworld myths; you go underground but return renewed. There is descent, but the process of descent heals and remakes you. In the play, LaShonda is moving through fragmentation toward wholeness. She's reclaiming herself and coming to terms with a painful past. It's both a descent and a birth story, both a disintegration and resurrection [*laughter*] . . . kind of piece.

Well, I know that you've talked about this piece as being in its infancy, but I wanted to ask you, in the places where you have performed, have you had similar responses from audience members, or have they illuminated something about the performance that you hadn't considered before? What kinds of audiences have come to see your work? I am sure you'll have many more opportunities to get more responses, but, so far, what kind of responses have you received?

The performance at Northwestern was only the sixth performance of the completed play. The finished play is still very new. I did staged readings throughout the developmental process, so a lot of different audiences have seen excerpts or earlier drafts of the piece. There have been a lot of different responses to the work. Some audience members have really enjoyed the structure of the play. One woman thanked me for respecting her. She said she thought the play respected her as an audience member by requiring her full engagement. Another audience member disliked the aesthetics of the play. She told me I should have a program note that prepared people. Maybe something like: "Get ready. This is a nonlinear, nontraditional story." Some black women have celebrated LaShonda's silly, goofy side. They've said they appreciate that she's quirky and not solely tragic. The play definitely seems to resonate with people who have dealt with loss, grief, and trauma. People have said that they feel affirmed by and reflected in LaShonda's journey.

That's the sense I got from the responses, after the performance, that I was able to see/hear. There was a lot of connection and appreciation, not just for the story itself, but also for your aesthetics, your voice, and your use of the space. There was so much that went into your solo performance with minimal staging; but still your voice, the lighting, your movement, the language and the delivery were the parts of the performance that people not only commented on, but also felt that you used in such a productive way. And although I saw it only in one place and each theater is going to have its own dimensions, its own sound, space,

and lighting, I felt like that [the audience's remarks] spoke to in the way in which you engaged the audience. They were paying attention to all [of it], echoing the multidimensionality [of the performance]. It's not just the words, it's not just the nonlinearity, it's all these things working together to create this piece that has, as you said, this multidimensionality, this tension—these ordinary, sometimes funny, sometimes more intense, experiences of trauma and, as you said, "the epic-ness of our everyday lives," which I love. I'll put that as the tag in my emails.

How great. One thing that was a little surprising to me, when I got to the point of finally being able to enter the play as an actor, is how completely I would have to engage my body. I knew the play would have movement in it. I wrote movement into the play but still some moments are challenging—for example, the moment at the subway where LaShonda can't move her legs. What is the physicality of her not being able to move? How is that expressed? That has been a rich exploration, discovering the physical life of the play.

And it requires, and asks, your viewers to participate in a way that's active. I'm speaking from personal experience but I felt that there was a sense of it being a collective experience, although you're doing most of the work physically and with your voice. I have one final question. I know I've exhausted you by now. When you were talking about memory and re-memory, I just kept thinking of Toni Morrison, and your interest in writing. I was wondering what you like to read or see? What kinds of stories inspire you and excite you or have in the past? And do you see your work in dialogue with any of it?

I'm a voracious reader. I read all different kinds of things. Zora Neale Hurston is deep in my heart. I can't even tell you how many times I've read *Their Eyes Were Watching God*. Toni Morrison's work has also affected me profoundly. Recently, I've been reading and thinking a lot about the work of Gwendolyn Brooks. *The Idiot*, by Dostoyevsky, is one of my favorites. I like creation myths. The last few years I have been trying to reread books that I read in high school that I don't have a strong memory of. I recently reread *The Scarlet Letter* and *Tess of the d'Urbervilles*. So many different books to love. I feel like my love of reading is that of a child. I read like I did as a child, full bite [*sic*], full delight. I have to read things more than once in order to be critical. To answer the other part of your question, I'm not exactly sure what my work is in dialogue with; it's an interesting question. Maybe I'm too close to the piece to know. Some people I've worked with have really influenced me. I got an opportunity to work with Daniel Alexander Jones, Laurie Carlos, and Sharon Bridgforth pretty early on in my career. They're all masters in the theatrical jazz aesthetic. Meeting them helped shape me and influenced the trajectory of my work.

And I'm sure, as you said, you'll be able to answer a lot of these questions in a different way, when you're in a different place in relation to your work. I also really appreciate that combination and that tension that you talk about, even in reading, with pleasure and critique. That tension is so much a part of consumption. OK, I'm consuming this. I'm enjoying it and I'm not critiquing it. But it's that layered engagement with material that [so many of us experience]. I think you're not alone [in the way in which you read]. I don't know if it's childlike or a real, full personhood way of reading and taking in works that we appreciate and enjoy, or return to. I will certainly return to your work. As I said, I feel fortunate to have been able to meet you and hear more about your work, but really to watch you perform and listen to the enthusiastic and laudatory comments, both from professionals in the field and students in performance studies in February [2011], when I viewed the play. I thank you for sharing your work and look forward to the evolution of your work, both as a playwright and as a performer. As you can tell, I'm winding down because I kept you for so long. Is there any last word or comment that you wanted to make, besides that there's more to come? It ain't over yet?

I like that. I think I'm going to start saying that all the time. It ain't over yet. Yes. That's a good way to dance in the world. It ain't over yet. That's right. Well said.

NOTES

1. Visiting Artist Stacey Karen Robinson performed her one-woman show, *Quiet Frenzy,* at Northwestern University's Annie May Swift Studio as part of the Performance Studies' solo/black/woman Performance Series on February 19, 2011.

2. The Bronx Council on the Arts sponsors the Bronx Recognizes Its Own award (BRIO). This award provides direct funding, in the form of $3,000 grants, to individual Bronx artists who create literary, media, visual, and performance pieces. Award winners also complete a one-time public service activity.

3. Professor George Houston Bass founded Rites and Reason Theatre in 1970, as part of the then Afro-American Studies Program at Brown University, influenced by the black arts movement. It develops work by undergraduates, graduates, and professional playwrights. It is one of the oldest continuously producing black theaters in the nation.

4. The prestigious Juilliard School is located at Lincoln Center in New York City. This private art conservatory provides artistic education/training for gifted musicians, dancers, and actors from around the world.

5. The Hourglass Group, Ltd., was founded in 1998 by Elyse Singer, Carolyn Baeumier, and Nina Hellman with the goal of developing and supporting innovative new plays. In 2005 they inaugurated a writer/performer lab for women solo artists.

6. Stacey Karen Robinson spent a semester living in Brazil while she was studying at Brown University.

7. This Egyptian myth tells the story of King Osiris's death. He was murdered by his jealous brother, Set, who dismembered and scattered his body parts across Egypt. Osiris's wife, Isis, found his body parts, reassembled them, embalmed him, and gave him a proper burial. Osiris then ruled over the afterworld as king among the deserving spirits of the dead.

THE BODY, TRAUMA, AND HISTORY
IN STACEY KAREN ROBINSON'S *QUIET FRENZY*

Nadine George-Graves

In *Quiet Frenzy* we bear witness to LaShonda's experience moving to the next phase of her life some time after the car accident that has killed her twin sister, Neecy. Life for LaShonda has become an abrupted process and the liminal space (that space ripe with possibility for performance, of course) is the arena for the 51-minute performance. In this space we are given vivid snapshots of insight into the character, but we are also given subtle, more opaque glimpses into larger implications.

As time is displaced for the main character, memory loops back, sometimes to the traumatic event, sometimes to an ancient death figure, sometimes to a nowhere space. Memory controls her body and memory takes possession of her body. Though we cannot locate memory, and though memory is not always reliable, it is the effect of the traumatic event lived in the present through memory that has paused LaShonda. Therefore, by focusing on LaShonda's memory of the trauma (personal and mythic) and its effect on her body, we are able to cut across critical race theory, performance studies, and psychoanalytic theory to lend critical insight into this piece. Three distinct themes of the performance allow us to analyze the piece along these terms.

The first and arguably the most salient is the body. In fact, within the context of *solo/black/woman* this is where we need to begin. These performances are all about black women alone physically present onstage and it is from here we should begin to understand *Quiet Frenzy*. LaShonda works through her ordeal by attending to the effects it has on her physically. Secondly, the piece asks us to consider the trauma the woman endures after the death of her sister. On the surface this seems to have nothing to do with being a black woman alone but, as this essay will show, trauma, race, and gender are inextricably linked in this show. Finally, LaShonda's relationship with a dead woman begs for analysis. Though not overtly stated, this ancient woman can easily be read as LaShonda's connection to the African diaspora and the larger, deeper, global trauma of historic and present black femaleness which must necessarily be part and parcel of LaShonda's personal trauma. Working through trauma by means of this spiritual experience has profound consequences for her sense of herself and the ways in which she ultimately learns to re-navigate everyday life.

THE BODY

Again, attending to the black female body onstage is probably the most important initial phenomenological experience we have with the performance. Since we are given her name only once and quite late in the piece (as her response to a flirtatious man who asks her name), she exists for us mostly as a black woman alone. The program begins in darkness and we hear her breath—hurried and frenzied. The first lines set the scene: "BOOM. My heart popped. A crack in time—All the stars snapped inward" (258) Even in darkness the body is evoked and in that evocation the mise-en-scène is presented as "a hole in history," to borrow from Suzan-Lori Parks. But unlike Parks, whose plays deal with History with a capital "H" (and probably all the other letters as well), Robinson is dealing with an individual's personal history (albeit with sizeable resonances). LaShonda leaves her own private light-draining chasm by going through the process we witness through performance—one might argue *because* we witness her process through performance. The traumatic event that we learn about later has exploded her heart. Her spirit, represented by the stars, has turned inward instead of shining outward. We understand the potential vibrancy of her personality later in the performance, which makes her interruption all the more tragic. Even though she might be out of linear time and her story comes to us in fragments, we still understand a process, a journey after which she emerges with a better sense of self—a journey after which, we presume, she can move again. In the first moments, the body, breath, and trauma converge to open up time so that where many of us go through daily life, she has to pause. But through the journey of the piece we come to understand this pause as a caesura—an opening in space, time, and subjectivity that allows us to delve into the deeper implications of this individual's life. This opening is not empty and silent—it is jam-packed quiet and frenzied, it moves and reckons and requires both audience and performer. When the lights come up on her we see that she is a stout, medium brown-skinned, bald woman. She later tells us that she has intentionally cut off all her hair, which can be read as an act to get control of her life through her body. In fact, we can understand the stages of this process for her by not only listening to the poetic language but also by watching what happens to her body.

Robinson also engages movement and stillness in important ways. For example, LaShonda gets psychiatric help after getting frozen on the subway platform. As she tries to go through daily life her body stops her—literally. Instead of embracing life she finds herself always holding her breath. She catches herself not breathing. These moments of stillness are replicated onstage with her arrested body. Terry McMillian's novel *Waiting to Exhale* might be considered too popular a reference, but waiting to exhale is a valuable metaphor here, and a number of scholars have found it useful especially for black feminist criticism in the late 1990s and early 2000s. It is helpful to think through LaShonda's pause using this metaphor as a touchstone. In these conversations, we consider race, gender, human connection, and healing because women (for our purposes, black women in particular) have certain gender roles created by history, narrative, stereotypes, and compulsory normalizing processes. As we work to expose and untangle these processes we think of black female identity as sitting in the inhale. Tense, held, and suspended even while daily life moves on. Like the ladies in the play *for colored girls who have considered suicide/when the rainbow is enuf,* Robinson uses poetry, movement, and humor to provoke the bodies, LaShonda's and ours, to exhale. All three are practical strategies for releasing tension, thereby allowing breath to flow.

In *Quiet Frenzy,* LaShonda's actual body means something semiotically and psychologically. Though not a stereotypically fat, dark, desexualized mammy figure, we should consider our initial expectations of the character given the history of representation. Whether we expected her to be the strong black woman, a mammy, a mother Africa, an Oprah Winfrey, a "magic negro," a lesbian, a force of nature, and so on, Robinson immediately defies expectations. Beginning in darkness is a good strategy here. The black female body has historically been used as public spectacle for a social satisfaction that, though shifting over time, ultimately leads to a kind of social death for the figure of the black female. Robinson resists this. So we are left to do something else with her image. She is girly, playful, and intelligent. She moves beautifully. She is sensual. She doesn't have all of the answers. Most importantly, she wants to love again and be open to being loved. But in order to do that, she must first establish her existence on a first-order cognitive and physical level. She says, "I thought I wasn't real. I thought I had ceased to exist because I have been here and nobody has said anything to me until you said 'hello.' Then I realized I'm still here. I'm really here. Right?" (262). This Althusserian hail does not mark her, however, like Fanon, as a Negro. It is not the state forcing her into a specific role nor is it explicitly linked to racial identity. She is not an Ellisonian invisible woman making a life in an overtly racist society.[1] Also, this moment in her life does not reference the *ubuntu* ethic linking existence of the individual to the wholeness of the group. Rather, she is simply ignored. Ignored, probably like many black women in many situations, but compounded with her personal situation this ignoring leads to an existential crisis of epic proportions. Even in her assertion of being, she has doubt and looks for confirmation.

Confirmation comes from the way her poetic language around the events of her life works her body. As in *for colored girls,* she moves fluidly, is comfortable in her body, and uses movement to move to a new place. It is not surprising that *for colored girls* is an important influence for Robinson. In her interview with Diana Paulin, she says of her early expereinces with performance, "I took an acting kind of 101 course, and I had this kind of experience with Ntozake's *for colored girls,* I don't want to call it an out-of-body experience, but some kind of special spiritual experience with performing the work. And I thought, I should think about performance."

Like the ladies in *for colored girls,* LaShonda is trying to find truth in herself. Although discourse around "authentic" black female identity is well-rehearsed, indeed overly so, the attempt on LaShonda's part to understand herself on a truer level in order to move on cannot be ignored. Late in the piece, in a humorous reminisence of childhood, she reminds us of the adolescent challenge to authentic being through the accusation of "being phony." Though performed humorously, allegations of disingenuous or somehow false identity cut to the heart of this performance. In another moment, we hear about a party she goes to where she unfortunately gets drunk and makes a spectacle of herself. At one point someone at the party talks about getting plastic surgery and she begins to wail. "Why are we taught to hate our body!" Were she not drunk this might have been a fruitful conversation about societal challenges to self-love.

Instead, she suggests a group samba dance, after which she strips off her shirt and vomits all over herself. She is made keenly aware of the disconnect between her intellectual ideology and her inability to reconcile what she knows with how she lives everyday life. She is even rather good at self-psychoanalysis. At one point she says, "I'm searching for a story outlines to existence. I have just one pure wish. I usedta be beautiful, remember? I was ripe full of scent before I knew what life was all about. I'm searching for a story to give me form. I haunt myself. I feel like I've been walking the earth searching for you but really I've been in this room asleep" (265). She believes that if she understands her story then she'll be able to be a whole physical person again. Several physical gestures allow her to attend to her body, particularly a hand around her head gesture in which she flutters her hand near the back of her head and draws it out and back as if clearing the clutter out of her brain to facilitate her search for Neecy. This gesture epitomizes how the body is at the center of the process toward healing because it is primarily the bodies of individuals that societal forces move as acts of ordering, categorizing, and ultimately controlling. The discursive site of the black female body as a locus of ideological debate seems always present in power negotiations. So it is not surprising that LaShonda, and other "colored girls," must attend to their physical presence in order to continue.

TRAUMA

Robinson also asks us to consider the trauma LaShonda endures after the death of her twin sister Neecy. Beyond missing her, or having survivor's guilt, LaShonda literally can't move on without her. Interestingly, the story is not about the physical pain of injuries she sustained (she was also in the car accident) beyond a fleeting reference to a scar, but rather the psychological pain of having lost her twin, ostensibly a part of herself. Despite her claim that "falling apart is so very mundane," the trauma of losing her sister is born on her body in a number of spectacular ways. Psychoanalytic and critical race theory, especially in terms of gender, seems apropos here though we must be careful around the slippage between persuasive theory and metaphor.

LaShonda is truamatized by the loss of her sister, ostensibly not by the institutionalized systems of racial or gender oppression. However, upon deeper examination, it becomes clear that because of the body she has and because of her spiritual and intellectual relationship with the past, trauma, race, and gender are inextricably linked in this piece. The key is in attending to more complicated matrices of historio-systemic trauma and individual trauma even in stories not overtly about Race and Gender with capital letters. Because of this, it is appropriate to analyze this work within the long history of black women navigating ways to articulate trauma, be it rape, torture, human trafficking, psychological violence, sexual stigma, or degradation. This is not the known cultural script with the usual suspects. Race and gender might not be the underlying cause of LaShonda's trauma as in the usual case studies, but it is part and parcel of her story and more so it is part and parcel of our phenomenolgical experiences as witnesses.

We should not assume the testimony in *Quiet Frenzy* operates only in the usual hegemonic spaces some scholars assume. We need to resist the totalizing spell of that rhetoric in this instance. One could argue that there is no way around it, but I find it unconvincing, especially from the several live performances I saw of *Quiet Frenzy* and from what I've gathered about other performances. Phenomenologically, one cannot ignore the actual venues and audiences in favor of the imagined uber-hegemonic audience. In terms of spectatorship, the spaces created by audiences for this piece I've experienced or heard about are generally affirming atmospheres that allow LaShonda to go through her process. Rather than an assumed heterosexual, male, white supremacist gaze, diverse spectators take on the important role of sanctioning the healing process. The spaces created by these audiences resist old assumptions about the power dynamics of performance, and it is vital to take into consideration how bodily and oral memory testify in these other spaces. Though arguably ever-present, the white supremacist, misogynistic hegemony was not a palpable force in these spaces. And that means something. As in performances of *for colored girls*, these spaces are constructive in terms of race and gender for the performer/character as well as for audience members. As witnesses, we audience members are made vulnerable, we become enablers of the testimony and we are responsible for it. When this happens in safer spaces, work to heal and move on (for all of us) takes important steps. As Uttara Coorlawala might say, it matters for whom you do solo performance work as a black woman.

This goes beyond having a refreshing story in which we are not bombarded with "The Man." Rather, it allows us to focus in on the intricacies of LaShonda's story. There is no obvious antagonist. There is no danger of black men being cast as the enemy (as Shange was accused of doing with *for colored girls*) to obscure our analysis. On the contrary, in many respects, heterosexual love with a black man seems to be part of the goal. Ultimately, Robinson asks us to give our full attention to this particular black woman and her particular trauma.

THE DEAD WOMAN AND EVERYDAY LIFE

That said, LaShonda's story does not exist in hermetically sealed isolation from the historical realities of being a black woman in the United States of America. Where we might think we are on sure ground, Robinson shifts the terrain when she introduces the dead woman of the past whom either Robinson steps into or who possesses LaShonda. Although the story resists the discursive limits of the overdetermined black female body, Robinson also gives us a figure through which we can recognize that the African American woman is always already a sufferer of trauma owing to the original sins of this country.

Like Robbie McCauley in *Sally's Rape,* LaShonda has to look to the past in a grand reckoning in order to move forward. She says "I can't get back to where the story begins" (268). At first she goes back to the day of the accident. Not enough to be the day her sister dies and she lives, insult precedes injury as she recounts that it was a particularly beautiful and happy day for them. "Even her [Neecy's] skin was breathing. We were eating sun" (272). With Neecy in the past, an angel, the performance becomes LaShonda's ritual to evoke her sister and make peace. But going back to the day of the accident is not far back enough. She needs to reckon with the dead woman of the past who visits her.

Not only a dead woman but death herself is stalking her, LaShonda thinks. LaShonda used to think she was the angel of death coming for her but then realized that she may hold insight. So instead of fearing the dead woman, she now seeks her out to learn her story—a story of a (if not "the") black woman "born into a curse forced upon [her] mother's hot pot." She begins speaking in tongues after the psychiatrist session to help her through her immobility and takes on who she thinks is the angel of death. Marked as her connection to the mythic past of black female identity, LaShonda calls her an "ancient mud mud dead dead cemetery dead dead-looking woman." And in her dream, the dead woman asks her, "What would you do with my story?" perhaps as a challenge to her need to go back to the beginning of the story. "You come for all this expecting to shake every secret from my hips, the key under all these rolls, this weight, this burden. Enter my tomb. It's empty. Ha!" (276). LaShonda's memory cycling back through Neecy to this dead woman points to the span of the cross-generational narratives that produce both collective and individual trauma. And the woman's tricksterlike denial of epiphany points to the holes in History (capital H) that may never be fully understood. Therefore, full understanding of the story (personal and historical) might not be the prescriptive key to healing.

Rather, a reckoning with the ghosting of the dead dead woman of the past, the ghosting of Black Female Identity writ large, and the ghosting of her personal memories of Neecy and what they had together are what LaShonda needs instead of the self-haunting that defines her day to day. Although a solo performance, she is not alone. There are many ghosts on the stage with her. Like LaShonda, we audience members must also reckon with the ghosts of performance onstage and in everyday life. And this reckoning must happen on everyday as well as spiritual levels. The weightiness of the dead dead mud dead woman collides with attempts to step onto a subway train, flirt, or attend a party. Though she tries to ignore the fact that she needed to attend to these ghosts and go on with her daily life, she soon learns that there are some things about which one has no choice. In the first story of her life that we hear, a brother on the street flirts with her, recognizing her stellarness by calling her "celestial." The compliment makes her day but when she sees him again later at a basketball game she is unable to reply fully. The interruption is brought on by what she thinks of as the angel of death. She tells us that the angel of death won't let her do basic things like ordering egg rolls and chicken wings. In this mundane act the dead woman peeks around the shoulder of the man behind the counter and says "Gotcha. Ya can't hide" (266). The dead woman forces LaShonda to attend to her own spirit, which she tells the doctor has left her and traveled across the chasm of time. Of course, without her spirit she cannot have her self. And this in turn can be extended to its larger implications. In the interview Robinson says of the Isis/Osiris myth, "It's a story that I used to think about a lot that really got inside of me. In one part of the story, Osiris, Isis's husband, has been killed and dismembered. Pieces of his body are scattered all over Egypt. Isis travels the country trying to gather the body, trying to recollect the discarded pieces of his body. There's something about that in my work, some mythos about recollecting the discarded pieces of oneself in order to come to wholeness, about having to journey to recollect and reclaim oneself" (299). On some level LaShonda knows this as well when she speculates that she is missing "the sacred symbol that animates." The dead woman could be that for her, but LaShonda runs from her until she stops moving. Only after she offers her self, her body, flesh, and emotions ritualistically and surrenders (ostensibly to the doctor but metaphorically to something larger) and tells the story of the accident is she able to allow the dead woman in.

Not only is her falling apart "so very mundane" that it reaches to the profound, it is also resolved in processes that reverse what we might expect. The dead woman says that rather than folding LaShonda into her story, she wants to be folded into LaShonda's story. In fact, they are part and parcel of each other. She prophecies that she will begin again gathering all the little pieces of herself because she has something to offer. LaShonda must grant the woman mercy before she can get her own redemption.

The resolution in *Quiet Frenzy* seems abrupt. She recounts her near-first kiss. Then she recounts the experience of riding down an elevator that happens to free-fall in the wind, which triggers an impetus as one passenger tells another who is upset by the free-fall to "get yourself together" (288). LaShonda simply takes this as the direction she needs in her life. She finally receives the visitation from Neecy that she so longs for, tells her she feels guilty, misses her, and then she's good to let her go and move on. Again, like the country western song LaShonda makes up, Robinson thwarts our expectations. There is no magic prescription.

In the visitation LaShonda also tells Neecy that she wants to love and be unafraid. She can't lose her grasp of reality like the old man who spent the last ten years of his life waiting for his wife to come home. She can't get stuck on the subway bench forever. She recognizes that she has much love to give but it is all directed to the past and to the absence of Neecy.

All she wanted to say was "I miss you" and "I love you." "Thank you for being mine." She then feels an intense connection in a mundane everyday experience of accidentally brushing the cashier's hand at the grocery store. She recognizes that she couldn't distinguish between who was who and where the cashier's skin ended and hers began. The meaning of life hits one during mundane moments—"life is on the move now." On leaving the supermarket she sees a little girl playing with the wind. She allows her free spirit to infect her. She allows her skin to feel good again. "Woke up this morning feeling good in spite of myself" (293). Feeling good for no good reason—we are again denied the magic formula. It simply felt good to be "in skin" for LaShonda. She allows herself to want life and open her heart to love. The performance ends with her touching herself saying "yesssss," allowing the exhalation to finally flow through her body as she moves to the end of her own rainbow, breathing out "yessssss" on the downhill side. The piece that paused in the inhale—the held breath, and sputtered with frenzied attempts to catch breath—finally ends in the exhale that we have all been waiting for.

NOTE

1. For more on these concepts, see Louis Althusser, "Ideology and Ideological State Apparatuses," in *Lenin and Philosophy and Other Essays* (1971), 121–76, 162; Frantz Fanon, *Black Skins, White Masks* (New York: Grove, 1967); Ralph Ellison, *Invisible Man* (New York: Random House, 1952).

WORKS CITED

Althusser, Louis. "Ideology and Ideological State Apparatuses," in *Lenin and Philosophy and Other Essays* (1971), 121–76, 162.

Coorlawala, Uttara. "It Matters for Whom You Dance: Audience Participation in Rasa Theory." In *Audience Participation: Essays on Inclusion in Performance*, ed. Susan Kattwinkel, 37–54. Westport, Conn.: Greenwood, 2003.

Ellison, Ralph. *Invisible Man*. New York: Random House, 1952.

Fanon, Frantz. *Black Skins, White Masks*. New York: Grove, 1967.

McCauley, Robbie. "Sally's Rape." In *A Sourcebook on African American Performance: Plays, People, Movements*, ed. Annemarie Bean, 246–64. New York: Routledge, 1999.

McMillian, Terry. *Waiting to Exhale*. New York: Viking Penguin, 1992.

Parks, Suzan-Lori. *The America Play and Other Works*. New York: Theatre Communications Group, 1994.

Shange, Ntozake. *for colored girls who have considered suicide when the rainbow is enuf*. New York: Scribner, 1989.

MILKWEED

Misty DeBerry

PRODUCTION HISTORY

Milkweed premiered at Links Hall in Chicago, Illinois, in May 2009. It was directed by Cheryl Lynn Bruce and coproduced by Misty DeBerry, Jane M. Saks, the Ellen Stone Belic Institute for the Study of Women and Gender in the Arts and Media, Columbia College, Chicago. The stage manager was Susana Pelayo, with lighting design by Margaret Nelson, set design by Tia Etu, audio design by Ramah Jihan, and image design by Jasmine Greer. Matthais Pierce was the video technician and Bryan Saner was the movement coach. Valerie Robbins was the production assistant for the performance.

CHARACTERS

[*all played by the same woman*]
Monarch, a shapeshifter. She is at once a narrator, a priest, a priestess, and an embodied soul riff
Stain, a student (mid-twenties)
Glow, a poet (late thirties, she appears at multiple ages)
Bernadette, a teacher (mid-fifties)

TIME

In flux

SETTING

A three-room apartment.
Sparse. Stain is in the living room, Glow is in the bedroom, and Bernadette is in the kitchen.

MONARCH [*opening*]: I am Madam Monarch.

Born in June I was part of the "summer generation" but come September I set out—no landmark in sight—for Mexico. Not everyone got to go; only those specially selected for the journey. Like the slave I lit out, the heavens my map, my north star was the sun.

When we finally arrived—me and ten thousand of my closest friends—we flung ourselves into the waiting arms of fir trees and slept . . . for nearly three months. You know a sister needs a nap after a road trip.

When we awoke, we made haste, searching for milkweed, searching for milkweed. Ahhh, milkweed . . . [*naughty laughter*]

Milkweed's a funky little plant with a bit of a bite [*beat*] seeing as how it's poisonous.

Toxic.

Venomous milk pumps through its veins. One bite's enough to take a life . . . save mine. Ha! This is what I snacked on to survive.

Next we girls laid about five hundred eggs . . . [*proudly*] apiece! Deposited each on the underside of a leaf,
a single leaf
a single leaf of milkweed where each little one will feast greedily, gorge itself.

A Thanksgiving Day three weeks long!
Got milk . . . weed?

To make room for their bigger bellies, they'll shed five times or more.
Then they'll stop.
They'll stop to spin
a final skin
and wait
for metamorphosis.

And now three tender souls summon me forth to bear witness and to bless their transformations. One's on the hunt for a prayer to believe in, one lays open a jealous heart, and one treads a fine line between pleasure and principle.

Know this—they will emerge bold, wings pumping warrior blood made from toxic milk. Poison, now a part of them, shows itself as blazing hues—a colorful defense foiling would-be predators.

Now, *that* is fashion forward.
They will be as I am—pure milkweed in flight.
A deadly beauty.
One taste of me will bring you to your knees and make confession of your last breath.
And let me be clear—I ain't bragging or dropping a threat.
Please. [*beat*] It's just how I roll.

[*Transition.*]

STAIN: Well, my mother named me Stain. I mean, you know . . . hey whatever—I like my name and all, you know, *now*. You know but, being in school, you know as a kid with Stain as your name is . . . you know . . . hell.

You know I don't even know how . . . how, how, how she came up with my name. She never would say, and it ain't like I didn't ask her. I mean a name like Lucy you don't really have to ask nobody about. You know you just, you know you just, you just, you just, you just figure, OK—she likes the name Lucy, or, or, or she likes someone named Lucy, or hell Lucy is like a—slick version of Lucky. Hell I don't know. But—OK . . . But Stain—you . . . want some extra information on Stain. But, let me be clear . . . my mom don't offer anything extra.

I don't know, I don't know . . . used to think that maybe while she was, was you know pregnant with me—maybe my dad took and punched her in her face one night and she got inspired by some new bruise coloring her face—maybe like some Rorschach shit she saw her unborn baby in that bruise and . . . "Stain!" You know what I mean? You know what I mean. I mean I don't think she was casual about it. Naming your kid is a big deal. I know if I ever had a kid . . . I mean I wouldn't just flip through a book—or pick some famous person I like. A person's name to me is a verb. I think a person's name sums up the one action that—that person is at their core. And Stain can be a verb—sure. But wearing this name I feel more like a pronoun. Like—there her is . . . just some shit my mom got stuck with on account of having to fuck my dad. You know what I mean? You know what I mean.

And besides I think your child will tell you what its name is—you know—while it's growing inside of you. Have you ever met someone and thought they sure don't look like their name? Well maybe 'cause that's not the name they wanted for themselves but they just been wearing it so long—they went on and got used to it.

'Cause I don't take personal ownership of my name. Rather—like my momma—guess I'm just stuck with myself. So what am I gonna do—give up my name? I don't know—all I'm saying is names should be like prayers—something you can instantly believe in.

STAIN: I first dug Sheila because she was cute—and she was the only one who never asked me to repeat my name. I was working at Bath and Body Works and she came in . . . And I'm not the physical type, I don't usually go for people because of their bodies really—I just feel things out you know. But she was fine. And so I chatted her up. Got her number. Called her. And we go out on a date. We go to see some play, some play where this dude thinks his wife is fucking his best friend, but his best friend is really fucking with his head, but he can't see through the setup, so he kills his wife . . . It was one of those . . . Shakespeare's. She was an actress, so. So we do that whole thing and we go to her place and you know I wanna do it, I want to do it! I'm so excited, I'm ready to go. But she wants to party a bit first. Fine. So we drink some. Fine. Put some music on. Cool. And then you know, we start touching on each other and stuff.

And I don't know, for some reason I got all nervous and stuff. And so I say "Wait." And I am not a "wait" kinda girl. I mean I have slept with a whole lot of people . . . And that's done for me what I needed it to do. The point is, I'm not shy and there I was suddenly shy for like the first time in my life. And so I'm say, I say "Wait" you know, "Wait."

And she's like, "No."

And I'm thinking, what do you mean "no"? "Wait." I say.

And she says point-blank, with such a calm in her eyes "No. You're gonna do what I tell you to do."

Then I started shaking . . . uncontrollably. My body's never done nothing like that before. So I knew—for a fact—that something wasn't right . . . because my body told me so, you know, not my mind.

And then it hits me . . . you know I don't know even where I'm at.

All I know is that I'm at her house.

I suppose I could have took her on. But she just put it in my head so simply that she meant to do me harm if I didn't do exactly as she told me.

And so I did. I went with it. It deliberately unfolded and I watched it almost outside of myself, like is this happening. You know . . .

So . . . well she just kinda does to me whatever she wants to do for the rest of the night . . . you know she's wearing one of those

[*She motions to her midsection.*]

and . . . and I just laid there—you know—in my head.

So I focused on the light in the room. And when I finally get all caught up in that light, when I finally leave my body—I cum.

STAIN: It's not like you hear, like it's not like I'm over here and my body is somewhere halfway across the room or . . . I'm, I'm looking down at it. No, it's more like I'm right here and my body is just two inches in front of me . . . kinda how it feels when you're on a crowded train . . . and a stranger is so close to you—you can smell their hair—that's more like what I'm talking about.

Last night I dreamed that I was, I was, you know touching myself.

Well it started that way at least. Then I, I, I was on the other side of me slipping my hand between my legs . . . examining——looking around and found everything to be in ridiculous order.

I mean there were numbers and codes . . . like a—what do you call those things . . . like a, like a, like a key. Everything stored neatly and accounted for—I mean my locker combination from eighth grade 18, 36, 18, my social security card, my bra size, my address——all connected to something or other. You know like my ovaries was my shoe size . . . really—my fallopian tubes tags with Size 10 w. My cervix—my school ID number . . . just, just things like that . . . Then I traveled through my chest, you know my lungs, my spine, kneecaps and ankles . . . all of me . . . not with any instruments—just, just me . . . like I'm rummaging through a yard sale inside my skin. When it was all over—when I was done—I, I vacuumed all of myself out . . . kinda like an abortion . . . of me . . . of my . . . and, and then set all of it on fire . . .

Then I'm walking down a, a long hallway—with no body—like I'm, I'm, I'm of no flesh. I am just the smell of, of, of a space made freshly hollow. Poison now a part of me. Through a window I see the insides of me strung loosely together and thrown over a radiator . . . drying?

And then a waterfall of, of letters—like those, those, those alphabet magnet letters starts streaming out of my mouth. They float up in the air and spell out "misspelled." And then I wake up.

[*Beat.*]

Rape is like carrying a hall pass during class. People just let you slide on by. I let myself slide on by. My girlfriend . . . this morning I found a heart shape bruise in the center of my back . . . I guess that means she loves me. My friends say I could leave her—go stay in one of those woman shelters. But how I'm supposed to hide in a women's shelter—from another woman—she could just check herself in during the middle of the night . . .

[*Beat.*]

People usually wanna, they wanna support you when they know you've have bad things happen to you. They wanna lean in close—place themselves next to you. I should be leaning into my own self.

STAIN: Tomorrow marks year seven. It wasn't a "date rape" . . . like somewhere within the night the date turned into a rape. This was a rape dressed up like a date . . . everything went according to her plan. She knew what she was doing.

Still I never did tell nobody—you know—legally. I never reported it or nothing like that. Anyway what I look like trying to prove I didn't want it time I came.

And anyhow—time says—time's up.

So I won't be going down to nobody's courthouse tomorrow to sign my name to some written account of the this and that of what she did. Be like making one more choice because of her . . . putting my name on an account of what she did.

[*Beat.*]

But I have been thinking maybe I don't got to be nobody's Stain no more . . . not even my own.

Maybe my momma got my name just about right.

[*A video of* STAIN *appears, where she is rearranging her name on a refrigerator with alphabet letters. She interacts with the video during the following:*]

I need a new beginning—say I start at the very beginning with the letter—"A."
Then relieve myself of one "S" . . .
Now keeping a record of the old me with one "N," "I," "T," and another "A." That could make one old Stain—Anita.
I need a, I need a new beginning—Anita.
I need a new spelling.
Anita—new name to sign to an emerging document.
I need a certain amount of grace this time.
Anita—a prayer I can believe in.

[*Transition.*]

BERNADETTE: My name is Bernadette. B-E-R-N-A-D-E-T-T-E. And I don't give a fuck. I don't give a fuck . . . I don't give a fuck—I don't give a fuck. What I look like giving a fuck about you—fuck you! People want you to think about their needs all the damn time. What I look like doing something for you before I do it for my damn self—fuck you. They even tell you that shit on the plane—with those damn . . . masks . . . deal with yo' shit first.

You know how they got that whole my space thing? Well this is my space. Fuck you and your space.

And don't nobody stay in your face like a curious well-meanin' white woman "*how does it feel to be a black woman?*"

Fuck you. It feels like fuck you. Or—"*what it's like to grow up without your black daddy?*" What . . . fuck you and fuck him too. Fuck him when I was four, fuck him when I was five, fuck him when I was six, fuck him when I was seven, fuck him come eight. Last thing my daddy gave me was a Peanut Chew—that sealed the deal. Something about peanuts and chocolate . . .

Got me a sweet tooth so bad it be like . . . In the mornings—I don't pack no damn lunch—I prepare my 'Sweet Bag.' I start the day with something hardy. I eat a good dinner. But all during the day—me and my sweet bag work the halls at that damn high school. It helps. I ain't got a problem with the school—I don't even got a problem with the policies—it's those damn trifling kids filling the classroom some sixty at a time. People got a problem with No Child Left Behind. Yea me too—my problem is some of them little bastards need to be left behind. The teachers give me all the kids they about ready to strangle. I don't like em anymore than they do.

[*Beat*]

I just call it as it is—if little Johnny can't read worth shit—little Johnny might not be much of shit. What I'm gonna do—save his ass between 2:15 and 3:45 on the days when he do show up. Please. I'd rather have a Twix. I'm serious.

[*Beat.*]

Sometimes they get to fighting in my class—I don't break fights up. Kids don't move like they did twenty years ago—they move like grown-ass men. The biggest lesson I ever learned was to fight your own battles. With a Principal showing up dressed like a pimp— driving his pimpmobile, already set up for failure. And they got some sure enough battles comin' their way. But most of em already a whole lot smarter than the people I know. But they bad—so folks wanna throw em in with the Special Ed kids. Huh—I teach art to sixty kids at a time—that's special ed.

[*Beat.*]

But I don't let that kinda thing get to me. 'Cause you really can't. Like I said—I self-medicate with—sugar. Can't smell it on my breath, I can drive and eat it, it won't have me nodding out forgetting my name—huh and I tell you what if I could E-Harmony myself a partner like they do in those damn commercials—I would create me. A big ole 6 ft 3 in mound of sugar, tattooed up like Tupak—reaching out for me—feeling up on my butt—squeezing me with big ole "I got cha" hands. I'd quit my job, padlock my front door and settle down with my sugar daddy.

BERNADETTE: I ain't never been bothered with dating nobody—not really. I don't give a fuck about that type of thing. I mean after I left my husband turned crackhead—I became a dyke. Best choice I ever made. I don't care what nobody say—I chose to be a dyke. 'Cause I could be with a man if I wanted to—but I didn't, so I chose otherwise. And it looks like dykes make more loyal friends than straight women do anyway. With the three dyke friends I got—we cook dinner for each other every other Sunday and don't get up in each other faces. They'll be my last witnesses when I grow old and sick since my kids are too selfish to look my way. Dykes don't let each other pass on alone. I need that—it's starting to get late and looks like I ain't gonna have me a . . . a partner.
Almost did though. Sharletta. I know. Where black women get these names from. I don't know. But a buddy of mine introduced her to me—talking about she wants to be a teacher.

[*Beat.*]

She at the university working on some big degree and she'd call—said she wanted to hear what I thought about this and that. Uh-huh. But I was starting to make good friends with her. And, yes, I do like younger women—'cause they too old to act a fool and too young to fool me. So—Sharletta. She calls me one Friday night—and this time only question she had was "You want to come over?"

[*Beat.*]

You gotta appreciate a mutha fucka that gets to the point.

So I say, "Ok."

[*Beat.*]

I get over there and turns out she done rolled us a joint about the size of a magic marker.

I ain't never been into that stuff—but . . .
There she was with her sweet little co-co brown fingers twisting and turning it . . . few minutes later she talking bout "*You feel good?*"

And shit yeah I felt good.

And we just sat there you know after that, real quiet. I could hear the house starting to settle down like it do once it figure everybody sleep.

I liked her quiet. You can't get that type of shit with just anybody. But I think you get at so much more with a person when the two of you can shut the fuck up—. Turns me on.

[*Beat.*]

I kissed her. Her skin so pretty and brown—her hair just smelling good.

She even liked when I yanked it, "harder"—she said.

Just held her little body. Said she never known nobody make her feel like that—safe, warm, and cared for . . . 'Cause you know, seldom a black woman can have all three in the same night.

She told me about her daddy and how he left her, how she been wrapped up in being left ever since. She got me to thinking about all my shit, and I don't think about my shit . . . 'cause I don't give a fuck.

[*Beat.*]

She fell on off to sleep. And I just laid next to her, studying her face all night. Touched her lips, her eyes, why her face dip right there like it do, wonder how she look with her hair wet and her skinny feet dangling over the armchair. I laid there till the sun made proper . . . then I got up and left. And changed my number that afternoon and never went back. That was too much. What I'm gonna do with a young girl really? My life is summed up by all that I have done—hers: by all she has yet to do. So. Best she figure I was just another vanishing act. 'Cause the quickest way to speak a black girl's language is to leave her.

NARRATOR [*as* BERNADETTE *at age twenty-nine*]: I was daddy's little girl. I'm the baby, the lucky one in the family. Everybody know the baby's main job is to be lucky.

[*Beat.*]

My mother married my dad, a Vietnam War vet who came back and beat the crap out of her—my brother. Fucked my sister but never laid a hand on me. I was daddy's little girl. Used to take me for long rides in his car, that fresh-cut grass smell rushing in through the windows.

I shared a bedroom with my sister. We slept side by side. Daddy would come creeping in at night and get to feeling under her gown while I slept. Guess she'd lay real still 'cause I never woke up to no mess like that. Still—I believe her. Somehow—that sound like my daddy. So . . .

My sister went and spilled the beans on account of watching two people rubbing on each other on some tv show she was watching with my momma.

[*Beat.*]

Momma packed us up in the middle of the night and we left. Never saw him again. Save for one time—like three years after that—my eighth birthday. He gave me a paint set and some candy. Then left . . . 'cause mamma told him to.

[*Beat.*]

My daddy beat her—she could take it. She could even take him beating on my brother. She couldn't, wouldn't take him making a lover out of her daughter. I get that.

She took us all west after that. Except for my brother. Him—she left behind with my father's mother. Maybe she just couldn't take looking in her son's face seeing her husband looking back at her. I get that.

But I don't remember much of his face. I don't remember much of him at all. Only his thighs—big and brown with two tattoos—an eagle and a fist. Used to trace over them while he held me between his legs, telling me something about . . .something. Daddy's little girl, the baby, the lucky one in the family. Everybody knows the baby's main job is to be lucky.

Funny how I grew up with my momma—but the love I remember is most my daddy's. Momma didn't look out for me the way she did my sister . . . like she about to cross the street by herself for the first time.

She didn't look out for me like that.

[*Beat.*]

But I was there too . . . I was there when he came into our room every night.
I was daddy's little girl—but he didn't want me.

[*Beat.*]

Wonder if I found him today—maybe he'd want me now.

Maybe he'd come back.

Poison now a part of me. It ain't what my daddy did to my sister, it's what he didn't do to me.

[*Transition.*]

GLOW: Well now Glow isn't my god-given name. It's Ericka . . . with a c—k—a—and while I thought I was extra cute growing up because of that detail by the time I was seven, I was calling myself Tina, convinced I was Tina. When you think of Tina—don't Tina Turner come to mind with those bad-ass legs, that crazy sexy voice. I didn't understand all those things at the time of course—but I think a person no matter the age can recognize a good thing . . .

[*Beat.*]

By the time I turned nine—"Happy Birthday Naja" was on my birthday cake. Naja was my best friend. We lived on the same block. All the kids on my block had the same curfew—soon as those street lamps began to flicker that meant time to take your behind inside. Not me and Naja. We knew those lamps had a few stages . . . it would go orange, then yellow, then green, cool blue—then white. We'd be outside my house making mud pies till the light made white.

[*Beat.*]

We were soul sisters. And we wanted to take things to the next level. But we were over the whole prick your finger—blood sister thing. We thought we'd do one better. So for our birthdays—two days apart—we gave each other our first name. I became Naja and she—Ericka with a C-K-A.

[*Beat.*]

Then one day—I was headed around the side of her house—I looked up and found the living room curtains gone. Through the windows—in the middle of her living room where her mother's rocking chair used to be laid a thin line of dirt—I guess what wouldn't make it into the dustpan. There one day—gone the next. And I never knew if she left with her name or mine.

[*Beat.*]

By the time I got to high school I was calling myself Red on account of my skin . . . three or four years of "Hey Red! What cha up to girl!?" Somehow Ericka—even with a c-k-a, wasn't quite right anymore. Then I met Ms. Debra Daniels. She was a bad-asss woman. Shot straight from the hip—Took to poetry like her lifeline. I wasn't into poetry—I was into her. First assignment—"Write a poem about your name."

Well hell—I had about five of them—never mind one poem—I had enough material to write a damn collection.

And so I did.

I wrote about what it meant to have a name—to want a name—to be a name. Thirteen poems I turned in—all on my names to date as well as the different names I thought of naming myself at one point in time. And for my last piece—I wrote that it wasn't so much that I was looking for a name so much as I knew my name was out there looking for me.

[*Beat.*]

They weren't bad poems—but they weren't so good either. But she read those poems like they were lost artifacts from Shakespeare. "Burn baby burn"—she said when she finished—"you can set a page on fire . . . ever think of calling yourself Glow?"

GLOW: I was always a good little girl. Five years old, standing in my mother's bathroom doorway, eyeing her eyeing herself in the mirror. I did the things that little girls do. I imagined my life beyond me—a full-grown woman with important things to do and say and the pretty colors I would put on my face before I did or said them. I imagined tapping my wrist with smelly goods after leaning from glass-doored showers, water spilling over my shoulder, strutting over my tummy, strolling over my thighs, rounding the knee, down the wonderful calf . . . Mmmmm, the ankle.

Standing in the doorway, I braced myself. Grabbing hold of the door frame with fingers each the size of pinkies, I pushed my belly forward, slowing crashing onto its coolness. A slow rocking of my belly, then my soup bowl of a pelvis pressing against the frame.

Then again.

And again.

Poom, poom, poom . . .

My mother smacked me one good one, right in the mouth.

Her eyes were serious and fixed.

(A mother knows how to look right down inside her child.)

I learned two things that day:

I had a body with its own mind for pleasure

and

that pleasure could be taken away.

GLOW: He wore dreads. One of those upright black brothas, he worked in the community—helped high school dropouts get their GEDs. I was mostly attracted to the fact that he was attracted to me. At that time you know—I hadn't, I hadn't . . . I hadn't figured out how fine I was. It makes a big difference in what's what sometimes, believing that you're fine . . . gives you perspective on your right to say no. But then, you know then, I didn't have much perspective. At the time the only men I tended to attract were conservative white men and closeted gay men. White men—'cause my skin's light enough for their friends and dark enough for cool points or at dinner parties. And gay men, 'cause, you know how that is.

[*Beat.*]

And I have always been insecure about my blackness. The amount of black I have in my skin . . . in my bones . . . in my soul. I mean slave master got a hold of many black women—so having a touch of white blood in my system is not an issue. I'm talking past all that . . . I mean the part of my being black that gets a grade-A approval in my black community. You know this story: the white kids couldn't connect with me, the black kids wouldn't connect with me. Too dark for one, too light for the other . . . hair too nappy for both.

[*Beat.*]

When I met Darren . . . it wasn't the first time I had dated a black man—but it was the first time I felt like I was dating The Black Man. You know.

With Darren I felt a bit like a white woman having snagged her first black man. Cool. Special. Validated. Better than my yesterday's me. He was long-awaited proof that I black enough for the black man.

[*Beat.*]

I absolutely couldn't stand him when I met him. He had bad juu-juu written all over him. We were in one of those swanky bars and he had a vibe so unnerving—it sent me running to the bathroom—splashing water on my face thanking God for the message about the asshole out in the front.

[*Beat.*]

But then drinks came and went—and came and went again and next thing I knew—I was drunk and hot and giving him my number.

But he tells me we should take our time. And I figured I was completely wrong about this wonderful gentleman. So we took our time over the next few months—talking late on the phone, writing lengthy mid-day emails, meeting up within groups of mutual friends. I wrote him a poem:

> *This is how I know closeness*
> *as pieces of lint*
> *in the corner of my side pocket*
> *giving my fingers ramblings of joy*
> *while I wait for the morning train*
> *thinking of you*
> *as sound on the*
> *tip of my tongue*
> *murmurs making*
> *like*
> *commas seeping from*
> *lungs*
> *climbing bountiful walls of*
> *the sweet cave*
> *embedded*
> *at the heart of your*
> *glorious rock.*
> *Roll me like fine lint*
> *into the corner of your pant pocket*
> *and tell me the bottom line.*
> *Make me*
> *mean that feels*
> *so good*
> *and*

give

us

a

reason

to

turn

off

the light.

[*Beat.*]

Then we planned our special date.

I was on a big fellowship at the time. So I decided to take him to the annual gala. This was a big deal event—hot ticket—gown, glitter, main floor kinda thing. He thought I dropped money on our tickets—but I didn't have it like that. I was basically privileged for a time.

Still—I look over throughout the night and catch him pouting.

[*Beat.*]

By the time we got back to his place I wanted to honor his black man-ness.
So when he poured me a drink—I drank it. He fixed a snack—I ate it. And when he asked me to join him outside in the backyard—I joined him. He told me that his neighbors weren't home. That since he met me—he had been wanting to fuck me on their patio.

[*Beat.*]

Ok, now I was letting him be the man and everything—but I wasn't down for that. Truth be told—I was a virgin when I met him—so that was 0 to 100 in 60 seconds.
I said no. And this is where it all changed. He didn't growl. He didn't raise his voice. Rather he got real quiet. Steady. A bank teller count-ing their drawer. He leaned in and said "if I have to hurt you I will."

[*Beat.*]

Whenever I think of a woman, especially a black woman defend-ing herself—she's kicking, screaming, punching. She's wild and quick and clever. But I was none of those things. I was quiet. I listened to everything he said. I was polite. I made believe everything was just fine.

[Beat.]

We all tell lies that we regret and usually something in our bodies betray us on the moment we tell them. But I'm a good liar. Guess that's why I'm still here. [Beat.] All night, then all morning—the sun came up kinda thing with me still making believe I was just fine.

[Beat.]

Then he drove me home. Said he'd see me later. I called my mother, told her what happened. She said, "That sounds strange," and went back to work. So that's what I thought for a while—that it was a strange date. Poison now a part of me—I went back to my life. I went to work in the morning. I met friends for drinks. I completed my fellowship. I made believe everything was just fine. But that kinda thing is like knowing about a gas leak while you're out shopping—or falling asleep at the wheel. It's the siren before the storm.

So I called him without a charge to make—but a gripe nonetheless. "What you did was wrong, it wasn't OK."

"No ma'am." He said. "You just don't know shit about being with a black man." [Beat.] And maybe he was right. Maybe if I knew how to be with a black man, maybe I wouldn't want to be with a woman.

Maybe.
Maybe.

GLOW: Sex became an argument with my vagina. It's dousing the living room walls with gasoline and striking a match. With my "strange date" behind me, I could trust again, I could sleep through the night again, but what I couldn't do was fix my broken pussy. It used to purr—hum at a perfect pitch—after my strange date it was struggling for middle "c." It wasn't always broken.

My clitoris was revealed to me by my babysitter. She solemnly promised I could play with any Barbie I wanted so long as I went down on her. Or she on me. She laid me down in the center of her bottom bunk—removed my dress and slid my panties over my little hips—our moist flesh would tap tap tap against each other. And then I was rewarded with the Barbie of my desire.

I kinda liked it. My body kinda liked it. What she did was wrong—I get that. But still I liked it . . . I like it.

[*Beat.*]

Hummmm my body as commodity . . . it doesn't have to be bad. It's simply a matter of perspective.

[*Beat.*]

Post "strange date" I wanted my body back and on my terms. I wanted what I found in the doorway of my mother's bathroom. Something was stolen from me as a girl and then again as a woman. And I wanted it back.

[*Beat.*]

So I gave my vagina a name—hell she earned it. I called her Molly. 'Cause Molly is so fun to say. Playful and sweet in the mouth, it dances off the lips just as cool as you please. Starts perfectly with mmmmmm then end with a slight flick of the tongue. Molly.
Moll: root for a prostitute or a gangster's girlfriend . . . hummm girl-friend? I made Molly my girlfriend and together we threw love fests. Women loving women. Women loving men. Women as men loving men as women . . . mmmmm.

[*Beat.*]

I harnessed myself to pleasure and got my needs met . . . and maybe help somebody else along the way . . .

Hell marching through the streets at take back the night rallies, oh no—I'll rally in my bedroom and take back the night my damn self.

People can get so bent outta shape about "alternative sex," not me. Way I see it alternative sex can lead to . . . healing.

I offer safe, tender, and fun at a nice price.

Mutual sex for an exchange of resources? Why not.

[*Transition.*]

MONARCH:

Dear
Brown
Girl—set on
fire—cinders
on the trail
ashes
scattered—dust
to
the wind.
You are a snap
shot/in a
thin article/
about
your
thinner body
with
no name.
You were not/
intended
for bold
face
print.

Make me
your
letter press.
Make
me your
canopy
and fruit.
Make me your/
small
clearing

towards
a clearer path.

Dear
Unidentified
Black
Woman/dead
in
the woods—
legs
stretched wide—
a pair of/
scissors
dropped to/
the floor.
Scattered along
94, lumber
yards, rain
forests and preserves—
you/and the Elms
a covenant
of
en.dan.gered
species.

Flesh/flesh
and
bark—earth's new
floor.
Trees
and
bodies—
deciduous mahogany.

Make me
your
Sycamore.
Make

me
your/morning
desk and
your
evening chair.
Make me your sugar luck,
your firm
lover
your
summer
shade.
Make
me
a
pair
of
tracks
stretch
s
t
r
e
t
c
h

s t r e t c h i n g
at/the horizon
Make
me
an article
specifying
the definite.

STAIN [*voice over*]:

I

am

a

narrow
leaf
not enough to shade
a piece of
anybody's
anything
I
stop to tie
double
knots
in
case
I
have
to
run.

BERNADETTE [*voice over*]:

I/am
tilt ing
coveting
the
fall.
I want
survivor
status.

NARRATOR [*as* GLOW *in voice over*]:

My body/is/
a
wrinkled
suit
sto len
from a muggy costume
shop.
Make me
the/time

it
takes
to lose//
track
of
time.

MONARCH:

O, SurvivoR
I have/pinned
your
name
to the/bottom/of
my hem.
O, SurviVor
I have/pinned
your
name
to the/bottom/of
my hem.
O, Survivor,
I have/pinned
your
name
to the/bottom/of
my hem.

[*Black out.*]

INTERVIEW WITH MISTY DeBERRY

Raquel L. Monroe

Where are you from? And how did you end up in Chicago?

I'm from Philly—I was born in Philly—later my mother divorced my father and put herself through nursing school—then joined the army. So I grew up moving around quite a bit, primarily along the East Coast—South Carolina. There I pretty much—you know—became the bulk of who I am. I guess you want to know these details . . . I usually skip over them. I started college up north anyway . . . a really small college—Westchester University—just outside of Philly. I was there for about a year. I wanted to spend time developing a craft as an actor. And I didn't feel like it had a tight enough focus. So I went to North Carolina School of the Arts, and I studied there for four years, which was a very intense process. It also influenced how I came to understand myself as a black woman artist in the world. And so—after North Carolina I moved to New York—was there for a while—studied some with Clinton Turner Davis at the New Federal Theatre. Then a few months later I landed a residency at the Kennedy Center in Washington, D.C.—which is, you know—where the incident took place—my date rape—and that's where Milkweed . . . the very small small fragments of it began . . . unidentifiable at that time. Two weeks after the rape—I moved back to New York—was there for about two years. There I began to develop an understanding around trauma—sexually based—or gender-based trauma . . . I was primarily concerned with dissociative behavior within intimate circumstances as a means for survival. A couple of years passed—I left the country for a bit—then landed in Chicago lured by the mission statement of Columbia College, Chicago. It's here I started pulling together the concept of really writing a piece about this evening in D.C. And that started in a few ways. I knew that I wanted to write about what that experience was, what it is. I knew that I wanted the writing to be particular, peculiar. I knew that I wanted to write about some of the things that were happening in New York around just being an artist and starting to find some type of understanding that I was some sort of a survivor or that I had been raped or even being able to use that word. So here in Chicago *Milkweed* came into full blossom in large part due to my relationship with Jane M. Saks and the Ellen Stone Belic Institute for the Study of Women and Gender at Columbia College, Chicago. They gave me a fellowship to develop the script. So my time developing the work under the support of the institute while completing an M.F.A. at Columbia College informed my process greatly. It also informed my role as a member of the Chicago community—in that way Chicago snuck up on me—became my home.

Putting together *Milkweed* . . . you said dissociative behavior, you obviously knew the term, so during that time when you were writing what things were informing your writing in addition to your own experience?

Sure . . . Well, my mother's a therapist—she's a social worker—as well as my sister—she's a social worker–therapist and so I came up with that type language around me and the arguments were just really interesting . . . But alongside of that, I got really taken up with this book by Dr. Judith Herman, on trauma and recovery. So I was reading a lot of texts that were both informed from social work theories, psychotherapy kind of theories and not so much art actually. I was also reading Dr. Charlotte Pierce Baker, a professor at Duke University—her work introduced me to the power of personal narratives—specifically where trauma is a key factor. What I really wanted to hear more of was the healing component within intimate relationships—how to reenter my body on my terms and invite—want—receive pleasure. I became more interested in the ways in which the body responds "involuntarily"—or responds out of sync from where the emotional/spiritual mind is—for me—deliberately seeking healthy pleasure is a fundamental part of reclaiming my body as a safe and resonant space. This is survival—being in charge of my presence in the world, especially when I'm engaged in an act of lovemaking—physical and beyond.

In the piece you say this out-of-body experience is not far away but like standing so close to someone on the train that you can smell their hair . . . So that's what that experience was . . . and that was the experience that inspired the other two women as well?

Yes—that's what the experience was. That's what that experience remains to be when at times I'm intimate with someone—and for some reason or another remaining present mentally-physically is unbearable. And that's part of my need for writing the play. Understanding that I could be intimate with someone years after the rape . . . and still have moments of just not being able to be there in the room with my partner whether I wanted to be or not. So I began deliberately listening—reading—documenting black women—black queer women's stories—not only what we said—what we didn't say and most importantly how we said or didn't say any of it about our love, lovers, loving—specifically where sexual trauma was underneath it all. Initially I wanted to write about these twenty-five nights that I could recall or piece together of checking out of my body, kind of odd experiences. So that's how it started, and I thought that I was working with about six characters, about six women, and then I went through this stage of just paring it down. For a while I was trying to understand the three women in relationship to each other . . . like the ego, id, superego kind of thing . . . just in their behavior.

So you said there were initially six characters in *Milkweed*? How did you end up with three?

When I'm writing or working—most times I will impose a structure on the work—or a construction—almost like an external environment as a way of allowing the work to respond in ways that are alive and potentially surprising—or refreshing in ways unforeseen. And then every once in a while I have to get real with myself and ask myself, "OK, is this construction serving the work or is it serving this clever little exercise you're into?" With the six women—which were actually seven really—it was this thing of wagging the dog. And so it's important for me to share that you're right—I ended up with three women because three women revealed themselves to be through following the voice of the story—and so I went with it. What's really interesting is I'd always knew that there was another voice—kept sensing a child's voice—and some of that voice came out through Glow—still I could never quite pin it down. But in working with Cheryl we totally developed this monarch character—I'd never even dreamed of having a butterfly as a character. And it was staring me in the face I suppose—still I had never even thought about it. It totally came 100 percent out of our partnership.

Your partnership with Cheryl?

Cheryl Lynn Bruce—yes—she directed the première at Links Hall and at Northwestern. She's fabulous—nothing short of it. I had seen her work years ago in Julie Dash's *Daughters of the Dust* and was blown away by her. After meeting her at a dinner one evening I was taken by her way of being in the world—in the room—and I wanted to work with her specifically for this piece. She's intuitive, quick, firm, and very gracious. I'm so grateful for our partnership because in deliberately developing Monarch—the play began to function in the live—the now. Also in understanding trauma and healing it's crucial to not think of it as a linear process whatsoever and I really wanted to express that in the writing of the piece—it was initially very very important to me.

To have it not be linear?

Yeah, *Milkweed* in its original script version—you'd hear a bit from one character, then another, then back to another—which is possible to stage sure. But Cheryl was pivotal in her vision of the piece in that she leveled me with saying—"Yes—that's all well and true—the experience is nonlinear but the audience needs to be able to follow you, my dear." I got that, I jumped on board with that really really fast 'cause it made a lot of sense. I just started to return to the whole anchor of the piece, which is generally how I answer all my work, I always find an anchor, and based on that anchor, I borrow structure from whatever that is . . . So the monarch being what it is and doing what it does to get through its life cycle . . .

The monarch . . . so the piece is called *Milkweed* . . . I want to know, if butterflies were not even in your realm of consciousness when you were doing this, or maybe it was in your realm and you didn't have the word for it, how did Cheryl then pull that out . . . you know, and make it the anchor, because it's a very strong, specific, compelling character that we only see at the beginning and then at the end?

Oh no—what I mean to say is—yeah butterflies were all up in the realm—I just never thought to personify one—to literally shape the voice of a monarch butterfly as literally a character named Monarch that is a butterfly come to life onstage. Almost like going to some magical realism place—a place that says—yea why not have a straight-up butterfly as a character in this play. That type of juicy play came from Cheryl. Though in the initial version of the play there was a narrator . . . the Institute and I had gathered a small group of loving fierce artists from all disciplines who directly help shape the work and the overall consensus in the room after the first reading of the script was that the narrator was there just kind of . . .

Narrating . . .

Yeah, that's pretty much what she was doing. So the monarch kind of became that voice in a way. But when I went back to the table right before rehearsal to figure out how we were going to put this thing up on the stage, which is a whole nother beast, I started thinking about the anchor being this Monarch and this Milkweed, and I just borrowed the structure of the monarch stage to stage to stage, and then those stages became the characters. So it was very very deliberate, Stain went first, you know . . . Before there was *Milkweed* or Monarch there was Stain. You know, when I began therapy because of the rape, one of my very first conversations was my therapist, or the therapist at the time, asking me how I felt about something, or it. And I said I just feel like I am at this wedding party and I have this stain on my dress, and there is nothing I can do about it. And she said, "Well do you need to?" And the thought of a stain being there, what it is and how it looks, what it does and not being able to hide it, remove it, and its persistency . . . and that's how Stain developed. And she became structurally the first stage that a monarch goes through. She as an egg laid on the milkweed plant—stuck—fixed—like her stutter—then she begins eating her way out of her shell—or skin—or name as we experience it in the play . . . then structurally again—Stain morphs into Bernadette. Bernadette is the incessant energy of the larva—eat, eat, eat—survive. And then the larva of course eventually spins a wonderful fine cocoon, if you will, which is Glow, a cocoon of spun silk like light—behold this extravagant thing—this is how Glow comes to see herself. It is important for me to highlight that in this way Glow is the cocoon—not yet the butterfly.

When you were constructing the piece, the play, did you have an audience in mind?

Yes. In deliberate ways I think of the women who gather at Pow-Wow—it's a spoken word collective—poetry juke joint really on the South Side of Chicago spearheaded by Chicago legends like C. C. Carter, Enina J., Jackie Anderson, Lucy . . . Most of the poetry in *Milkweed* I would read—test out at Pow-Wow and then I could always feel them when I worked on the script. And in other ways this is a black woman's play—a black queer woman's play . . . which isn't an essentialist point of view on what black feminist theater is or isn't—but how I understand where my work lives culturally. I wrote this for me—a black queer artist who has survived several experiences with sexual trauma—I wrote it for all other black/women/queer identified folk who can say—me too in whatever way "me too" means for them.

The craft of writing, all of your skills show up really well, and I mean that as a great compliment, the writing and the performance are so well done. So it's interesting to hear you talk about your journey and that grounding of structure and the technique of acting 'cause I think that it clearly enabled these three distinct women to manifest, and then the Monarch is completely different, yet the one that's in control of this sort of weaving. So I just wanted to acknowledge that. I'm wondering about audience testimony and trauma, have you had audience members share their experience of trauma, and the cyclical nature of healing?

Yes. The time right after the show closes for the evening is so special. All kinds of people have shared their thoughts—feeling—fears—hopes and most importantly they share their memories. In that way I feel as if for a moment we enter the work of healing—of becoming better together. And that's part of the point—how do we get by in this world together while healing from our various imprints—reconciling our memories—or reimaging ourselves.

If you don't address it's like you're trying to cover it up, trying to hide the stain. It seems like the play is addressing and articulating the voice of the stain, so to speak. And I think starting it off with Stain is really deep. What about the names of the other women? Naming seems very important because that's the first thing you say when you start the pieces.

Oh yes. And in a very real way naming has such a long history in black feminist thought and culture—and on a visceral level controlling—claiming one's name for one's own sake is *the* work of being present—alive and kicking with full intentionality and no apologies. Bernadette is actually my middle name and I had the greatest difficulty with accepting that name 'cause it just felt so grown, and I mean well into adulthood I was like, "I don't know how to put my foot into Bernadette." And one of my best friends, we were just kinda hanging out one day, and she's like, "I don't know what your problem is with Bernadette, to me, Bernadette is this black woman with this fro and some jeans, and she's walking down the street in the '70s. Bernadette is bad!" I was like, "You're so right. That's a badass name." And I feel like she just kind of repositioned that name for me. Since I was a little girl, Bernadette was so difficult for me to spell, and I could never get the "e-t-t-e," it took me so long to learn to spell my middle name, so when I was crafting Bernadette, which was inspired by my friend's mother, who is just an amazing character—just unapologetic, it didn't take any time. That was Bernadette. And Glow—which is not short for Gloria—but the verb "glow"—it came from just that—the physical act of glowing—seeing one's self from the inside out and setting that aflame as a means of light—protection—knowing. In the original script Glow says "Make me mean that feels so good and give me a reason to turn off the light." She wants to feel good—and potentially let go of herself—bloom. She's in love with language and her body—sensuality, and her view is a little questionable—still with this luscious urge to be present—and on her terms.

Yeah, that's made very clear in how it ends. You do something really interesting and kind of dangerous, something that people don't ever really acknowledge that much, and that's how pleasure and pain exist side by side, and the piece ends there. The vocal performance ends there.

Yes, deliberately I wanted to tap into—pleasure—pain—the sometimes ambiguity of engaging in mutually agreed upon sexual activity. Especially leaning into black/queer experiences—which if I was anxious about airing any type of dirty laundry, my biggest nerves came out writing about this type of ambiguity from a lesbian perspective. That seemed like . . .

How come?

Because the way . . . just along with outing this story and outing myself there too. I'm out, . . . but just the vulnerability factor, quite frankly, and in our community, you know, sometimes we kind of cut up. My work is very personal—my life is very private—and sometimes the two commingle and there I am in front of a crowded room dealing with it. And it's also so very important to openly work through—and talk about challenges and contradictions that exist within same sex or queer-identified relationships. With these things, the challenge as an artist for me is resisting the panic at getting it just right—while getting it just right. For Glow she's in the heat of figuring out where she stands in relationship to who gets to experience her body—how and on what terms—including herself.

That's not something that's addressed, and I can imagine that's something that you'd want to address, because it's already stigmatized and then . . .?

I wanted to flesh that out a little bit—how the body can experience pleasure without the spiritual/mind's permission—or vice versa. The body goes one way—the mind the other—then the impending overlap. And for me Glow, of all the women, is becoming very much aware of that dichotomy, for lack of a better word, and wanting to maybe control it, take advantage of it—how do these things work—how do they serve us— disserve us?

What is a monarch?

It's a butterfly.

Where are they?

Yeah, let me tell you the story. They fly and they migrate on a cyclical basis. They are everywhere—but can't survive the winters—so every year they migrate south to Mexico . . . It's just a really interesting story. So they all fly down to Mexico, and their sole purpose when they get there is to lay this egg on the milkweed plant. So they lay their eggs and then they go off and they die—they've done what they need to do. I've read and I've seen images of these monarchs literally coming in over the water into Mexico and the people wait for them and pull them in with nets. It's really an event. What happens is they flock to these trees, hundreds and hundreds of monarchs. I haven't seen it up close so I don't know it from my own eyes. But so they lay these eggs and they pass on, and then the egg sits on the plant and it begins to eat the substance for life—milkweed. And the substance is a poisonous substance—for any other insect that would ingest any type of milkweed, it would die, but it's something in the monarch's system that is sustained from it, quite frankly. So it goes through this whole process . . .

The poison on the tree or the poison that the monarch emits?

The poison from the plant, from the milkweed plant. It's a white milky substance, and they ingest that all through their whole maturation process. And once they come out of their cocoon, as you know, a butterfly, that whole story . . . the monarch which is known for the spots on its back—that's the residue from the poison and it's the one thing that ends up being its major defense system against predators. So when I first heard this story, it was very very simple, I was watching TV and it was something I heard on *Animal Planet,* and I felt like that's what black women do, you know, and women, for healing. We take in this substance; it becomes a part of us, and ultimately maybe defends us. The beautiful thing about the monarch, which I didn't quite explore in the play, is that not every generation gets to go—migrate, not every generation of monarchs fly down to Mexico. Typically they can live up to, maybe 45 days. But this particular generation, it lives a few months so that it can make this whole journey down to Mexico to lay these eggs and ensure the life cycle process of the species. And when I think about just the family structure of women and our culture, it just feels so right.

So do you see *Milkweed* as that kind of pilgrimage that allows the sort of survival, or gives voice to, or reminds us of women in trauma, and particularly sexual trauma, reminding us that they are here, we are here, and this is an experience that happens in our community?

Yeah, I didn't want the play to be this exclamation point; really I wanted it to be a comma, these things happen. Not these things happen "*and?*" but these things happen "and," . . . And definitely—my process alongside of the play was certainly a pilgrimage. I think I just kind of fooled myself in the process of writing it that I was in control of the script and therefore in control of the process, but that *so* was not the case, but yes that's definitely part of it, specifically from being in New York, and my very first attempt to put myself back together, or re-inform psychologically what had happened to me, coming out of this experience. I was just so taken aback by not seeing such a strong or any black presence at events like Take Back the Night rallies.

So it's a combination of your own creativity, your own experiences, and experiences that you heard. You can write something without having it be a live performance. What compelled you to explore these things in live performance?

Two very direct things compelled me to perform this play: one was the memories of that tragic experience, and the reality of how it exists, and wanting to put them some place visible and live. And two, I am an actor and a writer, and that's what I do and long to do—give myself work. So it came from both of those needs. I have no memory really prior to performing. It's just how I intend to be and participate in my life. Another part of what inspired putting it together was I want to be able to have the experience of going to a play and seeing something about this. I try to create things I want to see, that I want to experience, that I want to talk about.

WITNESS AND THE POLITICS OF READDRESSING BLACK PAIN AND PLEASURE: MISTY DeBERRY'S *MILKWEED*

Francesca Royster

I first had the chance to watch DeBerry perform *Milkweed* in a small theater on Northwestern University's campus. I was sitting in the front row, and I found it very powerful to watch her at work so closely: to watch her facial expressions, hear her intakes of breath, really listen close to the nuance of her word choices and the music made with words. DeBerry puts her body on the line by exploring difficult stories about survival as an ongoing and embodied struggle, a theory of the flesh interpreted through words, breath, and movement.[1] Because DeBerry inhabits her multiple characters/selves with such compassion and intimacy and complexity, she won over her audience. But we also left with the sense that we won her over, too, trusted somehow, in our powers of witness, to be part of this process of healing.

Naming black girls' and women's experiences, DeBerry's *Milkweed* is both particular and expansive, pursuing the shared dream of transcendence and healing with her theater audience. The rich if fraught inner life that the play conveys is something that has so often been denied black people, and in particular, black women, and flies in the face of myth and stereotypes that black women have to face, including the always-already sexualization of black girlhood, the criminalization of the black family and black sexuality, and the myth coming out of slavery of black women as either desiring rape or as unrapeable because of our inherent status as less than human. These stories of violence also reveal that creativity has always been a form of resistance for black women. The play speaks to the richness of black women's cultural responses, and also reminds us of our powers of reinvention.

Such work is part of the work of redress of past violence, and in the process, of transforming the history of performance. As Lynn C Miller and Jacqueline Taylor note in their introduction to their collection *Voices Made Flesh: Performing Women's Autobiography,* coedited with M. Heather Carter,

> The story of women's autobiography is the story of resistance
> to the disembodied, traditionally masculine universal subject,
> whose implicit denial of skin color, gender, sexual orientation
> (other than heterosexual), and economic disparity constrained
> many women as "others" with no voices or physicality. (Miller
> and Taylor, *Voices Made Flesh*, 4)

For those of us of color in the theater audience, *Milkweed* goes against performances that have typically offered the fantasy of escape or ironic distance of our own colored selves, or honorary identification with a white male subject.

DeBerry explores the ways that the experience of violence is always being processed in the body, that the body's knowledge must be trusted as we make sense of these experiences, and as we transmogrify them in our healing. Sometimes what can't be put into words can be put into movement: that body hugging itself in memory, eyes closed; the awkward shuffling from foot to foot as one tries to unwind a difficult narrative; an unblinking stare at the audience, neck outstretched, muscles tight, tendons popping; a quick shimmy that leads to undulation that leads to a wide, diva outstretch of wings.

For DeBerry, the stage is the chance to open up the crowded rooms that house our memories, to invite others in. Her sites are simple domestic spaces, and she uses small details to illustrate how we make spaces as a form of protection: a small lamp that warms and opens up a corner, a simple table that holds a journal, a beautifully colored orange scarf that we might use to soak up sweat one minute or drape over a chair, flourish over our shoulders as if in flight the next. The play asks, "What are the homes that we have made for ourselves, even in our pain? Are they expansive mansions? Or have we shrunk down our desires and expectations into the small space of a rented room, or the tiny leaf on which the monarch lays its eggs? Would it be possible to let others in? How would company, yours, ours, transform the room?" In its focus on shared transformation, *Milkweed* embodies the utopian potential of theater proposed by Jill Dolan in her book, *Utopia in Performance: Finding Hope at the Theater*. Dolan describes the moments of theater-watching that at their most powerful can take us out of ourselves and our solitary experience "in a way that lifts everyone slightly above the present, into a hopeful feeling of what the world might be like if every moment of our lives were as emotionally voluminous, generous, aesthetically striking and intersubjectively intense" (Dolan, *Utopia in Performance*, 5). These moments keep us returning to the theater space, even when witnessing stories of loss or sadness, because they provide for us "an affective vision of how the world might be better" (Dolan, 6).

The play opens with her own healing myth: the image of the monarch butterfly, the dramatization of transformation, and also homemaking. Milkweed itself operates as a double metaphor: as we are forced to live in the midst of poison, make our homes in poison, swallow poison, it speaks to the ways within a rape culture that we're forced to live within the reality of violence, continued violence against us. But it also suggests the possibility of adaptation, where we might even gain strength in order to survive by eating, consuming, making our home within poison. As DeBerry writes in her play notes: "I wanted to document the journeys black women make from trauma and recovery and the words used to construct the self along the way . . . As *Milkweed* is loosely based on the Monarch Butterfly, which consumes large quantities of poison from the milkweed plant to survive, this play ultimately speaks to journeys we take and our inherent will to survive. It asks how do we construct ourselves and our stories within our words—what we say—and what we do?" This becomes the framing story for the show, and the monarch, an anti-narrator of sorts.

The monarch, the play's mistress of ceremonies, makes a grand entrance—wide orange flowing scarves and kimonoed arms outstretched, ever-present sunglasses shielding her eyes from us, and perhaps, too, our probing eyes from hers, for the moment. Hers is the spirit of survival, the street-smart self we might yearn to be, toughened rather than broken by rejection and lack of recognition. She introduces us to the play's three characters, Stain, Bernadette, and Glow, in order to "summon a metamorphosis" that depends on our witness:

> They will emerge/
> wings pumping warrior
> blood
> begotten from poison-milk—
> poison

> now a part of them
> shows itself as blazing hues— . . . ,
> a colorful defense
> foiling
> would-be predators/
> dressed to kill. (318)

Each character tells her story distinctly—the story of her assault is included in the midst of stories within stories of self, desire, disappointment, and survival. Sometimes this struggle is set off by the stuttering sounds of electronic music. Grooving on dissonance, Stain, the first character, is hard, standoffish, yet her hunched shoulders draw us inward. Her voice is all baby butch shy, with threads of bravado and barely covered over vulnerability. She tells us of her assault by another woman, cutting across assumptions of gender, butch and femme, bottom and top. Stain shares her sense of betrayal, and the fear that her own body has somehow turned on her. "Rape," she tells us, "is like carrying a hall pass. People just let you slide on by . . . I let myself slide by" (321).

Bernadette is clearly older, takes up the space of the room with more authority. We have been invited into her kitchen, and we sense that we are welcome because she doesn't put away her dishrag, or untie her hair. Yet her words betray a sharp humor and defensiveness. "My name is Bernadette. B-E-R-N-A-D-E-T-T-E. And I don't give a fuck" (322). Does her anger hide a hidden hurt, or is it a source of strength, the sign of resilience, the insistence on self? In making us laugh in the midst of her pain, Bernadette calls attention to the ways we conventionally treat black women's anger as entertainment, or else as a sign of pathology. This stems from the history of chattel slavery. As Saidiya V. Hartman suggests, the control of black people's expressions of anger, terror, as well as pleasure, were central to the control of freedom, and were aspects of slavery's everyday practices (Hartman, *Scenes of Subjection*, 49–50).

Bernadette tells us of her world-weary struggles as a teacher, sidestepping fighting grown-bodied students in her class, and her techniques for "self-medicating" through the powers of Twix: "And I tell you what if I could E-Harmony myself a partner like they do in those damn commercials—I would create me a big ole 6 ft 3 in mound of sugar, tattooed up like Tupac, reaching out for me, feeling up on my butt with big ole 'I got cha' hands. I'd quit my job—padlock my front door—huh! get me some sugar in my bowl seven days a week" (324). Unexpectedly, the evocation of sugar as desire melts into a memory of the last time she has seen her father before he left under the cloud of suspicion of incest, the candy he left her, a peanut chew. Here, DeBerry evokes Toni Morrison's use of candy as both symbol and as the accessible resource of pleasure for young black girls in *The Bluest Eye*. In the novel, Pecola's trip to the store for Mary Jane penny candies becomes the site of desire and self-protection—the "orgasm of desire" of sugar as a guard against "inexplicable shame" and erasure (Morrison, *The Bluest Eye*, 49–50).

In Morrison's novel, the Mary Jane candy is a place of access to the consumption of whiteness, rightness, and pleasure. Yet DeBerry revises Morrison's move by showing the powers of Bernadette's resistant imagination. Bernadette refashions for herself a new man-woman made in sugar but different from the innocuous image of white girlhood of Mary Jane. Instead she claims for herself Tupac's black masculine resistance, Bessie's generosity, and spiritedness. But is Bernadette yearning *for* Tupac, and for the sugar daddy that might also be her own daddy? Or is she yearning to become him, to absorb his strength, his beauty, his deliciousness? Is she yearning to be comforted by Bessie's "got ya" hands, or to become her? With Bernadette, DeBerry challenges us to face the entanglement of tenderness and violence, the yearning for power, and the yearning to be loved, integral to this story of incest and memory.

Glow, though also an adult, is also deeply absorbed in the desire for both power and pleasure from childhood. She tells us first, "I was always a good little girl" and then tells us about how she was punished for her open sensuality, how she learned that the free pursuit of sexual pleasure was not "good." She tells us the story of being caught masturbating by her mother. This act of shaming comes to define her sexual identity. When she is raped by a date, a man held up in the community as a "good brother,"[2] as an adult, her mother dismisses her story by telling her that it is "strange." She describes her yearning to be accepted by her rapist; even while fearing him, seeking confirmation of her skin, body, and sexual desirability. Glow tells us

> I hadn't figured out how fine I was. It makes a big difference in what's what sometimes, believing that you're fine . . .

gives you perspective on your right to say no. But then, you know then, I didn't have much perspective. At the time the only men I tended to attract were conservative white men and closeted gay men. White men—'cause my skin's light enough for their friends and dark enough for cool points or at dinner parties. And gay men, 'cause, you know how that is. (330)

But by the end of her narrative, Glow reaches a place of self-knowledge. Finding a new name for herself, she discovers exactly how fine she is.

With all of these stories, we learn about the impact of the violence, but we also hear, in the midst of coping, the determination to flourish. Stain reclaims her name and becomes Anita. Bernadette builds a home for herself, not just the sugary male vision of a candy Tupac that she fantasizes about, but a network of female friends that she knows won't leave her. Glow decides that she will become the one who decides the value of her own pleasure, through writing, and sex.

DeBerry gives us a complicated vision of survival, where change is also registered in the body: we hear when Stain is stuttering, her breath moving toward a place of recognition; Bernadette's hard "fuck you" betraying a lonely, hungry child beneath. In this way, *Milkweed* captures moments of extreme discomfort and ambiguity. She does not glance away or idealize the experiences sometimes of desire, confusion, places where the body betrays us. These are also a part of reclaiming the body, and reclaiming the stories that others don't want to hear. In her book *Two or Three Things I Know for Sure*, Dorothy Allison tells of her commitment to telling "ugly stories." Allison helps us to understand how these prohibitions are linked to the experience of class shame, shame of women's bodies, and also racial shame—here, images of failed whiteness. In *Milkweed*, DeBerry heightens these elements of racial shame in the crucible of black authenticity, and the particular ways that issues of sexual pleasure, incest and father yearning, being a lesbian, and lesbian date rape might be understood within the already existing frame of racial shame. Her narratives' use of style and vocalization and reference help us to place her stories in a racialized context. Yet the elements of this shame and these ambiguities are both specific and open so that we might engage in them from multiple standpoints. And the empathy that she garners also helps others enter into the stories.

How does DeBerry keep these ugly stories from being alienating for her audience? First, she emphasizes these stories as not only about acts, but also about affective knowledge. These experiences, poisons, are—like the food on which the monarch butterfly feeds—part of the tools that we need to survive. So by the time we get to the violence, we understand the context, understand the depth of personhood, and can keep our eyes and ears on that full person at stake.

Her characters seek a full sexual and creative self that requires the voicing of pain and loss. And this process of healing is one that depends not just on the performer alone, but also on the audience. We must be part of the bargain. As she shows us how the body betrays and confuses, how it is vulnerable, how memory can sometimes be unreliable, we have to stay with her vulnerability. We cannot turn away. We *can't* leave them alone. This is foregrounded in the intimacy and sparseness of the set, the limited distance between character and persona, with the intimacy of the small theater space or stage, with the use of monologues that draw us directly into story.

Hers is a theater completely dependent on the rest of us, shaped by the conditions of performance, the live, the now. She demonstrates the ways that survival is a larger social act, even while it is an act that must heed our own timing, our own sense of safety, the particularities of our history. The relationship between audience and survivor is deeply personal, where the rhythms of our blood beats become the language in which one shares. This sense of interdependency is echoed in her last line: "SurvivoR, / I have/pinned / your / name / to the/bottom/of / my hem" (339). The distinction between "I" and the "survivor" ultimately doesn't hold—a reflection, perhaps, that we have all been forced to consume the poison.

CONTEXTUALIZING *MILKWEED*: BLACK WOMEN'S PERFORMANCES OF READDRESS

In her book *Wounds of the Spirit* Traci C. West warns us that the desire to turn away from black women's stories of violence tells us something important about ourselves: "Perhaps we are afraid that the destructive power will seize and overwhelm us if we open up our sensibilities too widely in empathy with them" (West, *Wounds of the Spirit,* 182). We are encouraged both to distance ourselves from individuals suffering from violence, and also from the forms of structural violence that have their beginnings in slavery, and which continue in the form of the current prison industrial complex. Indeed, such structures operate and succeed in their ability to encourage us to "other" ourselves from the other humans who are caught up in cycles of state violence. Indeed, we are all caught up in these structures through the dynamics of shame and forgetting.

Milkweed, like Sharon Bridgforth's play *delta dandi*, might be seen as redressive action—the "re-membering" of the pain and the intimate relationships structured by that pain that we've inherited from slavery. In her book *Scenes of Subjection*, Saidiya Hartman suggests that such redress must include the black body as a site of pain as well as a site of pleasure and eros. Black performance, as it is grounded in the remembrance of this history, "is an exercise in agency directed toward the release of the pained body, the reconstruction of violated natality, and the remembrance of breach. It is intended to minimize the violence of historical dislocation and dissolution—the history that hurts (Hartman, *Scenes of Subjection*, 77).

Here, the experience of rape is no mere metaphor, but a continuation of the history of enslavement. This is the outcome of a community's ingestion of black dehumanization, spat out into regimes of rape and shaming, violation and erasure. Significantly, though, *Milkweed* doesn't necessarily limit or even name white against black rape. Instead, the play paints a mostly black world of the exchange of violence. This is significant for *all* of us waiting here in the audience.

If Bernadette, Glow, and Stain's struggles to reclaim pleasure are historicized aspects of the lasting effects of the enslaved black body in pain, what does this drama tell us about the contemporary aftereffects of slavery? First, it forces us to consider the internalization of carcerate thinking and perhaps the perpetuation of pain as it becomes internalized, the punishment of the body out of bounds of the social. Second, the play is linked to the continued misreading of black pleasure that often accompanies the capitalistic exploitation and sale of black pleasure.

If, as Hartman suggests, black entertainment, including performance—song, dance, and story—is haunted by this history of black subjection, DeBerry's performance intervenes by bringing us back to the black body, and making it speak. And she does so by rejoining this body as it has been objectified and isolated to a community, led by the monarch butterfly, and peopled by ourselves.

It is the site of the ravished body that holds out the promise of larger cultural recovery, that "holds out the possibility of restitution, not the invocation of an illusory wholeness or the desired return to an originary plenitude" (Hartman, *Scenes of Subjection*, 74), Hartman suggests. We watch DeBerry's characters reach to their own dreams, their own flesh memories for the tools of their healing, and we learn our lessons that can heal ourselves, and even join us beyond the work of the two hours of the stage. In the sometimes not yet fully formed community space of the theater, in the process of our own witness, as well as in breech, we have the possibility for healing.

EPILOGUE: *MILKWEED*, WITNESS, AND COALITIONAL POLITICS

What I'd like to propose is a black feminist practice of theater as witness and as a site for community through accountability, generated from the embodied experience of watching *Milkweed*. Such a practice might provoke what Jill Dolan calls "affective rehearsals for revolution" (Dolan, *Utopia in Performance*, 7). As I just discussed, *Milkweed* invites a historicized consideration of the performance of the black body at its most vulnerable: in its state of pain and also in states of pleasure and yearning. DeBerry leads us from the embodied state of trauma to the moments of attempting to speak what has been erased. Our toolbox might include historical contextualization as well as deep listening, as well as somatic response, paying attention to the effects of the play itself on our own breath, vision, awareness of our bodies in space as we sit among others.

And thinking hard about our relationship to those others, a black feminist practice of theater as witness must also consider the "power lines"—the electric points of connection forced through struggle that potentially connect the performer with the community of the audience. In Aimee Carrillo Rowe's book, *Power Lines: On the Subject of Feminist Alliances*, she suggests that

> we tend to overlook the ways that power is transmitted through our affective ties. Whom we love, the communities that we live in, whom we expend our emotional energies building ties with—these connections are all functions of power . . . How might our subjects be constituted if we were hailed by

the needs and demands, struggles and joys, of those whose lives are excluded from the realm of our affective economies? (Rowe, *Power Lines*, 26)

I'd like to suggest here that theater might be such a space where, moved to the point of vulnerability and openness, we might also consider a space of belonging and power as figured by Rowe. Rowe's analysis speaks to the possibilities of pleasure and community beyond the lines of neighborhood or identity, and even beyond the boundaries of the performance: continued conversation and reflection, friendship and community, social action, including the inspiration of new art. Theater can and should change our relationships to one another by estranging our relationships to the usual ways of speaking, moving, and making sense. But, most importantly, theater can speak to this deep need for connection despite a history of shared pain. Such connection *is* also a site of struggle. In her essay "Eye to Eye: Black Women, Hatred and Anger," Audre Lorde writes: "It is easier to be angry than to hurt. Anger is what I do best. It is easier to be furious than to be yearning. Easier to crucify myself in you than to take on the threatening universe of whiteness by admitting that we are worth wanting each other" (Lorde, "Eye to Eye," 153).

Milkweed could be read both as a form of self-loving and as a model for coalitional politics—a mechanism for longing and belonging. It provides the opportunity for larger, deeper, and more loving understandings outside of the usual histories, the usual performances and stereotypes. The play teaches us an ethics of witness, listening, and reception. This is done through the exposure of vulnerability and by embodying the state of being vulnerable through breath, forcing us to look each other in the eye. But this is complicated because of the potentially diverse community of the theater audience, by our different positionalities and the ways we've received privilege based on our power or our ability to ignore others' abuses of power, and through our own internalization of pain through shame.

As an audience, we come together through multiple experiences: survivors and nonsurvivors and those who have been shaped by the culture of rape affecting the world (that means all of us), men and women, black and Latina and Asian and indigenous and white, young and old; an analysis of the differential relations of power might be a way of understanding and strategizing the multiple sites of connection, of what Rowe calls "differential belonging" (Rowe, *Power Lines*, 28).

As we belong in the theater audience, we necessarily belong differently. For this reason, we might bring as a tool an analysis of differential belonging. For me, such a lens might call up the experiences and constraints of my own various selves brought to the surface in watching DeBerry's narrative of pain and survival, vulnerability and healing: as a black woman, as the teacher, the writer, the lover, the dyke, the survivor, the daughter and granddaughter and great-granddaughter of survivors, the standard bearer, the trafficker/expert in Shakespeare studies, the good girl, the queer, the stranger, the friend. As I move across these positionalities, and I share this process with you, and you share yours, we are exposing the dynamics of power and the investments in that power that we might have difficulty turning loose. We might use the realization of the power in our own positionality to challenge things, to dismantle what keeps us distant. We might use the moments of recognition of shared selves to reflect back a fuller humanity, to confirm the humanity of each other.

This has particular resonance for black women, seeing eye to eye. As Lorde suggests:

> As black women, we have wasted our angers too often, buried them, called them someone else's, cast them wildly into oceans of racism and sexism from which no vibration resounded, hurled them into each other's teeth and then ducked to avoid the impact. (Lorde, "Eye to Eye," 167)

For white allies, this process might be the path out of the isolation, and out of knowing but not yet living changed by our knowing. *Milkweed* interrupts a tradition of centering whiteness by implicitly showing the implications of white violence on black bodies, but as it is ingested, acted upon, and reconstituted in black bodies. White violence as it shapes black violence against itself is one of the poisons that shapes the play as a whole.

For all of us, in the process, we might allow theater to remake us, undo us. This process can be done through watching, talking back, writing, performing. As a writer writing about performance, my own process as a critique is through the recognition of the beauty of this experience of undoing, embracing disorientation and trying to note its sensual effects through language, by respecting the "voice" and spirit of the writer in my own analysis and not letting myself become seduced by theory as a way of seeming smarter, sexier, more original, or more "right"; by including my own vulnerability, discomfort as it informs my analysis, by allowing myself to be guided by the desire to communicate, and through communication, my desire to create change; by imagining my voice as a part of a conversation, resisting the seduction of the idea of the "voice in the wilderness," the exceptional, the only One. Writing about performance may be one way to use theater not only to think about who we are individually, but also who we are in the world. Drawing from Aimee Carrillo Rowe and Audre Lorde, it is through this unmaking process that we are able to work through the historical experience of pain—as survivors, and as those implicated in that history. This process produces an experience of theater in which we are all very necessary.

For all of us witnessing this play, the willingness to be open to seeing each other in the play, as both victims and potentially, too, as perpetrators who have absorbed the lessons of black violence, is the purgative for our pain, the chance to draw it out of ourselves and to look at it, and then, like a milkweed spore, let it float away.

NOTES

1. In their landmark collection of radical women of color's feminist writings, *This Bridge Called My Back* (New York: Women of Color/Kitchen Table, 1983), Cherríe Moraga and Gloria Anzaldúa describe a "theory of the flesh" as "one where the physical realities of our lives—our skin color, the land or concrete we grew up on, our sexual longings—all fuse to create a politic born out of necessity" (20).

2. See Pearl Cleage's essay "Good Brother Blues," where she calls for black men to reject rape jokes, not hit their women, and to be "a good father/good husband/good lover/good worker/good warrior/serious revolutionary righteous brother" (in *Deals with the Devil and Other Reasons to Riot* [New York: Random House, 1993], 44).

WORKS CITED

Allison, Dorothy. *Two or Three Things I Know for Sure*. New York: Plume Books, 1996.

Cleage, Pearl. *Deals with the Devil and Other Reasons to Riot*. New York: Random House, 1993.

Dolan, Jill. *Utopia in Performance: Finding Hope at the Theater.* Ann Arbor: University of Michigan Press, 2005.

Hartman, Saidiya V. *Scenes of Subjection: Terror, Slavery, and Self-Making in Nineteenth-Century America.* New York: Oxford University Press, 1997.

Lorde, Audre. "Eye to Eye: Black Women, Hatred, and Anger." In *Sister Outsider: Essays and Speeches,* 145–75. Freedom, Calif.: Crossing, 2007.

Miller, Lynn C., Jacqueline Taylor, and M. Heather Carver, eds. *Voices Made Flesh: Performing Women's Autobiography.* Madison: University of Wisconsin Press, 2003.

Moraga, Cherríe, and Gloria E. Anzaldúa, eds. *This Bridge Called My Back: Writings by Radical Women of Color.* New York: Women of Color/Kitchen Table, 1983.

Morrison, Toni. *The Bluest Eye.* New York: Vintage International, 2007.

Rowe, Aimee Carrillo. *Power Lines: On the Subject of Feminist Alliances.* Durham, N.C.: Duke University Press, 2008.

Shange, Ntozake. *for colored girls who have considered suicide/when the rainbow is enuf.* New York: Macmillan, 1975.

West, Traci C. *Wounds of the Spirit: Black Women, Violence and Resistance Ethics.* New York: New York University Press, 1999.

ACKNOWLEDGMENTS

No project such as this could happen without the support of others. We would first like to thank the Mellon Foundation for funding this project and Northwestern University Press for agreeing to be a partner. We thank Donna Shear, then director of Northwestern University Press, who was instrumental in the development of the grant, and the current director, Jane Bunker, for supporting the project and nurturing it to its completion. Dean Barbara O'Keefe and the School of Communication provided the necessary infrastructure to make the project a success. We'd particularly like to thank Paul Riismandel, director of digital media and technology, for documenting all of the performances, talkbacks, and related events and Jane Rankin, associate dean of research, who assisted in the writing of the grant.

Support from Northwestern's Center for Global Culture and Communication allowed us to convene a summer institute where many of the artists and scholars included in this collection could workshop their essays and performances before an impressive interdisciplinary audience of graduate students from across the United States and Canada. We thank the center's director Dilip Goankar for allowing us this opportunity. We also thank the twenty graduate students who participated in the institute. They will find much of their provocative feedback and queries reflected in the final version of the materials here included.

To our research assistants, Jasmine Mahmoud, Colleen Daniher, Kemi Adeyemi, and Andrew Young, we say thank you for your work on this project. To our colleagues, D. Soyini Madison, Carol Stern, Paul Edwards, and Mary Zimmerman, thank you for supporting this project through your attendance at performances and engagement with the artists' work. Thanks also to colleagues Sandra Richards, Susan Manning,

Michelle Wright, Jane M. Saks, Gina Ulysse, Ann Orloff, and Mary Weismantel, who attended various performance events over the past three years.

To our partners, Stephen J. Lewis and Joel Valentin-Martinez, as always, thank you for your patience and support as we brought this book to fruition, even while on vacation!

And finally, thank you to each of the artists, critics, and interviewers who contributed to this volume. We are honored to have worked with all of you and we're so proud to feature your artistry to the world.

—*E. Patrick Johnson and Ramón H. Rivera-Servera*

CONTRIBUTORS

Bryant Keith Alexander is a professor and dean of the College of Communication and Fine Arts at Loyola Marymount University. He is the author of *Performing Black Masculinity: Race, Culture, and Queer Identity* and *The Performance Sustainability of Race: Reflections on Black Culture and the Politics of Identity.*

Renée Alexander Craft is an assistant professor of communication studies at the University of North Carolina at Chapel Hill. She is the author of *When the Devil Knocks: The Congo Tradition and Politics of Black Identity in Panama.*

Stephanie L. Batiste is an associate professor of English and black studies at the University of California at Santa Barbara. She is the author of *Darkening Mirrors: Imperial Representation in Depression-Era African American Performance.*

Lisa Biggs is an assistant professor of theater in the Residential College at Michigan State University. Her research investigates the impact of theater and dance programs for incarcerated women as sites of activism.

Sharon Bridgforth is an award-winning poet, playwright, performer, and activist. She is the author of *bull jean stories* and *love conjure/blues.*

Jennifer Devere Brody is a professor and chair of the Department of Theater and Performance Studies at Stanford University. She is the author of *Impossible Purities* and *Punctuation: Art, Politics, and Play.*

Edris Cooper-Anifowoshe has directed productions of August Wilson's *Piano Lesson* and the world premiere of Robert Alexander's *A*

Preface to the Alien Garden at Trinity Repertory Company in Providence, Rhode Island, as well as *Yellowman* at Curious Theatre in Denver. She has received awards for her direction of *The Old Settler* at TheatreWorks, Palo Alto, and WaterTower Theatre in Dallas.

NANCY CHERYLL DAVIS-BELLAMY is the founding artistic director of Towne Street Theatre in Los Angeles. She is an accomplished actor and playwright who has appeared in films and on television.

MISTY DEBERRY is a doctoral student in the Department of Performance Studies at Northwestern University. She is a Chicago-based interdisciplinary artist, whose work traverses the landscape of social behavior through language and the body as it pertains to gender-based violence, specifically against black women and girls.

ANITA GONZÁLEZ is professor of theater and dance at the University of Michigan. She is a director, choreographer, and writer whose work has appeared in national and international venues. She is a founding member of Urban Bush Women. She is the author of *Jarocho's Soul: Cultural Identity* and *Afro-Mexican Dance and Afro-Mexico: Dancing Between Myth and Reality.*

NADINE GEORGE-GRAVES is a professor of theater and dance at the University of California at San Diego. She is the author of *The Royalty of Negro Vaudeville: The Whitman Sisters and the Negotiation of Race, Gender, and Class in African American Theater, 1900–1940,* and *Urban Bush Women: Twenty Years of African American Dance Theater, Community Engagement, and Working It Out.*

E. PATRICK JOHNSON is Carlos Montezuma Professor of Performance Studies and African American Studies at Northwestern University. He is the author of *Appropriating Blackness: Performance and the Politics of Authenticity* and *Sweet Tea: Black Gay Men of the South.*

OMI OSUN JONI L. JONES is an associate professor of African American and African diaspora studies at the University of Texas, Austin. She is a coeditor of *Experiments in a Jazz Aesthetic: Art, Activism, Academia, and the Austin Project.*

RHODESSA JONES is the founder and artistic director of the Medea Project and co-artistic director of Cultural Odyssey. She has been developing work on incarcerated women for more than thirty years.

ROBBIE MCCAULEY is a professor of theater at Emerson College. She is an internationally acclaimed theater and performance artist. Her play, *Sally's Rape*, is a classic in the black feminist performance canon.

RAQUEL L. MONROE is an assistant professor of dance at Columbia College. She is a scholar, artist, and activist with a long history in academia and in diverse communities, engaging the ways in which dance influences and is influenced by social discourses on race, gender, sexuality, class, and culture.

DIANA R. PAULIN is an associate professor of English and American studies at Trinity College, Connecticut. She is the author of *Imperfect Unions: Staging Miscegenation in U.S. Drama and Fiction*.

SANDRA L. RICHARDS is a professor of African American studies and theater at Northwestern University. She is the author of *Ancient Songs Set Ablaze: The Theatre of Femi Osofisan*.

RAMÓN H. RIVERA-SERVERA is an associate professor of performance studies at Northwestern University. He is the author of *Performing Queer Latinidad: Dance, Sexuality, Politics*.

STACEY KAREN ROBINSON is a New York–based playwright and performer. She is the recipient of the 2009 Bronx Recognizes Its Own (BRIO) award in playwriting from the Bronx Council on the Arts for *Quiet Frenzy*.

FRANCESCA ROYSTER is a professor of English and Africana studies at DePaul University. She is the author of *Becoming Cleopatra: The Shifting Image of an Icon* and *Sounding Like a No-No: Queer Sounds and Eccentric Acts in the Post-Soul Era*.